44

A DUBLIN
MEMOIR

PETER SHERIDAN

44

A DUBLIN MEMOIR

MACMILLAN

First published 1999 by Macmillan

an imprint of Macmillan Publishers Ltd
25 Eccleston Place, London SW1W 9NF
and Basingstoke

Associated companies throughout the world

ISBN 0 333 75032 2 (hardback)
ISBN 0 333 76594 X (trade paperback)

Shadow of a Gunman from *Plays 2* by Sean O'Casey. Reprinted with kind
permission of Faber & Faber.
Waiting for Godot by Samuel Beckett. Reprinted with kind permission of
Faber & Faber and Grove/Atlantic, Inc.
'Not Fade Away' written by Norman Petty & Charles Hardin. Copyright ©
1957 MPL Comms. Inc. USA. Peermusic (UK) Ltd., 8–14 Verulam Street,
London WC1. Used by permission.
'Speedy Gonzales' by Ethel Lee, Buddy Kaye and David Hess. Copyright ©
1961 Budd Music Corp. Copyright renewed relating to Ethel Lee controlled by
Bienstock Publishing Company. Copyright renewed relating to David Hess 1988
and assigned to David Hess Music Co., Budd Music and Bienstock Publishing
Company. Lyric reproduction by kind permission of Carlin Music Corp, Iron
Bridge House, 3 Bridge Approach, London NW1 8BD; Memory Lane Music
Ltd., 22 Denmark Street, London WC2H 8NA and Budd Music Ltd., Midway
House, 27/29 Cursitor Street, London EC4A ILT.

3 5 7 9 8 6 4 2

A CIP catalogue record for this book is available from
the British Library.

Phototypeset by Intype London Ltd
Printed and bound in Great Britain by
Mackays of Chatham plc, Chatham, Kent

For Sheila my love

Acknowledgements

This book would have been impossible without the presence of Da in my life. He sadly left us in 1994 but his influence is undiminished.

Sheila has been by my side for over a quarter of a century and her love and support are the most important things in my life. Thank God for her punctuation and spelling skills, too, or I'd be lost entirely.

My children, Rossa, Fiachra, Doireann and Nuala have been patient with me throughout, even when I didn't deserve it. They are my fiercest and most loyal critics. Bless you for your love.

Each of my wonderful family, Ma, Shea, Ita, Johnny, Frankie, Gerard and Paul, has uniquely inspired me. Thank you for sharing your memories with me and then setting me free.

When this book was locked in my head, Deirdre Purcell helped me open the door and then cajoled and encouraged me throughout.

I want to thank Pat Moylan for so many things I wouldn't know where to begin, but mostly for being a great friend.

Darley Anderson, my agent, and his assistant, Kerith Briggs, have brought this book to places I never thought possible.

Suzanne Baboneau, Kirsty McKie and all the staff at Eccleston Place, thank you for your patience and good humour.

Thanks to Shane Connaughton for his critiques, his great advice, and his friendship. Lucy McKeever and Geraldine Kearney in the Abbey Theatre and Emer Dooley in Andrews Lane Theatre have given me continuing help and support.

Fiona Traynor is tenacious and doesn't take 'no' for an answer.

Paul McGuinness is one of the most helpful people I know and has a great staff at Principle Management.

Thanks to Hugh McCusker for his careful reading of the manuscript.

Fiona Killeen is refreshingly enthusiastic and knows how to throw a party.

Bill and Bob have no idea what they have done for me.

1

Dublin, New Year's Eve, 1959

Lodgings available. Centre city location.
Adjacent to RC church. All modern conveniences. Phone 41966.

Da read it back to Ma. She was proud of him. Proud of his
way with words. She looked at him and poured more tea
into his cup. She had a special way of pouring tea. She
poured tea like a countrywoman.

He started to count the letters. Tip-toed his pen from one
letter to the next like a ballet dancer, mumbling as he went.
Above each word he placed a number like a little crown.

—Will I milk your tea, Da?

He ignored her and continued counting. At the end he
stopped and gave her a look that needed no words.

—You're counting, I'm sorry.

He wrote down the word total and beside it the number
eighty-four.

—That's eighty-four characters all told. We won't get
eighty-four characters into two lines.

Jimmy Nelson was a character. He worked on the docks.
Every year for his holidays he booked himself into a suite in
the Gresham Hotel and never left the room. Not to eat, drink
or piss. For two weeks the world came to Jimmy Nelson.
That made him a character and people called him a character.

—What's a character, Da?

He looked at me over the rim of his glasses.

—The space a letter takes up is called a character.

I loved his way with words, just like Ma did. I loved Ma pouring the tea. I loved the two things about the same.

He pushed the piece of paper in front of me and asked me to delete words but keep the sense. I ran my eyes across the words. Across and back. I paused at the shortest word, 'to'. Adjacent to RC church. I said it in my mind and left out the 'to'. I looked over at Da. The pencil was sitting on the top of his ear, where most men keep their cigarette butts. A little nest of hair hung from his ear and the stubble on his face looked like ink dots on blotting paper. I took the pencil and drew a line through the word. I turned the page towards him. He looked at it and furled his brow. Then he took the pencil from me and put a line through the word 'available'.

> Lodgings. Centre city location. Adjacent RC
> church. All modern conveniences. Phone
> 41966.

I looked into his face and smiled. He put his great big fist on my head and rubbed it hard.

—You're a right little character. What are you?

—I don't know.

—A right little character. What are you?

—A right little character.

Not so long ago I'd have slapped his hand away. When I had ringlets. Blond cones of hair down to my shoulders. The morning of my first holy communion I stood before the mirror and worked my way up from the brown shoes. The knee-length socks with the yellow stripe. The fleck trousers and matching jacket. The white shirt and the green and white school tie. On top of all this a Shirley Temple head. I hated my hair, hated it more than any prison bars. I especially hated the oul' wans who slobbered over it saying how lovely it was. It was horrible.

I nearly fell off the chair from the force of Da's hand. I had a grown-up haircut just like his. I could rub my finger up the back of my neck and it felt like pin pricks. Dominoes falling. The quiff on top that stood up for an hour if you wetted it and all day if you used Brylcreem. I wasn't allowed Brylcreem because it stained shirt collars, so it was water all the way, except for the day you got it cut in Mickey Wellington's barber shop when he gave you a two-handed rub of his magic green lotion. Da never let 'foreign bodies' near his scalp. Jimmy Nelson wore so much grease (as Da called it) his hair was a solid mass. Didn't move in a hurricane. Just like the plastic 'nigger wigs' that Mickey Wellington sold in his barber shop.

Da pushed me so hard my head went all the way between my knees and onto the chair. I tried to loosen his grip but it was no use. I slid off the chair onto the floor and his hand followed me like a crane and I punched at him, with both fists.

—Come on, hit me!

I swung at him wildly.

—Have to punch harder than that.

Ma hovered with the teapot.

—Are you finished your tea, Da?

I managed to get up from the floor. I swung but missed by a mile. I could never hit him when he held me at bay like this. One day, I thought, one day my arms will be long enough and we'll see then.

My arms felt like lead weights. I concentrated all my strength into my forehead. I pushed against his hand. Hard as I could. He released his grip and I fell against his tummy. He wrapped his arms around me and squeezed me tight.

—You're a little terrier.

I looked up at him. His face seemed distorted.

—You finished your tea, Da?

3

I could see his hairy nose. His nostrils looked like rabbit holes in the dunes on Dollymount Strand.

—You've a drop left in this cup, do you want it?

Da let out a crisp, beautiful fart. He whistled with satisfaction. Ma beckoned to me.

—Come over here, son.

She lifted his cup from the table.

—There's still a drop in that, missus.

She handed it back to him. It was a crime punishable by two days' silence to take his cup with a drop still left in the bottom. He drank the dregs with colossal satisfaction.

—I'm going down the garage, son. Follow me down.

He gathered up his paper, pencil and the advertisement from the table. He started to undo his belt and headed for the back door.

'Down the garage' was Da's toilet. You got to it by going through the ordinary garage where he kept his tools and his biscuit tins. His bits of old bikes – wheels, frames, tubes, springs, saddles, pedals, crossbars, baskets, back carriers, all manner of spokes, front lights, back lights, dynamos, rust paint, white pump, black pump – and all of these spare parts secured to the wall with stays so that they looked alive.

Opposite bike parts and along one whole wall, pride of place, were Da's ladders. They were Da's other children, his twins. In winter they had their own blanket to keep out the dreaded frost and ice, which might cause them to crack.

The floor of the garage was taken up by two cars – one space rented by Father Ivers, a curate in Saint Laurence O'Toole's church and the other by Eamon Dooley, owner of the corner shop, the Emerald Dairy.

The entrance to the garage was by a small door from the backyard. At the furthest point from this door, beyond the parked cars and the wall hangings and the biscuit tins, was the remains of a building that looked like a hermit's cell. There were holes in it, all over. It was the holes that kept it from falling down. It had no door and no roof. An old timber joist stretched between two of the holes and this supported the cistern. The joist was eaten alive by wood-worm who had their own swimming pool because the cistern overflowed from time to time. Da put a sign up on the wall: 'Please pull up handle after use.' The word 'after' was underlined in red ink. Da was the only human being who ever sat down on this toilet bowl but nothing would convince him that intruders with fidgety hands didn't use it from time to time.

Lower down was the paper holder, designed and manufac-tured by Da. It was a coat hanger cemented into the wall so that it stuck out like a long spike. On to this spike, squares of paper, neatly cut from old telephone directories, had been placed in alphabetical order. He was currently wiping his arse with the Rs. Da claimed it was an inside toilet but in the corner was a lady's umbrella in case it rained. It was neither an inside nor an outside toilet, it was uniquely Da's.

As soon as I stepped inside the garage I could see him in jigsaw form through the holes. The smell was awful but I liked it. It filled the whole garage. It was amazing that a person his size, five feet six and a half, he said, but I'd say he was only five foot five (he always lied about things like that), it was amazing the stink he could make. Some day that power would pass to me.

I slid past the shiny black Volkswagen (Father Ivers') towards the portholes. The jigsaw changed like a kaleido-scope. I stopped, stepped back, it changed again. Past the Triumph Herald (Eamon Dooley's) and I could see his paper, opened at the racing page. He ran his pencil down the runners in the twelve thirty at Sedgefield.

—Bastard.

He wrote NWAF beside number six, Garryowen. It was shorthand for Not Worth A Fuck. It could mean the horse, the jockey, the trainer. Or a combination of all three. What was important was the system for picking winners. You were nowhere without a system. A wanderer in the desert. Lost, alone and abandoned. There are rules and there are fools. Some of Da's rules were: always back the outsider in a three horse race; never back in a race with less than six runners; trust your own judgement and never take advice; never refuse a drunk man's tip; never gamble beyond your means; beg, borrow and steal when your system clicks; never gamble on emotion; always go with your instincts; never, under any circumstances, desert your system. That was a cardinal rule, underlined in red ink. I knew not to interrupt him when he was studying form. That was a cardinal rule, too. You could get lynched for putting him off a winner. I didn't mind staying silent. I loved spying on him.

Most people covered themselves up all the time. Not Da. He didn't care if you walked in on top of him. He was the same on the beach. When other people were wrestling under towels he'd dry his hairy part to the heavens. He told me that the Fianna used to run around Ireland in the nude, over hills and through forests, and they wouldn't break a twig under foot.

He took a square of paper and blew his nose with it. The Reillys of James Street, Rialto, Kilbarrack and Raheny, met a snotty end. He dropped the piece of paper into the bowl between his legs and it landed on his thigh.

—You stupid pig's mickey.

He whipped off another square and mopped up the Reillys. The Reynolds were next. He took about half the families in Dublin and got up to wipe his arse. He turned around to check his stools in the pan (he was a great believer in checking your stools), when he looked up and saw me. He didn't flinch.

—I want you to take the advertisement over to the *Irish Press* on Burgh Quay.

He placed the piece of paper in the hole where my face

was. He pulled his trousers halfway up and fumbled in his pockets for money. He took out two half crowns and placed them in the hole.

—You'll need to go on the bike. They close early on account of it being New Year's Eve. Hurry.

I put the advertisement and the money in my pocket. I ran into the house and got my coat. By the time I had it on, Da had the bike ready at the back door. I threw my leg over and sat on the saddle. I could feel the hard lump of a penny under the soft skin of my bum. Da gave me a push start.

I loved going on messages up town. I loved the adventure. I loved discovering places and finding short cuts. I loved the oul' wans and the oul' fellas. I loved the statues and the buildings and the shops. I loved Dublin. I loved everything about Dublin. I wouldn't let anyone say a bad word about Dublin, especially country people. If Dublin was a woman I'd marry her.

The route to Burgh Quay? Up Emerald Street, right into Sheriff Street, left into Commons Street, right onto North Wall quay, left over Butt Bridge, right on to Burgh Quay and there. Easy.

In Sheriff Street I stopped at Mattie's, the best sweet shop in Dublin. Lucky lumps that were tuppence up town were only a penny in Mattie's. He had four different kinds of liquorice. He had sherbet sticks, loose rock, loose biscuits, penny packs of sweet cigarettes with red tips on them like they were lighting, loose marshmallows, honeybee sweets six a penny, everlasting gob stoppers, nancy balls (aniseed balls if you wanted to be posh), nougat, macaroon, blackjack and flash bars. The best of the sweets were lucky lumps. Soft, sticky pink sugar on the outside, and hard on the inside. If you were lucky there was a threepenny bit waiting for you on the inside and if you were less lucky you could get a certificate you could exchange for a free lucky lump. I looked in Mattie's window. There they were, staring back at me.

Bulls' eyes. I'd forgotten about them. They looked delicious. I loved the way your whole mouth went black eating them. At the end of the day, though, they were only a sweet. Lucky lumps were a sweet and a surprise.

I parked the bike outside and jumped down the three steps into the shop. I put the two half crowns and the penny on the counter and waited for Mattie. The bell tinkled and he came out of the house part of the shop.

—I want a lucky lump.

I ran back up the steps and out onto the street. I pointed out the one I wanted. I said a Hail Mary and went back in. Mattie held out the lucky lump. I went to pick up the money off the counter and it was gone. I was just about to scream when Mattie produced the half crowns from behind his back.

—Be careful where you leave your money, son.

I took the money and squeezed it. I squeezed it 'til my hand hurt. I jumped on my bike and I was in Commons Street before I realized I'd forgotten the lucky lump. I'd get it on the way back.

The girl in the *Irish Press* must have been going in for the Miss World Beauty Contest. She had more make-up on than anyone I'd ever seen. She read the ad. She seemed very satisfied with the wording because she purred to herself. She read it aloud.

—Where do you live?

—Seville Place. On the corner of Emerald Street.

—That's very handy. Seville Place. Tell me, do you have any big brothers?

—Yeah. Shea. He's bigger than me. He's thirteen.

Her face dropped. She started to write on an official looking piece of paper. She looked up and smiled at me.

—What age are you?

—I'm ten.

She flicked the hair back from her neck. I could see where the make-up ended. She pushed the form towards me and asked me to sign it. She spoke like the parrot in Uncle George's pet shop.

—Three insertions. Starting tomorrow. First January. Small ad in our accommodation to let. That'll be seven shillings and sixpence. Sign at the bottom.

I looked at her in despair.

—It's five shillings. My Da counted the characters.

—What characters?

—The characters in the ad.

—Now you pay the seven shillings and sixpence or you piss off out of here.

—I only have five shillings.

—You only have all modern conveniences or is that a lie, too? What are your bathroom facilities like? Are you deaf?

—We have two toilets.

—One not enough for you? Go home and get the extra half a crown and don't be annoying me.

I looked down at the form. I put a line through the word location. It seemed to make sense. I wasn't sure any more. I pushed it across to her. She counted the letters. She looked straight into my eyes when she was finished. She turned the form around on the counter and put a pen on it. She asked me to read it back to her.

—Lodgings. Centre city. Adjacent RC church. All modern conveniences. Phone 41966.

—Sign at the bottom.

I signed it in my best writing. I handed over the two half crowns. She smiled at me.

—Two toilets. How lucky can you get. I might just call.

I pedalled home like a madman. What would Da say if Miss World rang? We didn't even have a proper bath yet. Well, the bath was in position but it wasn't connected. We still used the metal one in front of the fire on Saturday nights. That wouldn't do for lodgers. Definitely not for lodgers. I should have crossed out the telephone number. It wasn't easy

9

when you were ten to make the right decision. I pulled on the brakes outside the Custom House and decided to go back. I'd take the ad out. Da might even appreciate getting the five shillings back. I was a fool. Miss World had the telephone number no matter what I did. She knew my big brother's name was Shea.

I turned the bike around and headed home for the second time. I hated Dublin. I hated everything about it. If Dublin was a football I'd kick it in the Liffey. I hated being ten. I looked at nothing on the way home. Not the Guinness boat, not the Liverpool boat, not the Isle of Man boat, nothing. All I could see in my mind was Miss World ringing our house and Da coming down from the phone with a beetroot face.

—You've destroyed me, son, you've destroyed me with a dame!

I went into Mattie's.

—Who died belonging to you?

—I did.

I put the lucky lump in my pocket. How could I suck happiness now? I would never be happy again for the rest of my life, I knew that.

*

At home there was great excitement. A big box covered in brown paper stood in the middle of the table. Frankie, the baby, though not a real baby, he was three, was climbing on a chair trying to get to it.

—I mant it.

My sister Ita who was twelve wasn't much bigger than Frankie. She was tiny for her age but she was a dynamo. She pushed the box across the table away from him.

—You can't have it, Frankie.

Frankie got down and raced around to the far side of the table and up onto another chair. Ita moved his chair away from the table. He was stuck in no-man's land. Ita moved all the other chairs as well. Now there were no chairs at the table. Frankie was flailing his arms about, grasping for a box that was miles out of reach. He looked pathetic. It made us all laugh.

—I mant it.

Shea was sitting in the armchair by the fire.

—You don't mant it, you want it. You can't have it 'til you learn to speak properly.

—I . . . I . . . I . . .

We all turned our eyes on him. Johnny, who was eight, crawled out from under the table where he'd been hiding but had now forgotten who it was he was hiding from. Johnny sang his encouragement to Frankie 'cos Johnny sang all the time.

—You wa . . . wa . . . wa . . . wa . . . what?

—I . . . I . . . I . . . I . . . want . . .

The word was loud and clear. We all went silent. Then a cheer.

—Hooray . . . hooray . . .

—Frankie said want . . .

—He said it perfectly . . .

Johnny stamped his feet and sang out in a chorus.

—I want I want I want I want I want I want I want.

Frankie took it up.

—I want I want I want I want I want I want I want.

They'd forgotten what they wanted. They were soldiers marching to war. Frankie nearly fell off the chair but Ita caught him in time. She was special like that. She could see things that were going to happen. She was tiny because she was so sensitive. It was like she didn't want to take up too much room in the world because she wanted to leave space for others. The body of a child and the mind of someone twice her age.

Da was disappointed she never saw who was going to win at the races. Ma said she had a gift that was not for material gain. Ita said it frightened her sometimes because she saw people who were going to die. Most people wanted to see into the future but I looked at Ita sometimes and I knew she was having a vision. She looked sad. I could see the tears at the back of her eyes. It made her beautiful, too. A doll with a human heart.

Ita lifted Frankie onto the floor and he ran out to the scullery shouting.

—Mammy, mammy, I mant the box on the table.

We all burst out laughing. Frankie started to cry. That made us laugh even more. He came back into the room shouting through his tears.

—I mant it, I mant it, I mant it.

He lay down on the floor and started to kick his feet like a helicopter. No one could get near him. He got so bad it wasn't funny any more.

—What's in the box? I asked.

Ita looked at me.

—Da won't say.

—I know but I'm not saying.

Shea always knew things like that. Ma told him everything. He was Ma's favourite and she never did anything to hide it. Shea always took Ma's part when she fought with Da. He was her little protector. She told him things she didn't even tell Da. Ma came in from the scullery with a big plate of buttered bread. The phone rang upstairs in the hall.

—Answer that, Seamus.

—Ma always gave him his full name.

—If I do they'll take my seat.

No one gave up the armchair that easy. Specially not when it was freezing outside like it was today. It suddenly dawned on me that it might be Miss World ringing about the ad. I ran up and answered it. There was no voice at the other end. I knew it was her.

—I'm sorry, we have no room.

There wasn't a breath. Nothing. Just someone listening.

—We're full up.

I pressed button A. The phone came alive in my hand. A machine-gun laugh at the other end. That meant it was Uncle Paddy. Uncle Paddy was normal in every way except that he couldn't stop laughing. No, he could stop but he didn't want to stop. To have a conversation with him you had to laugh. If you didn't laugh it looked like you were making fun of him. Paddy laughed before he said a word, in the middle of a word and at the end of a word, depending on the sense and the sentence.

I held the phone away from my ear.

—Is . . .

He chuckled.

—Is your . . .

He sucked for air.

—Is your Daddy . . .

He chuckled and he sucked.

—Is your Daddy there?

He went into total convulsions. Hysterics. It was an ordinary sentence but he made it sound like the funniest thing ever said. I knew he was going to be a few minutes laughing to himself. I read the instructions by the phone and laughed with him. 1. Lift receiver. 2. Insert coins. 3. Dial number. 4. Await reply. 5. Press button A. 6. To retrieve coins press button B. Beside it Da had written 'please comply'. On the phone his brother Paddy had stopped laughing.

—I think he's in the bookies', Uncle Paddy.

I knew he'd laugh at that. I read the instructions another three times. After about three minutes Paddy gave me a message for Da.

—Tell your Da the aerial has landed.

13

It was all secretive and hush hush.

—The aerial has landed, over and out.

I replaced the receiver and pressed button B. Sometimes money came out. Nothing today. I jumped the four steps down to the kitchen door. Soon as I walked in Ita looked at me.

—That was Uncle Paddy, wasn't it?

I didn't answer her.

—I knew. I knew it was him.

—Yous heard him laughing down here.

I looked at Shea. He shook his head. I looked at Ita. It was the sad look.

—I knew that was Paddy, just like I know that's a television set.

All eyes went to the box.

—A television set?

No one dared disagree. Frankie got up on a chair to have a better look.

—What's a tebibision, Mammy?

—It's a cinema in your own home.

The aerial has landed. Now I understood. I said it out loud. Everyone turned and looked at me. I said it again, this time with a smile.

*

—Get the ladders out!

It was Da's favourite expression. When Da said it you knew he was going up on the roof. It was his kingdom up there. On the roof, Da was king.

—Get the ladders out.

As far back as I could remember I was following him up ladders. I knew every blemish and paint stain on them. I knew each rung individually, the ones that had been repaired and the ones that needed repairing. The ones that escaped

14

the frost and the ones that didn't. I knew the respect they deserved and the respect they must be given.

—Get the ladders out.

'Get the ladders out' meant Da changed into his work clothes. Five days a week he wore a suit and tie to the booking office in the train station. Another three nights a week he worked at the greyhound track. They were jobs he did for other people. What he did in his own kingdom was missionary work. It was Da securing the battlements.

His work clothes were hand-me-downs from Adam. There were two slits in the seat of his trousers so that his arse peeked through every time the wind blew. There were slits at the front where his knees came through. Front and back, there were two perfect creases from Ma's ironing skills. The only original part of the shirt was the collar which had been turned at least twice. The tail was from a pair of pyjamas, the back was the front of a vest, the right sleeve was blue and the left sleeve was kind of pink (but now looked black), none of the buttons matched and only two of them closed. The jumper had no elbows and no back, only a front that looked like a baby's dribbler. His shoes had been brown once and were now colourless like the earth. The laces were white binder twine, saved from the bin months earlier. He wore two pairs of socks that were an insurance against foreign bodies inside the shoe.

The most important item was what went on the head. Da knew it from history and he knew it from personal experience. He knew it stretching back to the Greeks and from them through the Romans, the Vikings, Cromwell and down to the present day. Da knew that 80 per cent of body heat disappeared out of the top of your nut. You could wrap yourself in bear skins from the North to the South Pole but without cover on top you might as well work in your nude.

It was snowing. A light snowfall. All over Dublin people were getting ready to ring in the new year. Kids were trying to catch snowflakes in Seville Place, Emerald Street and Sheriff Street. High up on a balcony a drunken man's voice could be clearly heard singing a hymn to summer. He was praying for warm days and cold beer and something called 'pretzels'.

At four o'clock, Da said we'd be watching pictures from the BBC by five o'clock. Five o'clock in the morning, Uncle Paddy added and the whole house fell about. I laughed so much the shepherd's pie from dinner came up my throat and into my mouth. I got such a fright I swallowed it straight back down.

It was half eleven. The roof was like a scene from Mars. Da had rigged up his work light and had it hanging from the chimney stack. This cast huge shadows over the snow and along the terrace of roofs. Every time they moved the aerial it seemed that a giant centipede was about to enter our house through the roof. As well as the work light there were improvised lanterns – candles set inside disused bean tins. They were all over the roof and Da and Paddy used them to warm their frozen hands from time to time. They looked like zombies who'd been attacked by the abominable snowman. The drunken singer continued to croon in the distance.

—Fuck him and the days of summer.

—And double fuck him.

They had been seven straight hours on the roof wrestling with the aerial. They were beaten men. They made another adjustment to the brackets on the chimney stack. It was the tenth time they'd altered them. They looked at each other and knew it was the final throw of the dice. They got a good footing and gripped the aerial between them. Slowly, gently, they lifted it towards the receiving slots. One false move, one unexpected gust of wind and they'd sail clean off the roof.

I watched them from my perch at the top of the ladder. It was a long way up from the ground. Three storeys. I was safe where I was. I watched the two brothers lift the aerial.

16

They didn't speak a word. A word was a breath and a breath could upset their balance. Until they had the pole in the socket holes they were an accident waiting to happen. On the first try, they missed it altogether. They looked at each other and I thought I heard Da say . . .

—I love you, brother . . .

They went at it again and it slotted in like they were a circus act. They pushed it straight up into the sky. Straight and true like a plumb line. They stood up, too, like they were first cousins of the aerial, like they were saluting its achievement by saluting their own. Uncle Paddy's laugh returned and Da was humming along with the distant crooner.

In no time the coaxial cable from the aerial was lowered down the back wall, taken in through the kitchen window and plugged into the back of the television set. The entire family sat in a big semicircle and stared at it. Ma was in the armchair by the fire with Frankie asleep in her arms. Johnny was under the table as usual, wide awake, hiding from someone. Uncle Paddy told Da to turn it on and whatever way he said it we were all in convulsions in seconds. We didn't need a television so long as Uncle Paddy was around. No one could stop. Then Uncle Paddy got all serious.

—Come on, now, give your Daddy a chance.

Da reached out to turn it on. His hand was still blue with the cold. He couldn't grip the switch. He blew on his fingers and tried again. The click sounded like an explosion. A small dot appeared in the centre of the screen. It was magic. The dot disappeared and we all let out a sigh of disappointment. Just as quickly the whole screen lit up and we all sighed again with elation. It was a picture of snow. It filled the screen. From top to bottom and from side to side. It was snow outside and now it was snow inside, too. Frankie woke up and pointed at the television.

—Look at the moon.

It was like he'd had a vision in his sleep. Something in his brain had connected to something in the television.

—Look at the moon.

Ma shushed Frankie and turned to Da.

—You've done enough for one night. Leave it, Da.

He was so annoyed he didn't answer her. Never leave a job half done was one of his cardinal rules. Having risked his life and that of his brother, he was not about to abandon ship just yet. He'd prefer to float off the roof to his doom than leave a screen full of snow as his legacy to mankind.

He went out to the scullery, but it wasn't to drink tea. Whispers could be heard coming from it. We stared at the snow pretending not to listen. Finally, Da came back in followed by Paddy. He took off his woollen cap and threw it in my lap.

—Get that on, son, you're going up the aerial.

*

I knew not to look down. To look straight ahead, like Da told me. I was shaking with fear. I remembered the Greek boy. He didn't do what he was told and flew too near the sun. Disaster. Da and Paddy put a hand each under the cheeks of my bum and pushed me skyward. I reached with my arms and gripped with my feet. Now they put a hand each under the soles of my feet and gave me another push towards the stars. Each time I slid up those few feet, the aerial swayed gently under my weight. That was the worst part, worse than the snow going up my nose and into my mouth. I felt the fishbone aerial against the top of my head. I wanted to look down and see how far up I was but I gritted my teeth and kept my eyes straight ahead.

—Now, son, listen to me. Very gently reach up your hand, do you understand me?

I had never heard such emotion in his voice. I felt wrapped up in his words even though I was in the sky. He sounded like

18

a different father. A father who didn't care about systems, or logic or the old Greeks, who only cared about me, how I was and how I was going to be.

—Reach up your hand and turn the aerial towards England.

I'd have flown to England if he'd asked me. I reached up my hand and the aerial moved voluntarily. I turned it without looking. Then I stopped.

—Where's England, Da?

—Towards the river. Turn it towards the Liffey and hold it there.

I turned it in a straight line that connected Howth and Dun Laoghaire. Da sent the message down the line of communication he'd established.

—Have we a picture?

Johnny at the top of the ladder shouted down to Ita at the bottom.

—Have we a picture?

Ita ran into Shea who was in charge of the tuning.

—Have we a picture?

Shea turned the button fully one way, then the other. Word came back up the line.

—Snow.

—Snow.

—Snow.

—Snow.

The light on the roof changed. Out of the corner of my eye I could see Paddy's bald head as he took Da's worklight off the hook on the chimney stack. He pointed with it like it was a giant finger. Across the terrace of roofs.

—There's your problem. There's your problem, right there. The church is blocking your signal. The church stands directly between you and a perfect picture.

Da took the light from him and looked for himself.

—Saint Laurence O'Toole, bastard. That you were ever born, you pig's mickey.

Paddy reached across and took the light back.

—The church may be blocking your signal but it has to go somewhere. Coming from England, it's going to bounce over there.

Paddy turned the light northwards. Da saw it immediately.

—It's going to hit them houses and bounce over there.

Paddy turned the light southwards.

—It's going to re-form over there, do a little jazz dance and work its way into us from the direct opposite side.

The two of them shouted at me with one voice.

—Turn it around, son, turn it around.

I turned the aerial in the complete opposite direction. Word went down the line. Word came up the line.

—There's a picture!

—There's a picture!

—There's a picture!

—There's a picture!

I fumbled in my pocket for a spanner and felt the lucky lump. I'd forgotten all about it. I tightened the nut that held the fishbone aerial in position.

Half an hour into 1960 we all sat staring at the television. It felt very different to 1959. The sound was perfect. A man was describing 'traditional revelry' in Trafalgar Square. There was definitely something on the screen. Outlines that looked like human beings. I went right up close but all I could see were dots and lines. Paddy touched something at the back of the set and there it was – a perfect picture. Well, nearly perfect. Lots of snow but a definite picture. We all clapped. It was a woman on a horse. She looked majestic. She looked regal. A big silver sword in her hand.

—What do we need that woman for?

Ma was off. We tried to shush her.

—I won't be shushed in my own home. Not for that woman and her fat horse. She's not the Queen of this country, let me tell you, television or no television.

Ma left the room with Frankie asleep in her arms. Da threw his eyes to Heaven.

—Dames!

We stayed glued to the television. The music blared out and the Queen inspected the guard. Da and Paddy stood behind us. Their father had fought in 1916 and here they were stealing pictures from London.

I popped the lucky lump in my mouth and started to suck. I sucked as hard and fast as I could. I won nothing but it felt like it had been one of the luckiest days of my life. Maybe it was an omen. I couldn't wait for the rest of the sixties to begin.

2

The phone never stopped ringing for a week after the ad went in. We were bombarded with calls. Ma said it was worse than the North Strand bombing. She could turn tea into acid with her tongue but she was as nice as pie when she answered the phone.

—I beg your parding. Yes, we're fully approved. You're very welcome.

Soon as she replaced the receiver.

—Typical Cork bastard. Only short of asking did we have an indoor swimming pool.

By tea-time there was a queue at the front door. One behind the other, down the steps, along the railings. I watched them from the upstairs bedroom. People looking for a home. Lonely people. Hoping they'd get picked. Hoping they'd be part of a family. A man with a curly head of hair and a bald spot in the middle. Thick black glasses, too. The man beside him had brown moleskin trousers and turn-ups for catching money in. He had on a brown pair of shoes that were nearly red. The trousers and shoes didn't match but the shoes and his face did. He might be the typical Cork bastard.

They were like the lost souls. Country people queuing outside a Dublin house for lodgings. Every November you could get lost souls out of Purgatory and into Heaven by saying seven Our Fathers, seven Hail Marys and seven Glory Be To The Fathers. After you saved a soul you had to go outside the church for a few minutes before going back in to save more. The best feeling was when you were on the last prayer and the door into Heaven started to open. You could see it in your imagination. The lost soul could see it for real, only he didn't know who was opening it. He thought it was God. There were ten people outside our house and only one would get in. I wondered where the losers would go. There was nothing I could do about it.

*

Da had bits of newspaper with pimples of blood all over his face. He was in the scullery shaving. The blade was blunt and he was in a hurry. As well as interviewing the lodgers he had to go to the dog track at Shelbourne Park. When he came in from the scullery he was covered in a paper beard. One of the bits of paper was an ad for an electric razor. Safe and clean with twin sp . . . The last bit was missing. I think it was eed. Maybe ools. We thought it was funny but Ma was annoyed.

—You can't see anyone in that state. You look like Frankenstein.

—It's only a couple of nicks.

He looked around for support. We were afraid to speak. Shea broke the ice.

—You're worse than Frankenstein. He had an excuse.

Ma was dispatched to interview the clients while Da performed surgery on his face. She saw them in the front room. That was directly below our bedroom and it had two armchairs, a couch and a piano. We were under pain of death not to go up there so we watched snow on the television with the sound turned down and every so often heard Ma's laugh coming through the wall. Every time she laughed the reception got better. I noticed it first and told the others. We tried laughing at the television but it didn't make any difference. Da thought we were laughing at him. We told him about the reception but he just grunted and tried to fix his face. You could tell he wanted to be up in the parade ring with Ma, inspecting the runners.

23

The lodger would be an investment in education. Shea had started at the secondary school and each term there was a brown envelope that had to be filled with money and returned to the school office. The lodger money would fill that envelope. There were other envelopes, too, like the shoe club. I took that to a woman in Foley Street on the first of every month. It meant new shoes at Christmas from Griffith's in Talbot Street. There was the turkey club in the butcher's and the hamper club in the corner shop. But the money from the lodger would go to our education.

Ma met Da in the Liverpool Bar at ten twenty on dog nights. It was a ritual. She left our house at five past ten and walked to the North Wall. The pub was directly opposite where the Liverpool boat left from. Soon as Ma got there she ordered Da's pint of stout, which meant that when Da arrived he didn't have to wait for it to settle. Allowing a pint to settle was what gave it its magical taste. But having to watch it settle was torture for a man with a twelve-hour thirst.

At ten past ten Ma came down from the front room and dispatched me to the Liverpool. I was to tell him the interviews were still going on. I parked the bike in the corridor between the select lounge and the public bar and I searched for him. The pub was packed with dockers and cattlemen still in their working clothes.

There was a sing-song in full swing. The man in charge of it wore a blue suit with a silver shirt, opened so that his chest hairs were showing. He had a gold watch on his wrist and a gold ring on his little finger and they flashed every time he moved his hands to the beat of the song. He was singing 'Frankie and Johnny', one of my Da's favourites. There was something peculiar about it, though. When Da sang it you got the whole tragic story but this was like half a song. It wasn't that he didn't know the words, just that he deliberately left them out.

—Frankie and Johnny lovers.
Oh Lordy, did love.
Swore each other and the stars above.
He oh yes, man, done her wrong.

There was no rat tat tat with the gun like Da did. No moral about 'there ain't no good in men'. He was straight into the next song, 'Roses are Shining in Picardy', only he left out most of the words again. He had the whole song sung in under thirty seconds.

There was no sign of Da.

I saw Andy Griffin's mother. Andy was my best friend in school. He told me once his mother was an alcoholic. I asked her who the singer was.

—That's Christy Power, son. The man with the golden dick.

Her friend nudged her.

—He's only a boy, Molly.

—That's when they need to be told. Not right Christy Power having children by all them different girls. 'Course they fall for the voice, that's it.

Just then Da came in. I told him the news. He ordered a pint, swallowed it in two gos and got a half-dozen Guinness to take out.

Four men were having supper at the table when we got home. Two were moving in immediately. Mossie Sullivan was the one whose shoes matched his face. He was from Malla (Mallow) County Cork and drove his own cattle truck. John O'Mahony was the bald spot, not long out of a monastery in Kildare and now working for Offshore Oil. The Dargan brothers, Noel and Liam, were labourers from Tipperary and they weren't moving in until the dump room could be got ready.

Our family had doubled in size in one night. The problem was Ma. Ma had a terrible bark but she couldn't turn people away from her door. It all went back to her birth. Her mother died having her, so she had to survive alone in the world. It made her tough. A survivor. The flip side was that she wanted to be a mother to the whole world. And now the whole world was moving into our house. Where would they all fit?

*

Shea and I were at the top of the bed and Johnny was at the bottom. Every time I moved even close to the halfway line I got an elbow. Shea wouldn't let anyone touch him because he should have been in a single bed, a single bed that was now a lodger's bed. I moved away from him as far as I could. I listened to the gaggle of voices from downstairs and tried to stay awake. But it was no good. The heat in the bed was too much and I finally gave way to sleep.

I woke up feeling I was being gassed. It was Johnny's foot in my face. His little toe stuck in my nostril like it was trying to pick snot. I pushed his foot away and climbed across Shea on to the floor. I reached under the bed for the potty. I couldn't feel it. I moseyed right down and looked for it. Then I remembered we didn't have a potty any more because of the lodgers. In the hazy yellow light from the streetlamp on Seville Place, I headed for the door. I heard a voice coming from the other bed.

—Your oul' fella is fucking mad, you know that.

It was John O'Mahony in the single bed beside ours.

—This house is blessed. It's special. Go on to the toilet, don't mind me.

It was like he'd been lying there waiting to finish a sentence. He had his two hands behind his head and was staring straight at me through his glasses. I went down the stairs to the bathroom. I knew from the darkness of the rest of the house that it was the middle of the night. There wasn't a sound. I could hear the hiss from the light bulb over my head. Everyone was asleep. Everyone except this man, Mahony.

I got afraid. Out of the blue, I realized I was alone. It

was the middle of the night and I was standing in the bathroom on my own. Any lunatic could walk in behind me, and stab me in the back. Mahony could do it – I wouldn't even see him. If I was murdered it would be Ma's fault for taking out the potty. I dashed back up the stairs and into the room. Looking at nothing except the bed, I dived straight in and under the covers, panting. I lay as still as I could until my breathing got normal again. I was afraid to sleep. What if Mahony was a murderer? Why else would he be awake in the middle of the night? I had to keep my eyes open. If I fell asleep he'd smother the three of us – unless he fell asleep first. I decided to give him ten minutes and I'd check. Meantime, I tried to count sheep. They all had thick black glasses on. I switched my mind to Wembley and led Manchester United out for the FA cup final. I turned to the referee – it was Mahony. I couldn't wait any more. I leaned up on my elbows and looked across to his bed. He turned and looked straight into my eyes. I was terrified and spluttered out 'good night'.

—I'm an insomniac. I never sleep.

I slid back under the covers and started to pray. I prayed that this maniac would die, right there and then. I said seven Our Fathers, seven Hail Marys and seven Glory Bes. Soon as I finished I started over. I prayed and prayed until I didn't know what I was saying. I felt my lids getting heavy. I grabbed Johnny's foot and held it against my face. I held it there and thanked God for his smelly foot. I prayed for Johnny's foot. I prayed and prayed and prayed until I heard Ma shouting up the stairs for school and I realized I was asleep. I looked across and Mahony was gone. The bed was made but he was nowhere to be seen. I was relieved. He hadn't murdered me after all.

*

Mossie Sullivan always called me 'little fella'. He'd open his buckets of hands, scoop my little ones in and rub so hard I felt like two lumps of turf in the fire. Sometimes he'd do it to my ears 'til I thought I was going to fly.

—Where's Frenchman's Lane?

He always tried to catch me out. He didn't know I was Da's messenger and that meant I knew all the out of the way places. Frenchman's Lane was easy.

—Off Store Street beside McGowan's scrapyard.

He thought I knew too much for a little fella and he gave me an almighty tickling. Da used to tickle me when I was a kid but not any more. Now he only tickled Frankie. I didn't sit on Da's knee and since I learned to ride the bike I didn't take a crossbar either. It was nice to sit on Mossie's knee and feel the heat of his body coming up into mine. I loved the way he let me light his cigarette for him. If Ma wasn't watching I could blow the match gently and it would stay lighting. Lighting and lighting all the way to the bottom. I could lick my fingers and take it in the other hand and watch it burn 'til the whole match went black all the way to the tip. Burn and burn 'til the flame went out by itself. It was funny to think where flames disappeared to.

Mossie's fingers were a cross between yellow and brown. At the tips it was a black-yellow and on the palms it was a brown-yellow and in between it was my favourite colour in the whole world. I wanted that colour on my hands when I grew up. I watched him smoke. He pulled on the cigarette, let the smoke out in a cloud then sucked it back in like he'd fooled it. Then he chewed on it. When he finished chewing it he whistled it out through his nose like a dragon. I never tired watching him. I practised with sweet cigarettes, with matches, with rolled-up newspaper.

Before Mossie, I hated country people. All the teachers in our school were from Galway, Mayo or Kerry. They always seemed disappointed they weren't teaching country kids. If you were good in school they called you a smart jackeen and if you were brutal they called you a gobdaw. Why didn't they stay at home to teach? Why were they in Dublin if they hated it so much?

Mossie was built like a tank. He walked with his head slightly forward as if he were pushing air out of the way for the rest of his body to slip through. He didn't lift his feet off the ground, so he made a clicking sound as he shuffled along. It was a complete culchie walk, a culchie walk you could see coming from our house to the Five Lamps. He looked just like a farmer struggling through a wet bog. I was getting to like his walk so much I didn't mind his orange jacket and his moleskin trousers and his flowery waistcoat. I didn't even mind his culchie shoes.

Mossie always brought a bag home. He'd hand it to Ma and tell her it was a little something for the tea. Or the supper. Usually cream donuts or cream slices. Sometimes a flan or a jam log. He'd come in the back door, even though he had a front-door key and he'd give it to Ma in the scullery.

—There's a little something, Anna.

I loved the way he said Anna. I loved that more than the cakes. Him saying Anna in his Cork accent and her face lighting up like she was a girl.

—You shouldn't have, Mossie.

—Where's the little fella? Here, share them out.

He always gave me the bag of sweets to divide. At first he bought ones with their own wrapping but they caused too many fights about who got first pick. I told him one night to make sure the sweets were all the same, no wrappers, and he said back to me he'd have to stop buying sweets if they were causing so much friction. For one horrible second my heart sank. Then he tickled me so hard I laughed 'til I cried and he said he was sorry and he really meant it. It was the first time in my life a grown-up had said sorry to me like that. Even though my sides hurt and I was sore and I was really crying, he made me feel important in a way I had never felt before.

If Da was jealous of Mossie he never showed it. The way Ma fussed over him I thought he must be. Maybe Da hid his true feeling because Mossie had 'inside information'.

As far back as I could remember, Da always said that what punters needed to back winners was inside information. In the person of Mossie Thomas Sullivan of Malla, in the county of Cork, Da's dream had come true. Mossie's sister was the wife of a well-known and highly respected horse thief from Dunmeela in county Waterford. As such, Mossie had access to inside information. He could have called Ma Princess Margaret so long as he supplied Da with quality information that led to winners. All we had to do was sit tight and wait for Mossie to deliver.

*

On the nights he wasn't at the dogs, I helped Da get the dump room ready for the Dargans. It was hard to believe they were brothers. Noel was six foot four and had black hair as thick as a mop. Liam was five foot five and had fine curly blond hair. Noel hardly spoke, Liam never shut up. Most of the time Liam spoke, he spoke about his brother. Lots of his sentences started . . .

—Noel, do you remember the time you . . .?

Noel would look down and nod. He never smiled. Liam did the smiling for both of them. Noel did the living. They were complete opposites. If Liam was talking, you found yourself looking at Noel. When Liam stopped talking, you found yourself asking Noel questions to which Liam would make reply. It was strange.

Noel was a labourer, had been a soldier and wanted to be a soldier again. Liam was a plasterer, was never anything else, but wanted to be a drummer in a showband. He practised drumming with a knife and fork, any knife and fork. He practised before meals, during meals and after meals. By the time he was three weeks in the house Ma had only two small plates left.

His audition piece was a Buddy Holly song called 'Rave On'. One evening he really got carried away. He smashed both his plates, fell off the chair and toppled over the table breaking Mahony's plate as well. Noel gave him a big lecture. Two whole sentences, one after the other. He barred Liam from practising.

After a week he was at it on the sly. I was in the dining room doing my homework and I saw him. Noel and Mahony were there, too. He started off pretending to hit the plates. He did that for a minute. Then he barely tipped them. Every time he tipped one he'd freeze in mid air. When no one said anything he'd start again. He was working his way back to full strength. The tension was unbearable. He started to play 'Rave On', then he stopped. Started again. This time he used Mahony's plate as a cymbal. Mahony exploded.

—You're going to break the plates and we'll all be put out on the street.

Noel stood up from his chair, all six foot four of him. He looked down at Mahony, whose glasses were rattling on his nose.

—He was only making fucking music, you miserable bastard who wouldn't spend Christmas.

Noel looked at his brother.

—Play!

Liam started to play. It was a tense rhythm.

—Sing!

Liam started to sing. A song about the jungle and a lion going to sleep.

It only took him a minute to get into full swing. Ma came in with the dinners. Noel turned sharply to his brother.

—Did I tell you to stop?

Liam stopped immediately and apologized to Ma. She wasn't amused.

—You'll pay for any breakages.

I pretended to do sums. Noel stared at Mahony while Mahony pretended to eat his dinner. You could smell the fear in the room. Liam started drumming. He looked across to Mahony daring him to say something. He turned to me.

—Have you seen the scar?

I shook my head. He turned to his brother.

—Show him your scar, Noel. Show it to him.

Noel stopped eating his dinner and unbuckled his belt. Undid his fly and pulled his shirt up. Never took his eyes off Mahony for a second. I leaned over to look.

—He was in the Congo. You can touch it if you want to.

I reached my hand out but tried not to touch it. It looked like someone had used a tin-opener on his leg. Noel reached out and took my hand in his but he never took his eyes off Mahony. He rubbed my fingers all along the scar.

—Thirty-inch scar put there by a black man. Noel took his woman and rode her on a tombstone. She demanded money. Noel told her he didn't pay for sex.

—I don't pay for sex!

—He stuck his coward's knife in. Noel reached out with one hand and choked the life out of him. He still don't pay for sex, do you Noel?

Noel tucked his shirt back in and redid his buckle. Ma came in with the teapot and a plate of buttered bread. She reached out to collect the dinner plates when Mahony was on his feet.

—I'll do that, Mrs Sheridan.

It was an opportunity he had to take. With Mahony out of the room Noel turned to me and said:

—Don't tell your mother about the black man.

I shook my head and went back to my books. I was right, after all, we had a murderer in our house. I said a prayer that Ma wouldn't change the sleeping arrangements, that she would leave things as they were, now and for ever, amen.

*

Da couldn't hide his glee. He had an audience where he could test out his theories. His systems. His ideas. A gathering where he was the master of ceremonies. His own school where he could conduct what he called discourses, and what Ma called rows.

—Jesus Christ had twelve, how many have you?

He was off. He'd backed a few winners that afternoon and now he was invincible. God the Father on the throne, a bottle of stout for his crosier, and Ma in the scullery brewing tea for the full house in the kitchen. We were all there, apart from Frankie, who was asleep in his bed. Mossie had the armchair by the fire and I had Mossie's knee. The rest were in a circle around the table with Da at the head under the clock that never told the right time. He lifted the bottle of stout to his lips with great style. A great big arc of his arm, it never varied. Like a statue in a museum, it seemed frozen in time. The bottle glued to his lips, the river of sound in his throat and the slow drag of his mouth across the neck to finish. Then the best part, when he replaced it on the table and the surge of foam pushed itself out to let you know the volcano had life in it yet.

—How many do you have?

The question was directed at Mahony. Da could make an argument out of nothing, which made him a God, I suppose. I heard Ma saying that if she left him he'd argue himself to death. Da said he never argued, he discussed things. Mahony looked like he had an answer but couldn't get it out. I saw him looking across at Noel Dargan. Finally, he exploded into laughter. An hysterical laugh. Shea, Ita, Johnny and me all

33

laughed but we didn't know what we were laughing at. When it stopped, all eyes were on Da again.

—How many followers do you have? Do you have even one?

There was an eerie silence. Mahony nodded his head. He looked very impressive.

—Yes.

He looked around at the faces, one by one. His tone was priestly. Like he was turning water into wine.

—I have one who follows me. Follows me all the time.

Mahony blessed himself. We all blessed ourselves. It was an automatic thing. He picked up his glass of stout from the table and sipped it like a chalice. We were all bursting. Mahony kept the silence going. Liam Dargan couldn't take it any more.

—Who is he, Mahony?

—He's—

He looked out over his glasses.

—He's a—

He took another sip from his glass. Liam was lepping with curiosity.

—Who is he, who follows you?

Mahony drained the glass and turned to face us.

—He's a detective from the fraud squad.

The room exploded into laughter, most of it directed at Liam Dargan. Mahony was so convulsed he had to go out to the backyard for air. Noel Dargan wasn't laughing but he went out for air, too. Mossie coughed his guts up and spat them in the fire. Shea ran upstairs to the toilet – I heard him press the button B on the phone. Ita went out to the scullery to help Ma. I looked across at Da. He lifted the bottle to his lips and left it there 'til it drained. He took a full one from the brown paper bag and opened it with the satisfaction of a magician giving a genie her freedom. Mahony came back in holding his broken glasses in his hand. He was followed

34

by Noel Dargan, who had a look of satisfaction on his face. The night was young yet. Sometimes you just know.

*

I don't know why Da ended up on the floor with Noel Dargan. The ex-soldier made a remark about meeting fighting men in the Congo from every county in Ireland except Dublin. Da took offence at the slight to his native city. I could hear his voice rising up with every word. It was moving from a discourse to a row. They tried to settle it by arm wrestling. The hands went one way, then the other. Da knocked over the sugar bowl and Liam Dargan accused him of cheating. Da went beetroot. Next thing, it was shirts and vests off. They were going to settle it by Greek wrestling, once and for all. What were they settling? Da said fighting was the last refuge of a bowsie. Here he was wrestling with a murderer. I went out to the scullery. I wanted Ma to stop him fighting. I wanted her to know the danger Da was in but I didn't want to tell her all I knew. How could I tell her I'd seen the scar? That I'd touched it? Worse still, how it got there? I said nothing. I'd have to risk Da getting killed, that was the awful truth. I'd have to carry it on my conscience for the rest of my life. I went back into the kitchen to await the outcome.

They had each other in a headlock and were squeezing for all they were worth.

—Do you give in?

—No, do you?

That went on for ages. Ages and ages. They looked like dead jellyfish at the edge of the sea. Two lumps of blubber. I could see the crack of me Da's arse sticking out over the top of his trousers. It was embarrassing. The purple birth mark at the top of his shoulder was more embarrassing. It looked like it was alive, that it was growing there. You

35

couldn't see much of Noel 'cos he was covered in hair. Every so often when he rolled the right way you could see the top of his scar sticking out above his trousers.

—Do you give in?

—No, do you?

Mossie was the appointed referee but he got fed up after a half an hour and was back in the armchair by the fire. Liam was the only one still interested in the fight.

—Go on, Noel, go on ya boy, ya, think of the Congo.

Mahony was sitting at the table with a tube of glue. He was trying to stick his glasses together after the incident in the backyard. It was no good, he couldn't stick them without wearing them, and he couldn't wear them because they were broken. He asked Ita to get him Sellotape. Shea was looking up the football fixtures for the Saturday and Johnny was asleep under the table on a blanket. I was burning Mossie's matches and throwing them in the fire. Ma came in from the scullery with a fresh pot.

—Are you ready for your tea, Da?

—Do I look like I'm ready for my tea?

She stepped over the bodies on the floor and poured the tea. We all pulled our chairs in so that the wrestlers were on the outside. I knew Da would never give in. He was not going to let a jumped up culchie from Tipperary get the better of him. Mossie stood over the two of them.

—I'm declaring this contest a draw.

Neither of them budged.

—Anna's poured the tea, gentlemen.

He was humiliating them with manners.

—If you get up now, you're both winners. If not, you're both losers.

They'd been over an hour on the floor. Mossie reached out a hand to each of them. The temptation was too much. They started to drag themselves up from the floor. Mossie grabbed a wrist apiece and raised their hands in the air.

—The winner, ladies and gentlemen, is a draw.

We clapped. Da and Noel shook hands.

—You're lucky I'm not twenty years younger.

—I took pity on you because of your age.

Suddenly, they were at it again and pushed each other from one side of the room to the other. We scattered to the four corners as the dishes on the table started to hop. Ma came in from the scullery, very calm but very determined. She didn't even raise her voice.

—I'm getting my hat and coat.

It was a favourite of Ma's even though she never wore a hat.

—Don't, Ma!

It was a chorus of voices. Johnny woke up under the table and started to cry. It brought everyone to their senses. Da took his place at the table, Ma hung her coat back up and we all put sugar and milk in our tea. There was a silence. No one needed to fill it. And no one did.

*

Mahony was upstairs in bed when the word came through. We'd been waiting all Friday for the phone call. Ma answered when it rang. She came down from the hall and said it was for Mossie. My heart started to race. We all tried not to listen, but you couldn't help hearing Mossie's thick accent up in the hall. Even thicker now he was talking to his own. The bell tingled when he replaced the receiver. The humans were tingling too. He came in the door and Da handed him a stout.

—Tullow Lady runs at Tramore tomorrow. They can't see her being beat, can't see her being beat, boy.

I flew up the stairs to tell Mahony. I'd promised to bring him the news. He was in his usual position on the bed, staring at me from behind Sellotape. He'd heard the excitement downstairs so I didn't need to say much. I felt sorry he was alone. He didn't go downstairs much now if Noel Dargan was there, unless he was drunk. He was sober tonight, which meant he was broke, which meant he had nothing to put on the horse. I didn't know what to say. I asked him was he going to go to sleep.

—I never sleep.

I'd forgotten. I'd never seen him asleep. Not since he came to our house. I asked him when he'd last slept.

—Fourteen years ago.

I tried to imagine it but I couldn't.

—Means I don't miss a thing. I love it.

He gave his usual chuckle. He looked like a child. A grown up child. I didn't want to leave him on his own but my mind kept racing to what was going on downstairs. He read my thoughts.

—I know you want to go, it's all right.

I lied and sat on the bed. I looked at him and tried to imagine him in his monk's clothes. It was easy to imagine him in a brown habit collecting eggs from chickens in the middle of the night. An insomniac monk. I asked him what order he was in. He showed me references from Blackburn Abbey signed by the Abbot. They were glowing tributes to his character.

—Do you know who founded the order?

I couldn't think of a famous monk. In the end I said Friar Tuck. I could see the chuckle inside him rising up through his body. It burst out his face.

—I founded it. It's my order. I made me a monk and I kicked me out, 'cos I wouldn't go asleep when I was told.

He hopped out of bed and was halfway down the stairs to the kitchen before I knew it. I don't know what came over him. He didn't seem afraid any more. He bounded into the kitchen, declared he wasn't dead and offered to pour tea.

Everyone declined. Mossie called for hush and Da launched into the proper version of 'Frankie and Johnny'.

*

We spent all of Saturday morning spreading the bets on Tullow Lady. Small amounts in each betting shop. Large bets would only cause alarm bells. If word got back to the race course the odds on the horse would shorten and defeat what we were trying to do. Everyone, including the owner and the trainer, were backing it in the SP offices to ensure a good starting price.

I brought Mahony to O'Toole's Pawnbrokers on Amiens Street. He handed in his overcoat, his suit and his watch. The pawnbroker was examining the watch through an eye piece when Mahony dropped a silver cross in front of him.

—A memento from my days as a monk.

He turned to me and did his hysterical laugh. The pawnbroker thought he was crazy. He didn't even examine the cross. He offered thirty shillings on the goods and Mahony haggled with him but accepted the offer made. We went down to a small little bookie's shop in Killarney Street, beside the egg store, and Mahony placed the entire thirty shillings on Tullow Lady.

Tramore was only a small country meeting and didn't feature in radio commentaries on Saturday sport. Da was not to be outdone. From his contacts in Shelbourne Park he got the number of a public phone in the tote office at Tramore races. At a minute to three he made the call and got through. The contact in Tramore stuck the receiver out of a window so that we could hear the course commentary on the race. Mossie was elected to hold the phone and relayed the commentary to us as he got it.

—They're under starter's orders.

The crowd in our house were standing in the hall and sitting on the stairs. Nobody said a word.

—They're off.

Mahony sat beside me. His leg was shaking. I moved away. Da was leaning against the frame of the door. Most people had their heads in their hands and were staring at the floor.

—They're all in a bunch. Nobody wants to make the running. Gallic War is gone on. Two lengths in front. Four lengths. Starting to spread the field. Seven furlongs to race. Gallic War is six lengths to the good. Flash of Steel is in second place and the favourite My Bonny Girl is in third. Tullow Lady is in fourth and improving. They've three furlongs to run. Gallic War is starting to come back to the field. The lead is down to two lengths. One length. My Bonny Girl has joined Gallic War. Tullow Lady is coming with a run on the outside. They're inside the final furlong. It's My Bonny Girl from Tullow Lady. Two hundred yards to race. It's My Bonny Girl by a head. But here comes Tullow Lady.

The hall, stairs and landing started to vibrate. It was like a scene out of hell. Some were screaming the horse's name, others were screaming to hear, and some were just screaming a scream. Mossie's voice was booming out over all the mayhem.

—They're going to the line together. It's neck and neck. And at the post, they've gone by together. It's a photo finish.

Da was screaming for a paper to get the race numbers. Shea had it open in a second. He called it out.

—Our horse is number ten.

Mossie was calling for order.

—Here comes the result of the race.

It seemed like an eternity. We only wanted to hear one number.

—First, number ten.

I don't remember anything after that. It was pandemonium. Everyone hugged everyone. Da hugged Mossie. I hugged Shea. Shea hugged Ita. Ita hugged me. Johnny hugged

Frankie. Frankie hugged Da who was still hugging Mossie. The neighbours all hugged each other. Mahony hugged Noel Dargan.

It was a great advertisement for gambling. Tullow Lady was returned at one hundred to eight. That's twelve and a half to one. It was the biggest pay day ever. I had a shilling on and that was just me. I had thirteen shillings and sixpence coming back. We were all nearly millionaires. Mahony grabbed me by the shoulders.

—I told you this house was blessed, I told you.

I looked at Da. I had never seen him so happy in all my life. I looked at Mossie. He was a culchie and I loved him. I looked at Ma, the maker of it all. She would let Da think it was his doing. But she'd made it happen. Out of her own pain and suffering, she'd brought the lodgers into our house and with it the system to finally beat the bookies.

3

1961

The thing I hated most about school was being sent out for the 'mitchers'. Mitchers were boys who didn't go to school. They hung out down the 'naller', which was our word for the canal. On the far side of the naller was a broken ship left there by the Vikings who plundered and raped Dublin until they ran into dockers from Sheriff Street and scarpered. The Vikings settled up on Christ Church Hill on the south side. The native Dubliner stayed on the north side with the river for ever separating the two sides. Beyond the broken ship was the railway line to Sligo. Towering over these up on the metal bridge was the line to Drogheda, Dundalk and the North. To travel on any of those trains you had to buy a ticket first from my Da in the booking office at Amiens Street station.

There were boys who mitched occasionally and boys who mitched the whole year round. Brother Denehy referred to the latter as the hard core. We referred to Denehy as The Mongrel. The top of his little finger was missing. He'd had it bitten off by a German Shepherd dog. Andy Griffin said he was put out of the Gestapo for cruelty but got into the Christian Brothers with flying colours. In winter, the hard core hung out in broken down houses where they could light a fire to keep warm. Once Easter brought the resurrected sun, it was the annual pilgrimage to the naller. The ranks of the hard core swelled. They infected others, just like the

42

rotten apple in the barrel. The naller became an outdoor jungle where skinny Tarzans fought each other for supremacy of the broken ship. Every time a train went by they banged their chests with their fists and howled to the sun like demented apes.

I was sent by The Mongrel to request these boys to return to school. He informed me to inform them that Artane Industrial School (worse than any prison) awaited them if they refused to come in. They had one foot in the door, as he put it. It was the worst job in the world since Judas kissed Jesus. The mitchers were having a party and I was telling them to stop. Worse than that, I was requesting them to come to their own execution and be happy about it.

The Mongrel hated me because I did well in the exams. He hated the mitchers because they wouldn't come to school. He hated Lloyd George because he tricked Michael Collins into signing the Treaty. He hated Michael Collins because he signed the Treaty. He hated De Valera for signing the Oath of Allegiance. He hated Hitler for losing the Second World War. He hated America for joining up with Britain against Germany. He hated all foreign games, especially soccer. He loved some things just as much as he hated other things. He loved Gaelic football, the Irish language, the Gaelic league, anything with the word Gaelic in it, Connemara, Mayo, the Ring of Kerry, Sinn Fein, the IRA and most of all he loved 'nancy boys'. The nancy boys sat at the back of our class. During Christian Doctrine he would go over the Commandments with them, while he slipped his hand down their trousers. Nancy boys never fought back, which is what made them nancy boys in the first place.

Andy Griffin was one of the hard core. Denehy knew he was my best friend. That's why he sent me to get him. He liked the idea that he could force me to betray my friend. I might be the best in the class at reading, writing and arithmetic but there were other ways to cut me down to size.

When he called me to the front of the class he had his desk flap open. I could see the light of his mirror dancing across his face. He ran the comb through his hair, both sides, to make a perfect duck's arse at the back.

—Do you know where Andy Griffin is?

—No, sir.

He took the wrong end of a Biro, pushed it against his face and popped a blackhead.

—Do you know where the mitchers are?

He knew I knew. A denial would be seen as weakness.

—Yes, sir.

—We have a Cigire coming to the school tomorrow. If they're not here, he'll have them sent away.

I thought about Andy all the way to the naller. He didn't want to be sent to Artane. No one did. He just hated school. When he was asked a question, fear took over. He could only think of what would happen if he got it wrong. He couldn't think of an answer. He peed in his trousers once when The Mongrel asked him a question. It was a simple question. Which was longer, the radius or the diameter of a circle? There was an awful silence. The Mongrel took his silence for defiance. I hated it when that happened.

—Are you going to answer me?

It was fifty-fifty. I prayed for him to pick the right one.

—A rectangle, sir.

The class laughed. The Mongrel was frothing at the mouth with anger. Andy was in serious trouble. When he went up to get six of the best, I saw the pool of water on his seat. I put blotting paper on the wee and soaked it up.

Andy wasn't good at school but he was brilliant at finding money. He taught me the secrets of the trade. Shores were good. The dirtier the better. Money got clogged in the silt. If you went through it with a stick you could detect the metal sound. Afterwards you could wash it and shine it with bread. Bread made the copper shine like new. He taught me to carry cases, too. You waited at the bottom of the steps at Amiens Street station. You waited 'til you saw a woman falling down with too many bags, then you pounced.

—Carry your case, ma'am?

One time we carried to the Gresham Hotel and got ten shillings. We bought thirty penny bars each, went to the Elec cinema, sat in the soft seats and jeered the crowd sitting in the wooders.

I could hear sounds coming from the naller at two hundred yards. Screams followed by the splash of water. A silence followed by squeals and the splash of water again. It made me smile. It was a better sound than the school sound. It was free. There was no fear like in the schoolyard, it had its own voice. I thought about the prisoners in Mountjoy Gaol further up the naller. The Mongrel said the hard core would end up there. Artane first and then Mountjoy. I wondered if the prisoners could hear the water splash. Did it remind them of their school-days? Did they scream out of their cell windows for the screaming to stop because it hurt too much? Maybe they thought the hard core were laughing at them. Maybe they were screaming out warnings that smothered under the noise of trains and cars and horses and carts.

Soon as I came over the brow I could see Scissors Kane on the top of the broken ship, ready to dive. He froze when he saw me. I froze, too. Hard Head Hogan, Mickabird Langan and Mousey Mitchell were shivering on the bank. I didn't need to say anything, they knew why I was there.

—Fuck off, Shero, we're not going in.

Scissors Kane was in mid-air before he'd finished his sentence. Milliseconds later there were four bodies in mid-air.

—We're not going in!

Splash. They disappeared. I looked around. Four school bags. Four piles of clothes. No sign of Andy. The heads came out of the water gasping for air. I asked after Andy.

—He's up town looking for money.

I told them about the Cigire. Scissors dived under the water and stuck his arse up in the air. The others followed, like seals, in three-part harmony. I started to walk away. I heard Scissors' voice shouting after me.

—Tell the Cigire he can kiss my bleeding arse.

His words were ringing in my ear as I headed away from the naller back to school.

*

Ita had a dream about white smoke. It was belching out of the chimney and filling the whole street. Ma said it might mean a new Pope. Johnny said it was a train because Da worked in the station. Ita said there was so much smoke in the house we couldn't find our way outside. Ma said it was nothing to worry about. Shea said it was symbolic – the house was a coffin. Ma said she wasn't sure about that secondary school education at all. Da put down his paper and said that everyone had bad dreams only most people forgot them by the time they woke in the morning. The secret was not to wake up but stay asleep until they faded away into the subconscious. Ita said she couldn't stop herself waking up. Da said you could train yourself to do anything.

—The human brain is a limitless machine.

Da was perverse. There had to be an explanation for everything and he had to have it. Ita didn't want an explanation. She wanted a big person to wrap her up and make her safe. Da couldn't 'cos he was in the middle of an argument. Ma couldn't 'cos she had too many people to look after since the lodgers arrived. Ita was alone in a house full of men. I felt sorry that she had no sister to tell her secrets to. She had a sixth sense and she also had her own room which she didn't share with anyone. What did she do in the middle of the night when she woke up and there was no one there? I decided to marry her. It would save me looking for

46

a girlfriend and I'd know what to do when she had bad dreams.

Shea and Da were at loggerheads over the meaning of the smoke. Symbols versus logic. Mrs Scally from next door appeared at the window of the kitchen. Ma called her in. She produced a piece of yellow brick from her handbag and showed it to Da. It had fallen on her. In broad daylight. She was passing by our gable wall, minding her own business, when it hit her on the head. Hit her on the head and nearly knocked her down. God's blessing she wasn't killed. She held her hand out with the brick in it. Da was white in the face. He reached out to take it when Mrs Scally bent her head right down in front of him.

—Feel it for yourself.

Da felt the lump at the top of her head.

—That's an awful lump.

—I'm lucky I wasn't killed.

Ma made an ice pack from the fridge. Ita got out a china cup and poured tea. Da examined the piece of yellow brick from every angle. We all tut tutted about the yellow brick, but inside we were all wondering what the white smoke had to do with Mrs Scally's head.

I thought about it all the way up Emerald Street. Chimney pots, white smoke, yellow brick, Mrs Scally's head. I turned left into Sheriffer, past the boys' playground. A ball flew over the railings and bounced in front of me. A chorus of voices rang out.

—Shero!

I lammed the ball in the air, high as a chimney. It turned into a yellow brick. Someone headed it and it turned into white smoke. I couldn't think about football and I was captain of Sheriff United under 12's. I made my way into the flats. I paused at the bottom of the steps. I gulped in a bellyful of air and ran up as fast as I could. Even so, the tang of piss stole into my nostrils. Piss mixed with vegetables.

Why did kids piss on their own stairs? Why did people leave their rubbish chutes open? Was it because it didn't belong to them but belonged to Dublin Corporation? I could live happily in the flats if it wasn't for the smell.

Andy's hall door was open and voices were coming from inside. They were angry voices. I didn't like to knock. I stepped into their hall for a moment. I came back out onto the balcony. I waited. I don't know what I was waiting for. For something to happen. I don't know. For the talking to stop. For Andy to come out. I peeped in through the net curtain. Mr Griffin looked like he was dead. He was sitting with his head flat on the table and his arms awkwardly down by his side. His mouth was open. Andy was sitting opposite his father and beside his sister, Catherine. The five younger Griffins were seated around the table, silent with fear. Andy pointed at his father.

—See him, he's a pig. He's a drunken pig who drank our food.

A knob of butter came flying through the air at Andy, missed him and crashed into the wall. It stuck. Mrs Griffin appeared from the same direction as the butter and slammed a packet of Marietta biscuits down on the table. She stuck her face right up to Andy's and screamed at him.

—He's not a pig, he's your father.

Catherine plucked the butter off the wall and put it in the middle of the table. She picked up a knife and buttered two Marietta before pressing them together into a sandwich. Little maggots of butter crawled out through the holes. She handed it to one of the kids who licked the maggots off. Mrs Griffin swayed with the teapot. She aimed the spout at one of the cups but couldn't stop her arm from shaking. She rested the spout on the rim of a cup. She tipped the teapot up and started to pour. Steam rose from the cup before it toppled over and the liquid-brown river made for the edge of the table at speed. The kids pulled their chairs back just in time and it spilled over in a waterfall to the floor. Mrs Griffin tried to stop the flow with her free hand before Andy took the teapot from her and Catherine started to cry.

—Look what you're doing, Mammy?

Mr Griffin let out a big snore. Mrs Griffin turned on him.

—That pig made me do it. I should have poured the tea on him. Get a cloth, someone, a cloth.

I couldn't knock for Andy now. Not with all this going on. I'd have to write a note and drop it in his letter box. Explain about the Cigire coming. Maybe it was all a waste of time. Maybe tomorrow he'd have to go out looking for money again.

—What are you doing there?

Catherine was out on the balcony taking a floor cloth off the line. I felt like she'd caught me going through her underwear. I opened my mouth but nothing came. I stared at the outline of her definite breasts.

—Were you spying on us?

I couldn't tell her why I was there. I couldn't tell her without squealing on Andy. My only thought was that her breasts were mountains that formed a valley.

—Is Andy coming out?

Catherine retreated with her cloth and Andy came to the door.

—I can't go out. Me oul' fella's in here drunk. Me oul' wan's not far behind.

He didn't try to cover up the truth. That was the thing about Andy. He was tough but he was innocent. Much more innocent than tough. He'd say things that were shocking, but you knew they were true. Poor people took parcels from the Vincent de Paul but they denied it. Andy would tell me what the Vincents said when they were in his house. And the amount that was in the brown envelope. It was a great thing knowing you'd always get the truth from someone. It was the main reason why Andy Griffin was my best pal.

I could ask him things I couldn't ask another living soul. He'd never judge me. I showed him a scurvy patch on my willy and he asked me had I gone to the toilet in any strange place – like the men's metal cubicle at Capel Street Bridge. He thought it might be the pox. If it was, it would spread. I checked my willy fifty times a day. Andy started calling me a 'poxy bastard'. He winked every time he said it. It was a private joke. The scurvy disappeared but I didn't tell him 'cos I loved him calling me a poxy bastard when no one else understood. We were standing next to each other in the school toilets one day when he looked across at me.

—Are you still a poxy bastard?

He was concerned about me. Worried. He wasn't trying to be funny. He was just being a pal.

—No, I'm not.

He never called me a poxy bastard again after that.

I told him what Denehy said. Told him about the Cigire. He didn't seem to care. His mind was on other things like looking for money, I'm sure.

*

Da was inspecting the scene of the accident. Gathered around him were curious neighbours. Mossie and Mahony were there, too. Da moved back down Seville Place for a long-distance view. There was no doubting the evidence. The brick matched. The general consensus was that it had come loose during the erection of the aerial. Da didn't believe it. Not for one second. He'd been up and down ladders to the roof too many times to leave debris lying around in his wake. He was a meticulous cleaner upper. It was a cardinal rule. Cleanliness is next to godliness.

Da knew in his water it was more sinister. Directly beneath the chimney on the footpath he drew two chalk lines using a pumice stone. Along each line, in block capitals he wrote, KEEP OUT. After an inspection he went back and added the word DANGER. Within five minutes every kid in Seville Place and Emerald Street were dancing jigs between the white lines. Football, boxing, judo, wrestling and hop-scotch vied with each other for supremacy of the chalk square. Da knew he'd made a mistake but he couldn't admit it. He'd never admit it. Like King Canute he believed he could stem any tide. He got a bucket of cold water and threw it on the chalk marks in disgust. That was as near as he came to admitting a mistake. I could sense the rage in him building. I saw it in his eyes. I knew what was coming. I tried to shut it out but it was no good.

—Get the ladders out.

It turned out to be a scouting mission only. He measured the chimney stack from every direction. He recorded the figures onto the back of a bookie's docket. He inspected the chimney pots. Giant Georgian funnels. Works of art, he called them. He showed me the maker's inscription at the bottom. Blythman and Sons, Sheffield. He rubbed his fingers along the elevated letters. A gentle caress.

—That's when they had an Empire.

He stretched the cloth measuring tape around the chimney. I squeezed my finger where it met. Da recorded the number. I let the tape go. We repeated the process again. Measure twice and cut once. It was a cardinal rule.

The chimneys were coming down. Da unveiled the plan during supper. There was shock all around. The lodgers were shocked, the kids were shocked and Ma was shocked. Such was the shock that uneaten bread was left on the plate.

—Subsidence.

It had come to Da sitting on the toilet pan thinking of his old friend Archimedes.

—Subsidence.

I had never heard the word before. I wondered was it related to 'eureka'. That's what Archimedes said when he figured something out. Da always said he wanted to call Ita eureka only Ma insisted on calling her Ita after her sister. Da said it was a tragedy of Greek proportions in the making.

—Subsidence.

It was due to pressure. Gravity. Weight. Forces you can't escape. Why was it happening now, that was the big question? Why did subsidence wait to strike until the moment Mrs Scally walked by our gable wall? Weren't the chimney pots always pushing down on the chimney stack? The questions were coming hard and fast at Da. He was isolated at the supper table. Mossie winked over at me.

—I think you've got it wrong this time, Peter.

Mahony was straight in.

—You're a minority of one. Jesus Christ had twelve, you have none.

All Mahony ever wanted was an argument. Da loved an argument, too, but he hated anybody using his own quotes back at him. They were strictly copyright. Noel Dargan couldn't pronounce subsidence but he partly agreed with Da 'cos that contradicted Mahony.

—Sorry, you're a minority of two.

Mahony was treading on ice thinner than he could ever imagine. The supper table was stacked against the subsidence theory but Mahony was trying to rub salt into the wound. He was succeeding somewhat until Da produced his trump card. The aerial. 'Resistance creates an equal force but in an opposite direction.' It was an ancient law of science. Da explained that it wasn't the downward pressure of the pots but the lateral pressure of the aerial caught in cross winds that was causing the said subsidence. QED. I didn't understand it but it had a ring to it. Noel Dargan was smiling from ear to ear like he'd just won the Nobel Prize for physics. He stuck a finger in Mahony's face.

—QE fucking D.

There was instant shock at Noel Dargan's language, which he apologized profusely for using in front of the kids.

Cursing to win an argument was not in the rules. Mahony confided that he'd done science at school but he'd never heard of this law.

—Sounds like Sheridan's law to me.

Ma was getting irritated. She put on her telephone voice.

—You may go elsewhere for digs if you want an argument.

Mossie offered Ma a cigarette.

—Good woman, Anna.

Ma took the cigarette and Mahony offered her a light. It was his way to make peace. Ma took it and calm returned to the kitchen. Da launched into the story of the long plank. He claimed he could balance the world on a plank if the plank was long enough. Hard to imagine but it was true. Likewise, it was hard to imagine the aerial could be so destructive, but it was a fool who would underestimate it. That slip of an aerial on our roof could cause untold subsidence. And had, probably.

In the calm established by Ma, everyone was thinking of the plank.

—How long exactly would it need to be?

—Very long.

—A mile long?

—Much longer. From here to America maybe.

—Would need to be thick, too.

—Thickness doesn't matter, it's the length.

—Would it not break?

—Not if it was mahogany.

The discussion went on and on, just like the plank itself. Twenty questions. A hundred questions. A million light years. Hard-to-imagine stuff. Mind over matter stuff. Scientists in baths. In laboratories. In mad houses. Archimedes, Newton, Einstein. Seville Place Academy for Science. Da the president of. In his elemental. Current discussion, electric stuff. And still the question of the plank. No matter where we travelled in the galaxy it was back to the question of the long plank.

I stopped thinking about the plank and thought instead of the ladders. I was up on the roof. Up there with Da. Up there and wondering how he was going to get the chimney pots down. Up there and wondering what my part was going to be in their downfall.

*

Denehy didn't say boo to Andy. Normally he'd give six on each hand for mitching. He was nervous with the Cigire coming. He spoke nicely to us. His soutane was pressed, no horrible chalk marks on it. His shoes were polished. No sign of the leather in his belt. He wanted us to look civilized.

I felt proud. Andy had come to school. I knew the importance of school. All throughout history. Educate that you may be free. People risking everything for knowledge. A good education. Foundation stone for life, according to Da.

Andy overcame a lot to come to school. No food in his belly. No food in his house. His father with a hangover. His mother, too, maybe. He could have gone up town looking in shores. Or stood at the steps of the station waiting for a case. He'd come to school when his father would expect a cider home. Or a bottle of stout. He'd come to school. Maybe he was out to spite his father. I felt guilty that I felt proud. I had nothing to be proud of. Andy was afraid but he'd overcome his fear, that was the biggest thing. The Mongrel didn't understand fear, he caused it. He took pleasure in it. He loved it when boys became jelly in front of him. He slurped them up. He loved tears the most. He drank tears like a vampire drinks blood. Fear was his power. It allowed him to beat knowledge into us.

And it allowed him to fondle the nancy boys.

We practised for the Cigire's arrival. He got us to imagine a knock on the door. Denehy answered it. He spoke to the imaginary Cigire and brought him into the class. We all stood. Desks too noisy. We started again. We all sat. He told us once more to imagine the Cigire outside the door. There was a knock. Denehy turned on the class in temper.

—Was that you, Griffin?

—No, sir.

Andy's face went white. It was the tone in Denehy's voice. Rage. A volcano about to burst. He was about to launch at Andy when there was another knock. It was for real. He straightened his soutane and made for the door. He opened it and the Cigire came in. We stood without a sound. Not even the creaking of a seat hinge.

—*Dia dhaoibh.*

—*Dia is Muire duit.*

We'd been practising. The Cigire was impressed.

—*Suígí anois.*

We sat down. He turned his back on us and spoke to Denehy. You could hear the silence in Sheriff Street. They whispered in Irish. The Cigire wore black, just like a bus inspector but he wasn't here to inspect tickets, he was here to test our knowledge. If we failed he could have us put back a class or put out of the school altogether. Bus inspectors could put you off the bus for not paying your fare but that wasn't the only reason they checked your ticket. They were also making sure the bus conductor wasn't 'making the rent'. That was the bus slang for stealing. I heard it from Da. He knew a conductor who was sacked for making the rent.

I wondered if a teacher could get sacked. Maybe if the pupils knew nothing. It was a wonderful thought. We could give the Cigire wrong answers. On purpose. Five ones are four. Five twos are eight. Five threes are twelve. London is the capital of France and Paris is the capital of Outer Mongolia. I wanted to turn around and whisper it to the whole class.

—Answer everything wrong. Get Denehy sacked.

The Cigire introduced himself as Father Brown. He

wanted to ask us a few simple questions from our catechisms. Why were we having a Christian Doctrine test? We'd prepared all week for reading, writing and arithmetic. Even Denehy seemed surprised. Andy gave me a dirty look. I shrugged my shoulders. Father Brown asked a question.

—How many Persons in the Trinity?

Soon as he had half the sentence out Mickey Grey was out of his seat like a greyhound in Shelbourne Park.

—Sir, sir, sir, sir, sir, sir—

Spewed out in a continuous stream with his hand straight out in a Nazi salute. Mickey Grey always said the same thing if he was asked.

—Don't tell me, sir.

If he was asked his date of birth.

—Don't tell me, sir.

He'd wait for a prompt.

—I know it, sir, don't tell me.

He never got a prompt, we loved watching his agony too much.

—Was going over it with me brother last night, sir, don't tell me.

When he was given the answer.

—Why did you tell me, I knew it, sir.

Somehow he got away with it. Every time. He could make teachers laugh, that was it. He had no fear. Father Brown pointed at him.

—Don't tell me, sir.

—I'm not going to tell you because you obviously know it.

The whole class laughed. Mickey Grey put on his disappointed face and did his disappointed sit down. Denehy's face went from rage to laughter in the space of about one and a half seconds. Father Brown picked out Joseph Smith whose middle name was Mary so he was only ever known in Sheriff Street as Joseph and Mary. Joseph and Mary Smith cleared his throat and bellowed out the answer.

—There are three divine persons in the One God. The Father, the Son and the Holy Ghost.

Father Brown seemed pleased with the answer. He gave a satisfied look to Denehy. He asked how many of us knew what tablets were? Not the ones for a headache, he was quick to point out. He reminded us of the scene where Moses went up the mountain and came down with two tablets of stone. On the tablets were God's laws for us. How many laws were written on the tablets of stone? He looked around the room at all the faces. Some hands went up in the air. He told them to take them down. He pointed at Andy. Andy stared blankly back at him.

—Me, sir?

—Yes you, sir.

A shadow descended on the room as the sun went in behind the clouds. It got cooler. I could feel the bundle of terror sitting beside me. I could see Denehy straight in front of me. I could feel him willing Andy to say the right answer.

—How many commandments did Moses receive?

How could fear paralyse him so much? He knew the answer. He'd seen Charlton Heston get them in the Elec. We'd seen it together. God spoke to Moses and then the lightning came and burnt the stone. All he had to do was remember the tablets of stone. All that was happening was lockjaw.

—How many laws were written on the tablets of stone?

Denehy moved directly behind Father Brown. Andy was staring straight at him. He raised his two arms behind the priest's back. He raised them high into the air. He unfurled his fingers and splayed them. As he did the sun came out from behind the clouds and streams of light came in through the window. Denehy looked like the Holy Ghost descending on the apostles imparting his knowledge to the world. He was willing him, threatening him, terrifying him, cajoling him, instructing him, hypnotising him. In reality he was terrifying him, like he always terrified him, his chicken was coming home to roost.

Andy opened his mouth to speak. He didn't look at the priest. He looked only at Denehy.

—Nine and a half.

Father Brown couldn't believe his ears. He stared at the hole that was Andy's mouth.

—Nine and a half commandments? Where did the other half go?

—I don't know, sir.

—You don't know?

Andy shrugged. Denehy remained as he was, frozen in time, his hands in the air. Father Brown turned to him and the hands came quickly down by his side. The men retreated to a corner for more Irish conversation. It quickly turned into English. Denehy had been caught making the rent or whatever the equivalent was. He was in big trouble. Bad and all as that was, there was no word I knew in any language to describe the situation Andy was in.

When the Cigire left, Denehy stayed at his desk with his back to us. He looked like he was sobbing. No one said a word or took a book out. Denehy went to the cupboard and opened it. He took the leather out and put it in his belt. He went to the door and opened it. He stood there and called Andy with his finger. He didn't look at him, just called him silently with his finger. He left the room. His footsteps in the corridor sounded like claps of thunder.

Andy got out of his desk. He looked like a spastic. I thought he was going to fall down. His legs looked like they were taking him towards the door but his chest and head seemed like they wanted to fly out the window. I'd heard stories about men going to the gallows. Falling down in a heap and having to be carried. Men wearing nappies because they shat themselves with fear. Fear was a scent for Denehy.

It turned him into a mongrel with green eyes and froth on his lips.

We heard the footsteps move away from us. The key in the lock of the sports room at the end of the corridor. It was where the school jerseys were kept. The green and white of O'Toole's. Why was he being brought in there? The sound of the leather was unmistakable. It made me wince. A sharp sound. A rasping sound. It made me count. Two. White skin turning red. The leather lighting a fire. A fire that spreads. Three. Tears might put it out. You won't let them come. The arsonist wins if you do. Four. I'm not proud any more. Not of Andy. Not of me. Not of education. Not of school. Not of knowledge. Five. I want to burn the school down. Turn it into hell. Let it burn to ashes. Six. I want Denehy to burn 'til his flesh peels. For all eternity. No mercy. He gives none, let him get none. The sound of his footsteps again. He came into the class breathing heavily.

—Take out your jotters for a spelling test.

We rummaged in our bags. A quiet rummage. Andy appeared in the doorway. Closed the door behind him and made for his desk. He looked like an old timer in a cowboy film. His eyes were red and his legs were bent. He stepped into his desk but couldn't bend his knees. He tried several times to sit but he couldn't. Denehy stared at him, a hateful stare.

—What's the matter with you?

—I can't sit down, sir.

Denehy continued to stare at him like he was a fool.

—Stand in the corner, you amadán.

Andy hobbled across to the line like a scalded cat. Denehy called for quiet and the spelling test began.

—Disobedience. Break it up. Dis. O. Be. Dience.

*

Andy stood beside my bed with his trousers down. I had the cream Ma used for nappy rash. Sudocrem. She swore by it.

I picked up a blob with my finger. It felt cold. I looked at his pink arse and wondered where to start. The marks of the leather were visible all over it. I picked the worst spot and dabbed it with my finger. Andy jumped two feet in the air.

—Daddy . . . Daddy . . . Daddy . . . Daddy . . . Daddy . . .

I should have warned him it was cold. I told him to bite his finger 'til it hurt. He did that and I rubbed the Sudocrem all over. Gentle, gentle strokes of my finger across his tender skin. After a while he got used to it and didn't need to bite his finger any more. He relaxed his head back on his shoulders and closed his eyes.

—That's gorgeous. Don't stop. Ever.

I did it 'til the cream was caked on. No pink showing anywhere. Not even the soft baby hairs were visible. It looked like a map of the North Pole with a giant crack down the middle.

—Do you want me to do it to you?

—I'm not sore.

—Doesn't matter, it's gorgeous.

Why would I put Sudocrem on my arse if it wasn't sore? Why not if it was so gorgeous? I told him to pull up his trousers but he still couldn't bend. I pulled them up for him and gently slid them over his arse. He winced. I knew he wouldn't sit down for a few days yet.

*

I stood in McGowan's scrapyard with the letter in my hand. Mountains of metal all around me. Every colour and shape. Signs in gold lettering on green everywhere. Household scrap. Lead, iron and copper sought. Best prices. We pay more. On the paths between the metal stacks were pools of rust that never dried up. Men with carbuncle faces worked the scrap heaps. Men with hunched backs who never straightened up. They inhabited the bowels of the scrap heaps. Always dressed for winter. Long coats and mittens. No fingers. Woollen caps

60

and tap noses. Drip, drip, drip. They looked like they'd been bred for the job. By an iron father out of a copper mother. All the way back. They were born into the past. Outside these walls the city trundled on into tomorrow. In McGowan's it was always yesterday.

I handed the letter to a man they called Joxer. His nose leaked on to it but he didn't notice. He opened it out and started to read. '44 Seville Place. Dublin 1. 17th inst. Attention yard foreman McGowan's. Please supply the bearer with two only 24-inch diameter standard clay pots, or equivalent, and oblige. Fraternally yours, Peter J. Sheridan Esquire.' Joxer stumbled over some of the words. He called over his work mates. He handed me the letter and asked me to read it. I looked at the circle of dripping noses. I looked at the water smudges on the letter. I read out the address. The scrap men stood there with their mouths open. I felt like a circus act. I read the letter down to Da's name but left out the esquire bit. Joxer got all excited.

—You left out a word, you left out the last bit . . .!

I read it again from fraternally yours and finished with esquire. The scrap men repeated it back to me.

—Esquire . . . esquire . . .

One of them reached out and took the letter from me. He studied the handwriting, close to begin and then from far away.

—I thought Shakespeare was dead?

—He's alive and well and living in Dublin.

—Frame that, son, it'll be worth money in years to come.

I put the letter in my back pocket and followed Joxer. If only they knew. I had hundreds of letters like that. It was the first time I'd been made to read one out. It was going to be the last, too. In future I'd refuse all letters from Da. Shakespeare? I'd never tell a living soul.

Joxer disappeared in among the garden statues, door lintels and Doric columns. I stood in one of the rust pools like I was told. I could hear him pulling things around inside, then came the voice.

—You're in luck, Hamnet.

He emerged with a chimney pot. He put it down beside me. He disappeared and returned with a second.

—When can you deliver?

Joxer frowned. I knew the answer to my question.

—We don't deliver.

They had a sign at the front entrance, 'No deliveries'. It was Da's 'strategy'. Secure the pots and they might take pity on me.

—I don't live far. Seville Place.

—Show me that letter, Hamnet?

I put my hand in my pocket and felt it. What did he want the letter for? To make fun of me? Hamnet? He couldn't even get the name right. I went through my pockets pretending it wasn't there.

—Let me see your address?

I found it again. Joxer checked it and asked me to follow him. We wound our way to a small yard at the back of the offices. He pointed to a black cart standing against a wall. It was the strangest-looking cart I'd ever seen. Wheels that seemed too big. Two long handles that tapered at the end like a woman's hands. It had no side pieces and the floor was latticed. It looked like something from the Middle Ages.

—Do you know what that is?

I shook my head. I thought it might be an old pony trap but it looked too small.

—That's what they use to wheel baby coffins. In the cemetery. You'll bring it back, won't you?

Joxer loaded the chimney pots and I set off on the journey home. I cursed Da with every step. Sitting in his comfortable office in the train station. Selling train tickets to Belfast, Dundalk and Howth. The seaside. Normal people, doing normal things. I was going to have bad dreams for six months. A year. Nothing was more certain. I was wheeling my own coffin on a cart through Glasnevin Cemetery. My initials on the name plate.

I parked the cart at our back gate and went in to open the garage doors. I released the stay wires, another of Da's great inventions (protection against the unforeseen tornado) and pushed the doors back along their track. It took all my strength. I'd never done it on my own before. I went back outside to get the cart and there was Frankie sitting on it with his back against one of the pots, smiling up at me. I said nothing. I just beat him off the cart. Beat him with both fists until he ran crying into Ma in the scullery.

*

I finished a line of perfect writing and was wiping it with the blotting paper when the door of the classroom opened. Nobody appeared. Just a voice.

—Andrew Griffin in this class?

The voice sounded like broken glass. It repeated the question.

—Andrew Griffin in this class?

Andy shifted in the seat beside me.

—Yeah, Da.

Mr Griffin stepped into the class. He had on his Sunday suit and a trilby hat but his face was unshaven which made him look like he'd escaped from Grangegorman mad house. Denehy approached him cautiously and asked him to step outside the door. Mr Griffin ignored him.

—Come up here, Andy.

—Please, Da ... please ...

Andy curled up like a caterpillar beside me.

—Come up bleeding here.

Andy slithered out of the desk as Denehy got closer to Mr Griffin.

—You have no permission to be in this class.

Mr Griffin treated Denehy like he didn't exist. Andy stood before his father.

—Take down your trousers and show the class what that animal done to you.

—Ah, Da, please!

—Take down your bleedin' trousers!

Denehy turned away from Mr Griffin and came to the front of the class.

—*Teígí a codhlaidh anois.*

We put our heads down on folded arms. Within a second, however, every pair of eyes were locked on the top of the room. Denehy walked up and down the aisles whispering instructions which everyone to a man ignored.

Andy stood with his back to us. He unbuttoned his trousers and slid them down. He lifted his shirt and stuck his arse in the air. There was a collective gasp although I thought it was much improved. The marks of the leather were still there but not as pink as before. The Sudocrem had definitely done its job.

—Get your school bag and your books.

Andy pulled up his trousers and came back to his desk. He lifted the lid and took his stuff out. He didn't bother putting it in his bag. He just wrapped his hands around everything and headed for the door.

—You call yourself a man of God. You're not a man of God. You're a coward that beats up children. You won't be beating up my son any more, ya yella bastard.

Andy disappeared out the door followed by his father. I knew he'd never sit next to me in school again.

At Christian Doctrine we were writing out the Seven Deadly Sins. All I could think of was seven deadly ways to murder Denehy. Poison in his tea was my favourite, although after Mrs Scally's experience a rock from the school roof had a lot going for it, too. It had the vital element of surprise. The difficulty, of course, was hitting the target first time.

What a pity Mr Griffin hadn't shot him. A crime of passion over the state of his son's arse. He'd have gotten away with it, too. Now he was gone and the opportunity was lost. What could pupils do when Denehy had the leather on his side? I decided against poisoning his tea because I didn't want to spend the rest of my life in Mountjoy. I thought of walking out in solidarity with Andy Griffin. I'd stand up and make a speech. Like Robert Emmet's from the dock. The inalienable rights of school kids. I'd be impressive. Then I'd walk out the door for ever. The disadvantage was that I'd get killed twice if I did. First Ma would kill me and then Da would kill me. It was a fate worse than Robert Emmet's.

I'd write to Denehy. The pen being mightier than the sword. More lethal than any poison. I could be in the great tradition of Irish letter writers from Saint Patrick through Jonathan Swift and Edmund Burke down to my own father who was better than them all. I turned away from the seven deadly sins in high excitement. 'Dear Brother Denehy. What have you got against soccer? It's only a game!' The words were out without thinking about them. I read it back several times. I had to agree with myself, it was an outstanding start. Straight to the heart. It said everything. The more I read it, the more complete it seemed. Soccer embraced everything that separated Denehy and me. Soccer was Sheriff Street – that's all we played there. Soccer was working class. Soccer was ballet. Soccer was skill. Soccer made sense. Soccer was Manchester United. Soccer was the Busby Babes. Soccer was the Munich air disaster. Soccer was grief. Soccer was Spurs doing the double. Soccer was joy. Soccer was the past and the present. Soccer was Jackie Carey and Liam Whelan and Noel Cantwell. Soccer was Drums and Shelbourne and Shamrock Rovers and St Pat's. Soccer was Tolka Park on a Sunday with Shea and Johnny and Da. Soccer was Dundalk and Ma crying when they won the FAI Cup. Soccer was life itself so what had he got against soccer? What more did I need to say?

I folded the piece of paper and put it on his desk when he wasn't watching. I went back to the deadly sins. Pride. I sculpted it out of a rock. I coloured it green. I wondered about the colour. Pride should be red. I looked up and saw Denehy reading my letter. He read it several times. He was impressed. He had no answer. He put the letter on his desk and looked at me. A curl of his finger. By the time I reached his desk he was frothing.

—What's the meaning of this insolence?

I was going to be brave. I needed to be brave. My knees were shaking. I felt like I was stepping up to take a penalty in the Cup Final.

—What have you got against soccer?

He picked the letter up like it was a piece of dead fish. He held it for a moment between his fingers before he let it fall on the desk.

—Does your father know about this?

How could my father know anything when I'd only just written it?

—What would your father say if he knew about this?

—I don't know, sir.

I did know. He'd kill me. The teacher was always right. A cardinal rule. You don't give cheek. I was sunk. Lost for words. Beaten into pulp. All the soccer matches I ever played for Sheriff flashed through my mind. I thought of Macker, our manager, shouting encouragement from the line. The half time talk. Express yourself. Don't be shy. Take the fight to them. We're not beaten yet. Let's not lie down. Sucking oranges to restore our strength. The second-half assault. Playing down the hill, the wind at our back. If we got a penalty it was my take. Pedro the peno king, that was me. The day I missed one in the Cup semi-final against Lourdes Celtic. On our own ground, too. Fairview Park. I was facing

Denehy with the ball at my feet. Defending the team's honour. Sheriff United. Macker's honour. My honour. Andy Griffin's honour. There was no passing the chalice. I had to sup.

—I don't know what you have against soccer. It's only a game, just as good as Gaelic. Or any other game. Macker was studying to be a priest. He runs our team. He was a deacon. So what have you got against it?

My heart was thumping like a lambeg drum. I saw Denehy's lips move but I couldn't hear the words.

—I beg your pardon, sir?

He spat them in my face. After each word a heavy pause.

—Judas . . . was . . . an . . . apostle!

I had no answer. Just four words and I was trampled under foot. Denehy showed no mercy. He pointed at the door.

—Get out of my school.

*

I sat on the apex of the roof and watched Da ascend the chimney stack. He tied a great big Guinness rope around one of the Georgian pots. He threw the loose end to me. It landed a foot or so from my hand. I picked it up without conviction. I held it without conviction. I was without conviction of any sort. I wouldn't get a job as a messenger boy having been expelled from school. How could I tell Da I'd brought disgrace on the family? What did I expect for standing up to a teacher? I was twelve years old. I wouldn't get rights 'til I was eighteen. If only I had those minutes back. I felt like chopping off my hand. Or Da might chop it off for me if I was found out. He got down off the stack and retreated towards me. He wrapped his hands around the rope a few times and told me to do the same. He pulled the rope until it was taut. I followed his moves. One foot either side of the apex for balance. Squat position. It was a

67

tug-o-war with the pot. The important thing was to feel a movement towards us. Any movement. Once she started to move we were three-quarters of the way there. To shift her from her housing was vital to success.

Da gave a one, two, three and we tugged. Tugged, grunted and tugged. I grunted myself and it felt good. The first time ever. We relaxed a moment to draw breath. We went at it again with louder grunts and tugs. I could see Da's body shaking with the effort. I thought I could will it to move. I imagined the pot was Denehy. In my mind I said 'move'. It didn't budge. We went at it again, this time grunting before we tugged and while we tugged. I stopped pretending it was Denehy. It still didn't move.

Da took off his shirt which had stuck to his back. He wiped the sweat off and offered it to me. I declined. He swung his arms windmill fashion. He swivelled his hips. He flexed his two shoulders and cleared both nostrils of their snot. I asked him what he was doing.

—I'm taking on the pots. Man to man.

He got up on the stack and loosened the rope. He took it off the pot and put his head in the noose. He worked it down over his shoulders as far as his waist. He pulled it fast until he was satisfied.

—My life's in your hands, son. Keep the rope taut.

He stood between the pots and looked down at his feet. He raised his right hand and placed it against one of the pots. He raised his left hand and did the same.

—Taut, son.

I leaned back and felt his weight in the tension of the rope. We were tied together by this umbilical cord. At any moment I could release it and let him slip away. No one would ever know. It was a powerful feeling. Let him slip away. It was so powerless being a kid. When would I have this power again?

Like Samson in the Temple, he started to push with all

his weight. Victor Mature. The crowds jeering at him because he'd lost his strength. From somewhere he gets power and brings down the columns. Smothers the mob in their own ignorance. Cheers and roars in the Elec. Victor victorious.

—Yeh . . . eh . . . es!

Da roared like a lion as the pot moved an inch. Maybe half an inch.

—We have her now, we have her.

He hugged one of the pots to his chest and nestled his head against her. Like he'd taken possession of her. He jerked the pot from her bed and freed her into the air for the first time in over a hundred years. Suddenly, the rope in my hand was steel rod. I felt myself sliding along the apex. I looked at Da who was about to take flight with the chimney. His body was leaning off the stack at a forty-five degree angle. My only instinct was to pull on the rope but I was heading for a collision with the chimney stack when Da opened his arms and released the pot into orbit. The giant bird of clay took flight. It glided majestically through the air and as it did, Da cupped his hands around his mouth and shouted out . . .

—Fore.

There is a law for the speed of a falling body. It's a lie. There was first the echo of Da's voice.

Fore . . . fore—

There was the whistle of the pot through the air. Da straightening up with his hands over his ears. My body coming to rest against the base of the stack. After all that came the bang. The loudest since the German Air Force dropped two tons of bombs at the Five Lamps in 1941. I wondered what they shouted on that fateful night. Did they shout fore?

The chimney pot exploded to the four corners of the parish. It seemed like it was raining chimneys. Fragments came flying over our heads on to the roof. When the dust had settled my head felt like it had the mumps. I put my hand up and pulled the shrapnel from my hair.

Da got down from the chimney stack and knelt beside me. There was a trickle of blood from his ear running down to his neck. I noticed his hands were shaking. When he opened his mouth to speak I could see his lips quivering.

—Say a prayer, son. Say a prayer there was no one down there.

He blessed himself and bowed his head. We knelt on the roof opposite each other. His eyes were closed. I closed mine. I realized in that second why he had held on to the pot. He didn't know what was below. Surely we'd have heard kids playing. Then I remembered Joxer's funeral cart and suddenly I was worse than Da. I blessed myself double quick and looked over the roof into Emerald Street. There were people standing at every hall door. At the top of the street a crowd had left the Ball Alley pub, including Mr Griffin. I moved across to the other side. It was the same in Seville Place. People coming out of doors and wondering what had happened. Debris was everywhere but there were no bodies. It was a miracle, pure and simple. It was a blessing, too. For the moment, at least, my expulsion from school faded away under the weight of the Georgian chimney pots.

4

1962

The man in the shiny suit cut open the cardboard box like a magician. I watched him through the window from the yard because the scullery was jam-packed. As well as Ma and Da and all of us there were the neighbours – Scallys and Hogans and Bakers and Dowdalls. They'd made a kind of circle and were watching the man at work. First he cut off the top and gave it to Da who was like his assistant. Da held on to the cardboard – he would find a use for it no doubt. He cut away one of the sides. I couldn't see a thing, I just heard the neighbours swoon.

—Mrs Sheridan, it's only beautiful.

—It's a dream machine.

—You won't know yourself.

—Look at the shine off it.

He cut away the other sides and asked everyone to stand back. He revealed his magic trick. The white enamel box with the blue top and the blue hose. A twin tub. Ma's twin tub. Paid for by Da's dog money. His nights at Shelbourne Park. Just like our education was paid for by the lodgers. Everything in its place. Books and socks. Laundry and education. Knowledge and Daz. Not that it mattered a washing flake to me. I was expelled from the future. Brought down by the sin of pride. Lucifer's sin.

Shiny Suit made an address on behalf of the twin tub. You could put your complete trust in her, she was the housewife's friend and more reliable than a husband. Shiny Suit got very emotional. Like he didn't want to part from her. She was his slave and he didn't want to sell her. He pulled himself together and cleared a path for her final journey to the sink. Da and he nursed her into position. Shiny Suit attached the hoses to the taps and plugged her into the socket. He flicked the switch. A red light came on at the front. He turned on the taps. Everyone listened intently. Listened to the sound of water they could not see. It was like Irish dancing on the radio. You could hear the taps but you had to imagine the bodies. The sound of the water hissing into the twin tub had everyone on tenter hooks. I was sick, sore and tired of water. Water, water, everywhere. Dirty naller water. Water mixed with rats' piss. I swam in it every day since I was expelled. Swam with the mitchers. They didn't believe I was expelled at first. They thought I was working undercover as an informer.

—You're Denehy's rat, Shero.

For an hour or two they wouldn't come near me. Like I was diseased. The more I protested, the more they stayed away. When I told them about Andy Griffin's arse, though, their attitude changed. They all got out of the water and went up town looking for him. They wanted to see his arse for themselves. I spent the rest of the day swimming on my own. I got bored. After a week I never wanted to see the naller again. I was bored wetless.

The twin tub was pumping water through a white hose and into the sink. At the same time it was spinning so fast I thought it was going to bore a hole in the ground. Shiny Suit was shouting at the top of his voice above the noise. He was telling everyone it was coming to an end. It would soon spin itself out and be over. He sounded like a preacher predicting the end of the world. We might not know it but we were in the final cycle. We'd soon be hanging out to dry before our Maker. The days of slavery were over. It was goodbye to drudgery. Washboard, mangles and scrubbing brushes, we could offer them up to God. The lifesaver had arrived. Available for cash or on the never never. Before he left our house Shiny Suit had orders for another two. While he took the details, Ma had her lifesaver twin tub in full flow. I was delighted we had something new, something that worked, something that didn't need Da's intervention. As Shiny Suit pronounced before leaving our house:

—All moving parts well oiled and bearing an equal strain.

*

I took the bull by the horns and decided to humble myself before the almighty Denehy. I bounced into the class and went straight across to his desk. He pretended I wasn't there so I launched straight in. I apologized for the letter. Apologized for my insolence. I promised it wouldn't happen again. I told him I'd confessed it to a priest (which was a lie). I grovelled. I squirmed. I licked arse. I did it with gusto. I felt like the twin tub. Spinning out of control. My mouth couldn't keep up with my brain. Images were spinning in my head and sounds were pumping out of my mouth. I felt I looked like the machine. I felt I was the machine. I couldn't unplug myself. I needed intervention. Divine intervention. I prayed that The Mongrel would snarl at me. Bark at me. Walk on me. Paw me. I was coming to the end of my cycle. I was spinning out, out, out. Denehy looked at me. My mouth stopped working. I could hear the lambeg beat away in my chest. He told me that from now on I would play Gaelic football for the school. It was compulsory. Our matches were Saturdays, our training Wednesdays after school.

—I can't play Saturday mornings, sir.

—Can't or won't?

Did he know I played soccer on Saturdays? Of course he knew. I was captain of Sheriff United under 12's. I led my team, home and away. I called when the ref flipped the coin.

Heads or harps? I was a harps man. It was an even money chance. Odds never changed. They were fixed. Certain. I was responsible for my team. Represented my team. Now I was being cast out of soccer heaven by the almighty Denehy. I would have to learn brawn and unlearn skill. Out of my life was dribbling, back heels and flips. Into my life was handling the ball, jersey pulling and shoulder charging. Gaelic football was faction fighting under the guise of running after a ball. A Gaelic match without a fight was a poor spectacle. The supporters watched it for the mill, the players played it for the mill and the referees refereed it for the mill. It was the association for organized milling. In return for a seat back in the class The Mongrel was forcing me to embrace it. I didn't have much of a choice. If I remained loyal to soccer, I stayed expelled from school. If I stayed expelled, Da would eventually find out and I'd be dead. I wanted to stay alive.

My only problem was Macker. He was a gentle person. A caring person. Sheriff Street was his vocation now. Only for Sheriffer he'd have gone on for the priesthood but he couldn't let the kids down once he'd found them. Macker found a new family when he found us. There were others who could take my place. I sat down in my desk and reassured myself that I was back in the educational system. I had brains to burn and I was going to burn them. The Mongrel would never forget me even if, for the moment, I had to live out my life as one of his Gaelic footballers.

Macker danced on hot coals when I told him. He cursed curses I'd never heard before. He called Denehy a neanderthal nutcase.

—He should be stoned to death with balls of his own shite!

Da would have been proud of that one. When jockeys threw races or horses fell fifteen lengths in front, Da could summon Lucifer. Well, Macker looked like the devil with his foot dance. Just as quickly as he lost his temper, he calmed down again. He apologized for cursing in front of me and blessed himself. Da never did that. No, Da in a rage could last for twenty-four hours at least. Macker hadn't lasted twenty-four minutes. We went out to the playground and played a five a side but my heart wasn't in it. I went home at half time and got into bed. I fell asleep and dreamt my favourite dream. Manchester United in the Cup Final. Me as captain. I was magnificent as usual. Second half turned into a faction fight and by the end all twenty-two players were stretched out dead in the centre circle of the Wembley pitch.

*

Andy Griffin never went to school after his father took him out. He was supposed to attend Rutland Street Primary, which was better known as the red-brick slaughterhouse, but he never bothered. The schools' attendance inspector called round to his house several times. His mother pretended he was sick. His father pretended he was staying with an uncle. The inspector insisted on seeing the sick Andy. Mr Griffin backed down and told the truth. Andy was instructed to appear before Justice Kennedy in the children's court. I went around that afternoon to find out what happened. Soon as I got within distance I could see a crowd gathered on the balcony. Mostly kids. On the ground, backed right up to the stairs, was a black car. There was a figure sitting in the back. I could see the white of the collar. I knew it was a Christian Brother. The car looked out of place. The Brother in the back even more so. The windows were rolled up tight. I could see his breath on the glass as I passed. Maybe he was saying the prayer for Edmund Rice. Every day in school we said the prayer for the canonization of Edmund Rice. He founded the Brothers to give the poor children of Waterford city an education. The Brothers spread everywhere. I hoped he would be canonized soon and we'd get a day off school.

At the very least. Maybe even a week. The Brothers needed three miracles to convince the Pope. If Andy Griffin could escape his present trouble they would definitely have one.

The kids on the balcony were pestering the Garda to produce handcuffs. Little hands and fingers were crawling all over him. Nothing he said would convince them he was clean. One of the kids was certain he was concealing them under his cap. They climbed up window ledges and rubbish chutes trying to knock his cap off.

In the hallway, Mr Griffin had a bottle in his hand. The attendance inspector shook his head in stony resignation. Mr Griffin insisted they discuss the situation over a drink. The inspector kept showing him the paper in his hand.

—I have a warrant for his removal, Mr Griffin. There's nothing to discuss.

I'd only ever seen a warrant in the pictures. The FBI flashed them all the time. There was no discussion. They broke down doors. They poured into buildings. Pulled people out screaming. They didn't hang about in hallways. No one dared offer them a drink. Mr Griffin introduced me to the attendance inspector as Andy's best friend.

—He's from the houses in Seville Place. His father runs the train station.

I tried to explain that he sold the tickets in the booking office. It was no good. Mr Griffin was not about to be contradicted.

—His father knows where the mystery train goes every Sunday. Isn't that right, son?

—Yes, Mr Griffin.

The mystery train left Amiens Street station every Sunday morning for a destination unknown. The passengers bought their tickets from Da, took their seats on the steamer and wondered with every turn of the wheels where the train would stop. Some passengers on the mystery train were privileged. They had prior knowledge. They came through our back door from Thursday on, all with the same question on their lips.

—Where's the mystery train going this Sunday, Mr Sheridan?

Ma said we should hang a sign on the back door. Shea said we should charge for the information and we all thought that was a much better idea.

Mr Griffin raised his voice. He stuck his finger into the inspector's chest, for emphasis.

—Very few people in this town can tell you where the mystery train goes. Am I right or am I right?

The inspector smiled at my embarrassment. I half excused myself and went into the kitchen. Mrs Griffin was sitting at the table crying over a glass of stout. Catherine was berating her.

—Stop crying, Ma, he has to go away.

Catherine was crying, too. They didn't notice I was there. Normally, Mrs Griffin would wipe a chair and tell me to sit down. She'd offer me a cup of tea. Or a biscuit. I always refused. She always insisted. Tonight they didn't seem to care, they had other things on their mind. I backed out of the kitchen and into the boys' bedroom. Andy was sitting on the bed. His kid brother, Christy, was standing at the window with a sheet in his hand.

—Come on, Andy, I'll lower you down.

Andy laughed nervously. It was a hopeless situation. Andy brushed his brother's suggestion aside. Christy was not about to give up. He came over to me.

—Hold this with me?

Out of politeness, I held the sheet. Christy urged his brother to give it a try. Andy picked up the loose end and looked at us.

—You want me to get out the window holding this?
—Yeah. Hurry.

Andy tugged at the sheet. It started to tear. Andy dropped it on the floor. Christy's face took on a look of horror.

—What are you going to tell Ma about the sheet?

—I'm telling her nothing. I'm being sent away.

There was a tone in Andy's voice I'd never heard before. It was an accusing tone. Venomous. He blamed his mother. Was she responsible for what was happening to him? I thought he would have blamed his father for taking him out of school that time. Maybe it was his mother who made him confront Denehy? Mothers and fathers were funny. The way they had power over each other. Men proving they were men. Mothers proving that they loved their children. Whose fault was it that Andy was going to Artane? Was it some fault in him that he'd been born with and could never escape? Or was it the adults who were to blame? Mrs Griffin? Mr Griffin? Brother Denehy? The attendance inspector? The Garda? Andy was surrounded. It was the Alamo and there was no way out. All we had was a torn sheet. We didn't even have a Gatling gun. A torn sheet, the white flag of surrender. Andy had spent his whole life trying to avoid the Christian Brothers and now he was being sent right into their clutches. Twenty-four hours a day he would walk in their shadow. By day he would sit in their desks, by night he would lie in their sheets. He mitched out of fear, now fear would face him every second of the day. Perhaps that would cure him. If he learned to overcome his fear they would let him go. Something good might come out of it yet.

—Walk me down to the car.

Andy took off his belt and wrapped it around the brown suitcase that wouldn't close. We walked out to the hall. Andy opened the door to the kitchen. Catherine was putting some biscuits and an apple into a brown paper bag. Mrs Griffin put her glass down.

—Where did we go wrong, son?

—Don't start, Ma.

Catherine came over and pushed the bag into Andy's hand. Mrs Griffin went at Andy with a clothes brush. He held out his hands for her. When she took out a comb and started doing his hair, Andy pulled away and tossed it with his hands. I knew exactly how he felt.

—Don't come down the stairs with me, Ma.

—Goodbye, son.

Soon as the words were out Mrs Griffin went hysterical. As Catherine tried to calm her down, Andy and I retreated onto the balcony. The kids swarmed us. The Garda was delighted with the reprieve. Andy took the brown paper bag from his pocket. He took the apple from the bag and asked the kids did they want a 'grush'. Usually in a grush you threw money. Outside the church at a wedding the best man threw a handful of coins. Grushing an apple was very unusual. Andy drew his hand back and threw the apple as far as he could. The kids scurried like so many rats to find it. It would end up in mush, I thought. I said it to Andy. He showed me his hand. He hadn't thrown the apple at all. That was the great thing about Andy, the way he was full of surprises. I loved him for it.

The inspector stood between Mr Griffin and the car. Mr Griffin was pointing at the Brother in the back.

—If he lays a hand on my son I'll hold you responsible. I'll come looking for you, true as God's my judge.

Andy froze when he saw the white collar. It was like the reality of it suddenly dropped on his head out of the sky. His hand opened and the apple fell on to the ground. I picked it up and cleaned it as best I could. I put it in his pocket. He didn't respond. The Garda opened the back door of the car and the Brother looked out. Andy didn't move. I shouted across to the Garda.

—He'll travel in the front.

Andy looked at me and almost smiled.

—I'll write to you.

He walked over and got in. As he did his father shouted, loud enough for the Brother to hear.

—Don't let them touch you, son.

The car pulled away and came to an immediate stop. Kids were on the ground in front of it looking for the lost apple. It was safely in Andy's pocket but Andy was anything but safe. He was safe for the present in the front seat. How long would it last? The Brothers were experts at smelling fear. If he could control his fear he might have a chance in Artane.

The car moved forward again. Kids were now attached to it. They held on by the back bumper, the front bumper, the door handles, the running boards, the wheel guards. They held on to any part that stuck out. It was a moving ant hill. The driver stopped the car and got out. The kids scattered. By the time he was back in his seat and moving it was an ant hill once more. It continued like that all the way out of the flats and on to Sheriff Street. It was as if they were trying to hold on to Andy. They were waging a guerrilla war on the car. Tactics invented by the Irish. Art McMurrough to be precise. He never engaged in battle. Picked off the enemy from the rear and the sides before retreating into the forests. The Sheriff Street kids were too young to know they were repeating history. I wanted to attach myself to the car but I was afraid. A good observer, that was me. I was sick of being a good boy. I watched Andy splutter away from me and I cursed myself that I ever told him to come to school.

*

Ma's twin tub was turning into a disaster worse than the *Titanic*. Every time she turned it on it leaked. When one source was plugged it found somewhere else to leak from. I thought maybe it was a test model from the factory that was supposed to develop leaks and we'd been given it by mistake. Da modified a timber pallet he had hanging up in the garage. This acted as a kind of bridge that got us from the kitchen to the scullery without drowning. We were living permanently in wellington boots. If things continued, a raft was next. The leaks by themselves were bad enough but they would have been tolerable if it wasn't for the epileptic fits. I didn't know machines could suffer from epilepsy. When it went on to spin it lost complete control of itself. It jumped two feet in the air and bounced wildly from side to side. It was so bad we thought it was possessed. Father Ivers blessed it to no avail. It smashed every dish that was in the sink and it tried to jump in after them to make sure. Da reduced the fits by means of a concrete block but it still required a physical presence to stop it getting completely out of hand.

Ma was determined about one thing. She wasn't going back to hand washing in the metal bath. She would put up with all manner of attack from the lifesaver – physical assault and floods – but there was no going back to the stone age. No matter what the problems were with the bitch from hell, as Da christened her, Ma was digging her heels in as deep as General Custer. It was shaping up for one hell of a row. Ma's determination versus Da's stubbornness. Ma won the early exchanges and sickened Da when she suggested getting Shiny Suit back to check how we were using the machine. That hurt his pride and posed a question mark over his ability to follow instructions. I knew him, what he was thinking. He'd delivered television pictures into our kitchen. He'd performed Samson on a chimney stack and saved it from certain collapse. It was now forgotten. Worse was to follow. Ma suggested we get an expert plumber to check out the hot-water tank. She might as well have said that the Acropolis was built crooked. Da and Uncle Paddy had plumbed in the water tank. They'd worked through a Saturday night and into Sunday morning to finish it before the first lodgers arrived. It was more than Da could take. He went on an immediate hunger strike. For four consecutive days he refused all of Ma's cooking. Breakfast, dinner and tea. Ma

end up in debtors' prison where not even a hunger strike would save him.

We were under pain of death not to mention the lodgers in front of Shiny Suit. He was an outsider and outsiders were dangerous. Ireland had the worst record of informants of any country in the world. Informing was a national pastime. Da did not want his name added to the list of the betrayed.

Shiny Suit looked funny in Da's wellingtons. At first he thought the house had been built on a well. He took the back off the machine and gave it a thorough examination. Just like a doctor. He put it all back together, connected the hoses to the taps, turned on the machine and waited for it to wash the clothes. Da reminded him of the concrete block. He flatly ignored him. It was a fatal mistake. Within seconds the twin tub took a fit and physically attacked Shiny Suit. He ran from the kitchen in terror. Everyone started screaming. Da was the only one to hold his ground. He lifted up the concrete block and put it where it should have been from the start and immediately the jerks and spasms subsided. It was round one to Da, all three judges, and he was smiling from ear to ear.

Shiny Suit made a bold move at the start of round two. He switched the machine off at the plug. He produced a spirit-level, just like the one Da had hanging up in the garage. He put it gingerly on the machine and slid it around. He inspected it like a doctor with a thermometer.

—No wonder she's sick . . . sick, sick, sick . . . sick as a parrot . . .

Da was very uncomfortable with the insinuation. Shiny Suit slotted timber wedges under the legs of the twin tub. I watched the bubble in the spirit-level move like a baby crawling along the floor. A blob of flesh, slowly moving, then belly flop, smack between the lines. Shiny Suit told Da to remove the concrete block. Da didn't like the tone of his voice. He performed the task in silent protest. Shiny Suit switched on the machine, it gave a hiccup to start but then settled into a quiet, gentle sort of a sway. The epilepsy was gone. It was like a cat purring. Round two to Shiny Suit.

The final round began cautiously. Shiny Suit circled the twin tub and examined it from every angle. Da copied him in the opposite direction. Shiny Suit turned his back on it, bent down and looked at it from between his legs. Da mirrored the move just as if he did it every day. Shiny Suit moved towards the sink. He bent his ear close to the taps and listened. He listened for ages. He told Da to turn off the machine. What was Shiny Suit hearing? Was there more than water in the water? Had the twin tub been poisoned? Is that why it spewed out its guts? Shiny Suit slowly, deliberately straightened up. He looked at Da. He called Ma in to the sink. He put his hand on the twin hose and started to pull. The rubber made a kissing sound as it parted company from the taps. Water trickled into the sink. Shiny Suit pointed at it. It was a decisive move, you could feel it in the air. Da looked sheepish, Ma looked bewildered.

—Is there something the matter with the water?

—Look at it! Look at it!

Ma looked at it. We all looked at it. Da put his hand under it and felt it between his fingers like a priest at Mass. He rubbed the tips of his fingers together. Frankie squeezed between my legs and pushed himself up onto the sink with his elbows. We watched it trickling for an eternity.

—You have no water pressure. Your problem is water pressure!

Da was out for the count. KO, round three. Shiny Suit had delivered a clean, crisp uppercut. There was no way back for Da. He'd been hit with a haymaker. Water pressure. It was a text book knock out with a pedigree stretching back to the Marquis of Queensberry. Worse was to come for Da. Shiny Suit sat him down and went over the whole thing round by round and blow by blow. We all sat and watched

Da being crucified. You could see the wounds in his face. He bore them as clearly as Padre Pio bore the stigmata. Ma offered Shiny Suit a cup of tea, which was a terrible betrayal and for which she would no doubt pay. To round off Da's miserable day, Mahony came home early from work, burst into the kitchen and declared in front of Shiny Suit that he was a paying lodger. Blood pressure. Water pressure. Da was about to explode. Da was about to drown. Da was very quiet. Da was thinking ahead. When Shiny Suit left, Ma asked Da what he thought. It was a stupid question. It didn't matter what Da thought, our world as we knew it was coming to an end. Shiny Suit was back in his office talking to the tax man, Da was contemplating a life in prison and Shea, Ita and me would have to leave school and find work. Da got up and went to the back door without a word. I knew he was heading for his toilet to figure it all out. He beckoned me with his hand.

—Come on, son, we're going to have to get to the bottom of this.

*

Every time there was a ring at the door it was the same awful wait. Ma got up to answer it. She was following Da's instructions. He believed every knock was a tax inspector. When Ma came down and said it was Catherine Griffin my heart started to race.

—She has a cream cake for you, anyway.

Everyone at the table started to laugh. I went scarlet. Did they know I dreamed about her? Did Shea suspect that when I snuggled up to him at night, I snuggled up to her? It was nice to think about her, that was all. I could never be with her. She was from the flats. She was older than me. She had breasts and I had only six hairs on my willy and I didn't shave. She had a part-time job in the Kylemore Bakery with her own uniform. She would be made permanent the day she left school.

—Bring her into the front room.

Ma's advice turned the laughs into jeers. I wanted to cry but I couldn't let them see the tears that were trying to burst out. I wanted to smash their faces, turn the table upside down and spill their fried rissoles on the floor. I wanted to run up Emerald Street to the Ball Alley pub and tell Mr Griffin to bring his daughter and her cream cake home. I didn't care if he threatened me with a saw. I was outside the Ball Alley on the night Andy was taken away, when he threatened Mrs Griffin he'd saw her in half and all the men had to hold him back and all the women held Mrs Griffin at bay as she screamed.

—Saw me, let him bleedin' saw me.

I was less afraid of Mr Griffin than I was of his daughter standing at our hall door with a cream cake in her hand. I thought of the front room and the communion photograph of me with ringlets hanging on the wall. That was it, I was running up to the Ball Alley pub. I headed for the back door when Ita stood up.

—Come on, introduce me to this girl.

I was saved from humiliation. Catastrophe. Ita knew Catherine, of course, so I didn't need to do that stupid stuff. Ita kept her talking at the door while I slipped into the front room, removed the photograph off its nail and hid it behind the armchair. Ita and Catherine never stopped talking. I didn't read the *Bunty* or the *Judy* so I didn't know about the Four Marys. All I could do was listen. They sounded like oul' wans. They were the two most important girls in my life and I was being completely ignored. Sometimes, Andy and I could go for a whole ten minutes without exchanging a word. I'd know what he was thinking so I wouldn't need to talk. I loved when that happened. I looked at Ita and

86

Catherine talking and I wondered could it ever happen with a girl.

Ita went to the toilet (I think she was deliberately leaving us alone) and Catherine handed me the Kylemore box. She handed me a brown paper parcel tied with twine. It was soft to the touch. She asked me to give them to Andy. I wondered why she asked me to do that when he was locked up in Artane.

—I won't be seeing Andy.

—Yes, you will.

I didn't like to contradict her. She was more developed than I was. She could make me go red at the drop of a hat. That gave her power over me. I could only ever be her slave. How could I disappoint her over this?

—You're playing Gaelic for your school tomorrow?

—Yes.

—You're playing against St Ciaran's?

—Yes.

She looked at me wide-eyed. Broke into a smile. Waited for my reply. I didn't have one.

—St Ciaran's is Artane, ya dope.

*

We got off the bus on the Malahide Road outside the big gates with the arc of iron letters. Artane Industrial School. The gates were closed. The gates were always closed. Denehy put down the school kitbag with the jerseys in it. He put his hand up and pressed a bell. You'd never see it unless you knew it was there.

We stood outside Artane. Twenty Gaelic footballers from Laurence O' Toole's. Some people knew our school. Everyone knew Artane. They knew it 'cos they wanted to avoid it. A training ground for prison. Artane. Mountjoy. St Ciaran's. Only those with inside information knew it was called St Ciaran's. Denehy lit a cigarette. He was agitated. He hardly ever lit up in front of us. Because of the vow of poverty. Where did he get money for cigarettes if he was poor? He smoked Sweet Afton. That was also the name of the cup. The Sweet Afton Cup. Ma smoked them, too. Her butts always wore lipstick. Flow gently Sweet Afton. A gentle stream. Today a river of blood. Doing battle for the cup. Laurence O Toole's versus St Ciaran's. Both teams trained by the unchristian Brothers. Gaelic football. A game for bowsies played by bowsies.

The small gate opened and the lodge keeper ushered us through. Once inside I could see the white railings and the path that led to the grey building with the steps in front. The building looked alive. The front door was a mouth that could gobble you up. All around it were fields. Cattle stopped to look at us, they must have known we were visitors. I wondered as we walked along if Andy was watching us from the grey building. I had the brown parcel tight under my right arm. The cake was safely tucked away under my shorts in my bag. I made room for it by taking out my boots which I carried around my neck like a stethoscope.

It was miles from the front gate to the grey building. It was probably only a half a mile but it felt like ten times that. In the distance a group of boys, all dressed the same, were gathering up leaves from the path. Their jackets and trousers matched the colour of the building. When we got up close they stopped what they were doing and waited for us to pass. They looked down at our shoes like we were their superiors. I didn't recognize any of their faces. Soon as we passed they were on their hunkers again removing leaves from the path.

Denehy swerved left at the grey building and we followed him around to the back. A path led to another big gate by way of a white railing. In the middle was a pitch completely surrounded by trees. I'd never seen one like it before. Straight lines of trees on all four sides. There were trees in Fairview

Park and the Phoenix Park and Bushy Park but they weren't organized. They were haphazard. The trees in Artane made the pitch look like a prison. I suppose it was deliberate. Even nature hemmed you in. Next to the pitch was a pavilion. There were three dressing rooms in it but no sign of the home team. No sign of the home supporters either. Were they all dead or what? Denehy placed the kitbag in the middle of the room, untied the stays and started to root for the goalkeeper's jersey. It was a light purple colour. He found it and held it up.

—In goal—

Mikey Grey was at it already.

—Sir, sir, sir, sir, sir, sir, sir, sir—

Denehy looked at him. He caved in and threw the jersey at him.

—In goal, Michael Grey.

Mikey Grey was about to say 'don't tell me, sir', but stopped himself in time. Denehy continued to throw out the jerseys. I got the green number six. Centre-half back. In soccer I played at number four. I hoped my opponent wouldn't be too tall. In soccer, height didn't matter too much but in Gaelic you couldn't catch a ball against a player six inches taller than you. Our biggest player, Daddy Kelly, was five foot ten. His real name was Billy but even Denehy called him Daddy. I was eight inches smaller than Daddy Kelly, who couldn't kick a ball but he was great to have on your team. That was Gaelic football.

Denehy's pre-match talk was passionate. He reminded us of our duty to our school, to our parish and to our country. He reminded us of Fionn MacCumhaill, Cuchulainn and the brave Fianna warriors; of Michael Davitt, Michael Cusack and Bishop Croke; of Parnell, Casement and Padhraig Pearse; of the proud tradition of Mayo football (his county) and the West's awake; of the proud tradition of Dublin football (our county) and Snitchy Ferguson, Kevin Heffernan and Lar

Foley; he reminded us most of all of our duty to ourselves; we had a debt to the past but we owed it to the future to excel ourselves; what would we want our children and our grandchildren to say of us, that we surrendered or that we fought to the death? Make no mistake, Artane will want to kill you; remember dead men don't fight back; if you can't get the ball then for Christ's sake get the man; get him with your fists, get him early and often; if you get out of here with a win, we'll have a half day tomorrow; now get out there and compete for every ball.

We ran out of the pavilion looking for players to kill. There was the sound of polite applause. On three sides of the pitch were the inmates of Artane, all dressed the same, all clapping. They'd taken up their positions without a noise. A minute earlier they had been in the grey building, now they were lining the pitch staring at us and clapping. Hard chaws, criminals and misfits. Clapping politely. It didn't seem to fit. The sound of women's voices broke the atmosphere.

—Come on, O'Toole's.

—Come on the Larriers.

In the distance, a group of women and children waving green and white flags were making their way towards us. Our supporters. I could see Mikey Grey's mother and two of his sisters. And Daddy Kelly's mother, you couldn't miss her, she was six foot four. They'd come to cheer us in the first round of the Sweet Afton Cup.

All politeness vanished when the home team appeared. They came out a door in the back of the grey building. A Brother with a head like a turkey, silver hair sticking straight up in spikes, was running beside the boys and shouting into their faces as they went. He carried a ball and bounced it so hard I thought it would burst. They came tearing on to the pitch, shaking their fists at us as their supporters bayed for blood on the sidelines. The polite Artane boys looked like they'd been released from a dungeon in hell.

Their colours were almost the same as ours. Green jersey with white shorts. Only difference was they had a yellow hoop on the chest. It would be important to look before passing. Didn't want to face Denehy's firing squad. Daddy Kelly kicked the practice ball to me. I jumped up to catch it when I heard a voice behind me shout.

—Let it go!

It was Andy. In his uniform. Just like all the rest. Except he wasn't like all the rest. His voice seemed softer than before. He motioned with his head and we moved a little bit away. I moved to the sideline and did exercises while Andy talked to me in his new voice. I was conscious all the time of being watched.

—I heard my mother and father were killing each other outside the Ball Alley?

I tipped my toes with my hands and looked at him under my legs.

—Yeah.

I could see the anger in his lips. The way they curled up.

—I have something for you.

—What is it?

—It's in the dressing room. A cake and a parcel.

I got up and made a move towards the pavilion.

—Leave it there. I'll get it myself.

The referee blew his whistle and I headed on to the pitch. I took up my position and before the game started I got an elbow in the ribs from my opponent. I ran after him but he ran away like a good coward. I was determined not to let him get a touch of the ball. I needn't have bothered. From the throw in it was all Larriers. Wave after wave of attack. In five minutes, we had five scores. Three goals and two points. Artane were no score. The game was as good as over.

It wasn't over on the sidelines. The war of the chieftains. The Mongrel versus Turkey Head. Up and down the sidelines they charged hurling abuse and encouragement across the pitch. Turkey Head had it for volume, The Mongrel had it for passion. After twenty minutes of play it was five goals and six points to one point. The Artane supporters were still cheering their team like victory was within their grasp. The referee did his best to encourage Artane. He gave them frees for nothing. The Mongrel was incensed. He screamed at the referee.

—Put on a yellow jersey, why don't you?

From a free kick, Daddy Kelly caught the ball. The referee blew and gave a penalty to Artane. It was the worst refereeing decision I ever saw but I was glad for the opposition. The Artane captain stepped up and sent the ball wide. The referee blew for a goal. There was complete chaos. The Mongrel started digging a hole with his foot in the pitch. Turkey Head ran around like a headless chicken shouting:

—Goal . . . goal . . . goal . . .

In the midst of all this the referee kept blowing his whistle and pointing at the pavilion. It was half time. He hadn't given a goal. The Artane supporters went quiet but Turkey Head was still running around. We had to wait for him to stop before leaving the pitch. It was sad.

Denehy went crazy in the dressing room. His big gripe was that we had them by the throat but we were afraid to finish them off.

—I want them buried in the second half. Six feet under? I want them ten feet under. I want goal after goal after goal. I want the Sweet Afton Cup. I want it back in O'Toole's. That's our destiny.

We were out on the pitch for five minutes before Artane appeared. This time there was no spring in their step. They all had their hands tightly jammed under their armpits and some of them were crying. They'd been slapped at half time. They'd been slapped because they were losing the match. The referee prepared to throw in the second-half ball. The Artane players couldn't even pretend to reach up and catch it. The referee couldn't bring himself to release the ball. The Artane players tried to shake the stings from their hands while Turkey Head ranted on the sideline. We all stood there as part of this angry circus. Word quietly went round the pitch.

—Don't score. Kick it wide. Miss the goal.

For fifteen minutes the worst misses ever seen in Gaelic football were witnessed. Heroic misses. Wave after wave of Larrier pressure yielded nothing. We shaved the post, we hit the bar, we missed openers, we went for goals when points were there, we did everything but score. Denehy issued death threats to several of our players. I thought back to the day he left cowardly marks on Andy's arse. How I'd rebelled but later backed down. How much worse would I fare against this Turkey Head? Andy had to face him every day. A brute who slapped his team. He was the galley master and the boys were his galley slaves. Did he have a drum to keep time while he lashed them?

A high ball came towards our defence. I took it on my chest and it dropped nicely at my feet. My opponent came at me, I put it through his legs, skipped round him and met it at the other side. I dribbled forward a few yards, then sent a blade cutter in to our number nine. Immediately I heard Denehy's voice.

—Cut out that fancy nancy soccer. That's a nancy boy's game. Pick it up in your hands and kick it like an Irishman.

Fancy nancy. The words kept going around in my brain. Fancy nancy boy. Was he looking to put his hand down my trousers in Christian Doctrine? Did he want me to be one of the silent ones? Was that the price for eating his humble pie? Play Gaelic and stay silent.

I fielded a high ball. How fancy nancy was that? I sucked it right out of the air. I began a solo run. Ball to toe and catch. I side-stepped one opponent. Then another. An opponent tackled me. I clean shouldered him right out of my way. Ball to toe and catch. I was possessed. I was determined. I was brutish. I was Irish. I was Gaelic. I was brilliant. I threw the ball in the air and never took my eye off it for a split second. It dropped for a perfect half volley and I sent it screaming to the back of the net. I'd scored a goal. *Cúl, cúl agus cúl eile.* In the back of the cúl. Goal *iontach maith.* I'd scored a goal for Artane. Mikey Grey sat on his arse and smiled up at me. Daddy Kelly stood with both hands on his hips and stared at me, bewildered. I didn't care. I was exhilarated. Alive. On fire. The Artane supporters went demented. I looked around for Andy but he was nowhere to be seen. What I did see was Denehy running towards me. My first instinct was to run. Where was there to run to? This was a prison. I turned back and faced him. He came at me like he expected me to back away. I stood my ground. He knew every pair of eyes in that ground were on us. I looked at him and for the first time in my life I didn't care what he did to me.

—Get off the pitch. You'll never play for this school again.

It was the proudest moment of my life. My Gaelic football career was over after three-quarters of a match. I went into the dressing room to change. There was a girl with her back to me in the dressing room. She was bent over pulling up her ankle socks. I told her she wasn't supposed to be in the boys' dressing room. She half turned towards me.

—Are you looking for something?

—Yeah.

She sounded hoarse. She took off her head scarf and I could see it was Andy. I didn't know what to say. I looked at him.

—Did you eat the cake?

I don't know why those words came out of my mouth.

—No, I didn't.

—Are you going to eat it?

—No.

—It's an awful waste.

—I'm trying to escape. You eat it.

I checked my bag. It was still there. I tore off a corner to see what it was. A jam roll. Ma served it with custard on a Friday. I couldn't believe I was thinking about jam roll and custard in the middle of an escape. Maybe I was trying to stop myself thinking about the reality of it all. The reality if it went wrong. It was easier to think about the jam roll. I looked at Andy and he was fixing the wig on his head. It looked cheap. He put the head scarf back on. It looked deadly.

—Why did Catherine give me a cake to bring up?

—If you'd known what was in the parcel you might have gotten nervous and given the game away.

How was I going to learn things like that if Andy was locked up? I was glad he was escaping. I might suggest to Ma to take him in as a lodger. He was wasting his time in Artane.

We went outside and watched the closing minutes of the match. O'Toole's failed to score in the second half, which was a mystery to almost everyone. Still, we trounced them. Artane were out of the Sweet Afton Cup. I'd scored their only goal and I was retired from the game. We stuck close to Mikey Grey's Ma and his two sisters. Andy blended well into the company. After the final whistle we rambled down the path with our supporters, were ushered out through the gate and got on a bus bound for the Five Lamps. It was simple. Oh, so simple. Until the bus conductor asked Andy for his fare and wouldn't believe him when he said he didn't have it. The bus conductor wanted to know how 'she' got out to the match if she didn't have the fare. He gave his name and address with great confidence. Almost too confident, I thought. The trek down Seville Place was good practice for Andy's female walk. He was becoming a proper little dame, as Da would say. When we got to our back door he shouted out in his best voice.

—Where's the mystery train going tomorrow?

—Donabate.

Andy headed off up Emerald Street and I headed in for my dinner. Ma was mopping up from the twin tub.

—Who was that girl with the funny voice?

—Never seen her before!

I emptied out my dirty nicks and socks and gave them to Ma. Her face dropped. She'd just done a wash. I gave her the jam roll and her face brightened up again. Funny, the armchair by the fire was free. I plonked myself in it and waited for the classified soccer results. I was back in soccer heaven after my nightmare in hell. I waited for the United result. They were still playing at Old Trafford. While I waited, I pictured the scene in Andy's house as he sailed through the door to the kitchen dressed as his sister.

5

Andy Griffin practised being a girl by going to the shops for his Auntie Kathleen. He stuck to Sheriff Street where he was safe and where everyone called him Mary. Andy didn't pick that name. Some oul' wan started it and the others all followed. It showed great community spirit. Everyone treated Andy like a girl because the world was watching. Everyone played their part in the conspiracy.

He was living with his Auntie Kathleen in Phil Shanahan House at the far end of Sheriff Street. He went home to his own flat on Sundays. The rest of the week he holed up in Phil Shanahan. He made occasional forays to the shops. A trip to McIntyre's for bread and butter with Catherine doing a dummy run first to make sure the coast was clear. After that it was Mattie's and Christy Dooley's vegetable shop. Then he progressed to the same trip with no dummy run. In no time, Andy had the freedom of Sheriff Street. McIntyre's, Christy Dooley's, Mattie's, Cuddy's Butchers, the Ball Alley pub and the playgrounds, both the boys' and girls'. He was even looking for money again. On his way home from the shops he never failed to drop in to the shrine of The Little Flower, light a candle and say a prayer. It was a peculiar thing to see him kneeling in front of the statue of Saint Teresa in his girl's clothes and putting money into the brass box when he spent so much of his life figuring out ways of taking money out of things.

I wasn't sure I liked the new Andy. In learning to play a girl he wasn't the Andy I'd known. We both knew he couldn't stay being a girl for ever. He was trapped being a girl. It was like a seed had been planted in him and it had become a flower in a prison cell. If he went back to being a boy it was Artane and different bars, but the same. So we pretended things were great.

—What does it feel like being a girl?

—You really want to know?

—Yeah.

Andy grabbed my hand and held it against his chest. I could feel the stuffing inside his bra. Tissues. Not like real breasts. How could they be?

—You fancy my sister, don't you?

I pulled my hand back. I instantly regretted it. It was a complete give away.

—You'll never get a feel off her. She's too holy.

It was written on my face what I was thinking. I tried to stop myself thinking of Catherine. I thought of Saint Teresa. The Little Flower. Great devotion to her in Sheriff Street. All the oul' wans. Going to the shops. Coming back from the shops. Pennies in the box. Some oul' fellas, too. Dockers, cattle men, coal men. Now Andy. On the mahogany kneeler in front of the statue with the fresh flowers.

—There y'are, Mary!

—Grand day, Mrs Power.

It was Christy Power's wife, the man with the golden dick. They were separated. Drank in different pubs now. He in the Liverpool, same as Ma and Da. She in the Ball Alley, same as Andy's Ma and Da. They'd barred Mr Griffin for a week after the attack with the saw. Mrs Griffin pleaded with them before they took him back in. They were a united couple again, now that Andy was free.

Andy wasn't free. He was playing a part. The part of Mary Griffin. He couldn't stop playing her. He'd grown into her. Soon as he stepped out of his Auntie Kathleen's house, he became her. When he called for me at our back door he put on the Mary Griffin voice. I told him he didn't need to

98

and he stuck his chest out, put his nose in the air and walked away from me in a huff. Just like a girl. I called him back and he kept on walking. He wiggled his arse. It was stupid. He stopped all of a sudden, turned around with his hands on his hips and asked me what I was looking at. Not much, I said, and I burst out laughing. Andy couldn't see the joke. Didn't want to see it. He got annoyed with me.

—What are you laughing at?

—Nothing.

—You're laughing at me, aren't you?

—I'm laughing at Mary Griffin.

Andy ran at me, grabbed me in a headlock and wrestled me to the ground. I scraped my hand along the cement but I didn't care. I was delighted Andy wasn't Mary any more. I laughed right into his face with delight.

—You're laughing at Mary Griffin, are you?

—No—

I was so convulsed I couldn't get the words out.

—You won't be laughing at Mary Griffin when I'm finished with you.

I didn't try to fight back. I couldn't fight back. I wanted to hug him because he was Andy again. I wanted to kiss him. Andy Griffin was my best friend. I didn't share him. He was mine. He didn't belong to the world. He belonged to me. We were from the same nest. I laughed at him because he was Andy. I laughed at him because he wasn't Mary. I laughed at him, 'til I didn't know why I was laughing any more. He sat on my chest and pinned my arms to the ground with his knees. I hadn't the energy to fight back. He dropped a slow spit from his mouth towards my forehead. I turned my head but it caught me in the temple. I laughed because he spat at me. I laughed because it struck. He brought another torpedo to his lips and dropped it right into my eye. I struggled onto my side to shake off the spit when I got pinched in the thigh. I thought it was Andy. Then I realized it was my Da's teeth. I had the two halves in my trouser pocket with a note for the repair man. I got a surge of energy from the bite and pushed Andy right off me onto the ground.

—I'm heading up town. I'll see you.

—Let me come with you?

—You can't.

—Why not?

I could think of a hundred reasons. All to do with Mary Griffin. I didn't like to say, now that he was back to being Andy.

—I'm going on the bike.

—Give me a crossbar. I'm light. I'll give you one on the way back. Come on.

I hadn't seen that look on his face for ages. Like the day in school when he begged his father not to show his arse to the class. An Andy look. Andy the beggar. Pleading eyes, begging me. Me the giver. I liked playing God. Will I or won't I?

—I don't know if I can.

—Please . . . I don't need a crosser. I'll run beside the bike.

We walked up town side by side. Andy's first time out of Sheriff Street since his escape. We kept our eyes peeled for attendance inspectors. Christian Brothers. Gardai. Black cars. And money. Always money going up town. The race to find money. At the bottom of the steps at Amiens Street station, Andy quietly bent down and without a word picked up a tanner and showed it to me. He didn't shout. He just pursed his lips and exploded quietly on the inside.

We crossed the road and passed the Elec. Store Street Garda station was only yards away. We picked up speed. Past Railway Street and Phil Shanahan's old pub. The flats were called after him. The pub was a safe house for IRA men during the Troubles. We bounded on. Two Gardai came round the corner of Gardiner Street towards us. We ducked right into Mabbott Lane and kept walking.

We listened out for heavy steps to follow but none came. We walked down the lane and drank in the spray paint that seeped from the lock-ups right and left. We emerged into Sean McDermott Street and headed for O'Connell Street in the distance. I felt in my pocket for the teeth. They were still there. Split in two. I felt the note. A Da special. I got that feeling in my stomach. Not butterflies. More like bats. The note was on bookies' paper. Three sheets pinned together. He stole it from Bet with Security in Guild Street. A few sheets at a time. Kept it on a shelf above the kitchen door. I once counted over four hundred sheets. I suppose Da paid for it in lost bets. He used bookies' paper for notes because he thought people would take pity on him and charge less. There was always method in his madness. I took out the note and looked at it. The top right-hand corner had our address. Under it the date plus the word inst. On the left-hand side he'd written, 'My reference: enclosed teeth.' I felt like I'd been stabbed in the chest with a screwdriver. I felt like the child of a vampire being sent to have his father's dentures sharpened, bearing a note. I knew I'd be christened son of Dracula. I was about to be humiliated in front of Andy. I crumpled the note up and threw it at the outstretched hand of a statue. Charles Stewart Parnell. Another man who'd been humiliated. The note fell at his feet. Andy went to retrieve it but I managed to march him onward to our appointment. In the distance I could see the red letters on the white background painted on the front of the house – SHARKEY'S DENTAL REPAIRS.

It was a spooky house. The hall was almost completely dark. There was no light bulb, just naked wires hanging down. The remains of an old chandelier sat in one corner. On the bare floorboards was the reflection of the fanlight. There was an old painted sign on the wall. NO DANCING, BY ORDER. The letters had once been red and yellow. Now they were dark brown like the walls. I tried to imagine people dancing. Vampires. Skeletons. Sons and daughters of Dracula. Toothless old people dancing between the cobwebs. Beneath the chandelier. Under the baton of the famous Mr Sharkey. The gummy orchestra who took their dentures out to play. Gave them to Mr Sharkey. Now he had them upstairs in his laboratory. For repair and destruction. Teeth that once chattered now powder. Ground down and scattered to the wind. Whistling around the world. You could hear it at your window at night, rattling to get in. We walked slowly because of the shadows. The stairs creaked and the banisters rattled. On the handrail knuckles of wood every few feet. I showed them to Andy. He ran his hand across them.

—What are they for?

—To stop kids sliding down.

Andy froze in mid-step. I could see his brain working. It was like looking at an X-ray. I loved when that happened.

—What mean bastard thought of that?

—Someone who didn't like kids.

Andy didn't need an invitation. He hopped straight up onto the handrail and started to slide. At the first knuckle he won a bravery medal. You could see it separating the cheeks of his arse. At the second knuckle he stopped himself and jumped over it. He repeated this all the way to the bottom where he leapt off and came back up the stairs holding his crotch.

—He wasn't a mean bastard, he was a clever bastard.

We reached a set of double doors. One said 'Private', the other said 'Please enter'. We did as it bade and entered a small corridor. An arrow on the wall said 'This way'. We followed it. It was like entering the maze in an amusement arcade. The corridor went on and on. If you got lost here, no one would ever find you. Still it went on. We came to a door. We opened it and were right back on the landing where we started. We stood for a minute looking at the two doors. Maybe the signs had been switched? I checked 'Please enter'.

It was well stuck on. Andy bent down and peeped through the private keyhole. His voice went all serious.

—I'm getting out of here. Mr Sharkey is dead. Look.

I bent down and looked. A skeleton suspended by a wire danced over a powdered table. I heard Andy laugh behind me. A figure in a white coat passed by the keyhole. I jumped up and pointed at the door.

—There's someone in there.

Andy didn't hesitate. He knocked on the door. A voice boomed back.

—Go in the other door and follow the arrows.

We entered a second time and proceeded with caution, as Da would say. We noted every arrow along the way. Followed them around in a circle. Back towards the door we came in. Just to the left of it was an arrow we'd missed the first time, pointing up to the ceiling. Embedded in the wall was a tiny white enamel bell. I pressed it and heard it ring. A hatch in the wall opened and there at last stood Mr Sharkey. The only thing to notice about him were his teeth. They were like Bugs Bunny. They were more tusks than teeth. He didn't open his mouth to speak, he just lifted his teeth from their perch.

—What can I do for you?

It was a voice to match the teeth. I wanted to say, what's up, Doc? I bit my lip. I handed him the two halves of Da's teeth. He took out an instrument with a sharp point and tapped on the plastic. He held them up to the light. He put the two halves together and held them out for inspection. He took them apart and scraped at the edges with the sharp point. A black substance rolled off it into his hand. He held it out for Andy and me.

—You know what that is?

We hadn't a clue. I didn't do science at school. There was a formula for plastic. Shea knew it. You learned that information in secondary school. You had to pay for that kind of knowledge, of course.

—That's Bostik.

He was right. Da had tried to stick it together with Bostik. He got food poisoning from it. He blamed Ma first and said it was rancid butter on his bread. He went on hunger strike for a day. It was Shea who figured out it was the Bostik. Ma was proud as punch. She said the money being spent on his education was worth every penny. Shea loved the praise and Da was jealous. He was head of the house and didn't like sharing the limelight. With all eyes on him, Shea unveiled a mathematical secret – he could prove that one and one didn't equal two. Da leapt off his chair. He'd had enough. He raised his fist in the air and demanded a retraction. Shea was as cool as a cucumber. He had the formula. I could tell by the way he didn't flinch. Da was steaming, Shea was ice. Ma was in between them trying to keep the peace.

—That fella's trying to get my goat up.

Ma was insistent there would be no violence.

—One and one always equals two.

Ma was the best referee I ever saw. Da in a temper was a bull. Ma, a matador. Shea leaned over to me and whispered.

—Bostik is all that's wrong with him.

Mr Sharkey wanted to know why Da hadn't brought the dentures in himself. I explained about the passengers in Amiens Street needing tickets for their trains. He wasn't impressed. Andy threw in the mystery train for good measure. Mr Sharkey asked me if the dentures were tight or loose in the mouth. I thought he meant my mouth. He started to get annoyed. He was becoming more like Jerry Lewis than Bugs Bunny. He was chopping holes in the dentures with the pointy thing. I was getting afraid of the nutty professor.

—How can I repair them if I don't know whether they're loose or tight. I need instructions. Do you have instructions?

The instructions were crumpled at the feet of Charles Stewart Parnell. I took a gamble in the best family tradition.

—They're loose. He told me they're loose.

Mr Sharkey pulled himself together with a series of short breaths. He smiled a goofy sort of a smile.

—Come back in two hours, folks.

We stepped back out into the sunshine and I saw that we were opposite the Rotunda Hospital where I'd been born. I got this strange feeling that I was responsible for my own birth. I'd come from an idea in my own head. Sometimes those kind of thoughts frightened me. Not today. If I'd been born a few years earlier I knew I'd have invented Bugs Bunny. I just knew.

Andy did his nutty professor walk up one side of Parnell Square. I remembered the Moving Crib was near here. I found the basement where it was. Andy didn't want to go in. I told him it was free. He wanted to go to Walton's instead. We started arguing. An oul' wan told me to stop shouting at my sister. I laughed at her. Andy immediately started to cry and told the oul' wan I'd stolen his sixpence. She opened her bag and gave him a shilling from her purse. She stuck out her tongue at me and walked off. I begged him to come to the Moving Crib. I wanted to see Trixie, the dog who had saved three people from drowning in the Liffey. He was stuffed now and part of the crib. Andy said he must be a stupid dog to end up as part of a moving crib when he was stuffed and couldn't move. I jumped on him and caught him in a headlock. He agreed to toss me for the moving crib or Walton's. The shilling came down on its side and started to roll down the hill. Past Sinn Fein it went and the Galway Arms Hotel. We ran after it, waiting for it to fall. It was against the rules to touch it once it left the hand. It bumped off the path and slowed down. It staggered for a second before it fell over. It was heads. Andy won.

We stood looking in the window of Walton's at the array

of musical instruments. We were standing on the railing ledge with our feet squashed between the uprights and our hands holding the spikes. I was so delighted I digged Andy in the side. Not too hard, just a nice gentle dig. He digged me gently back. When he won the toss I thought he was bringing me to Walden's. Walden's was a garage further up Frederick Street on the other side. It had nothing in the window except batteries and tyres. It was nothing like Walton's even if it sounded the same. I was never so delighted I'd lost a toss.

Walton's window had an electric organ that took up nearly the whole space. There was a stool in front of it covered in red satin and standing at the back was a cardboard man smiling from ear to ear. He had a black moustache and a sign in his hand – yours for as little as a pound a week. The cardboard man was delighted with the offer.

Andy shimmied along the railings to a second window. I followed him. It was given over to accordions. Whole families of them. Daddy ones and mammy ones. Second-hand and new ones. Open ones and closed ones. Accordion heaven. Accordion hell. I started to count. I got to twenty-six when I felt Andy's fist in my side.

—I hate accordions.

Andy pushed open the door into Walton's. A man came over and asked us what we wanted.

—Just looking.

—Just looking.

We made our way through the Aladdin's cave. The instruments were fixed onto walls, dangled from ceilings, sat on chairs, rested on floors. There were wind, stringed and traditional. Signs everywhere. Piano-tuning on request. Learn to play the zither. Credit terms available. Maurice Mulcahy shops at Waltons. Nurses Dance, Saturday, National Ballroom. Ask for assistance. Accompanied children only. I pointed it out to Andy.

—We're not children, come on.

A song crackled out all over the shop. It was Stone Age music recorded in the cave. The song came to an end and a man's voice beamed out . . .

—Remember, listeners, if you feel like singing, do sing an Irish song.

I'd heard him on the radio at home. Tommy somebody. He only played singers with RIP after their name. Dead people. Dead music. Dead culture. It was big among the corpses in Glasnevin Cemetery. We came to a flight of three steps with an archway at the bottom. A sign over it read 'popular instruments'.

We entered in and were greeted by a drum kit. Bass drum, side drum, snare and cymbals. Microphones, amplifiers and speakers. Acoustic guitars and electric guitars. Four strings, six strings and twelve strings. Gibson, Hohner and Fender. Tremolo arms were everywhere. A wah wah pedal just arrived from England sat on a shelf by itself. On the wall, Lonnie Donegan, Joe Brown, Cliff Richard and The Shadows. I knew this was special. We'd left the land of accordions and diddle de di and stepped from the past into the present.

Andy sat on the chrome stool and picked up a pair of drumsticks. He struck the snare drum once. It reverberated around the room. He struck it again. Louder this time. He waited for the echo to stop. When it did, he attacked the whole thing, hitting every drum and smashing every cymbal. He lost himself completely. He looked like a wild woman, a wild woman who'd invented sound. A man from Walton's leapt in and danced in front of him like a demented ape.

—How much are the drums?

I thought the man was going to drop dead on the floor. Andy stood up and held out the sticks.

—How much are these?

I heard the man say a shilling, but the words seemed to come from a space behind his head. Andy repeated it.

—A shilling.

The man started to point the way out. Andy took the shilling from his pocket and offered it to him. I noticed that one of Andy's breasts had flattened out. It looked peculiar. One proper breast and one flat one. The Walton's man just kept pointing. We paid for the drumsticks and went out on to the street. I told Andy about his breast.

—Shit.

We ran around the corner into a pub opposite Barry's Hotel. Straight to the gent's where we both peed and Andy fixed his bra stuffing. All the men were staring at us when we came out. I heard one of them say, 'Jesus, that's the best yet.'

Sharkey had the teeth ready. He showed us where he'd welded the two halves together with steel pins. Four of them. Sunk right into the plastic so they wouldn't grate against the roof of the mouth. He took us into the workshop and showed us how he clamped the two halves in a vice. There were teeth everywhere and an assistant who was deaf. Mr Sharkey spoke of the teeth like they were people. After five minutes in there I felt they had souls. I asked him how much for the dental surgery.

—Twelve shillings and six pence.

He said it without conviction. He wanted companionship, not money.

—I only have ten shillings. I'll have to go home for the rest.

I took the single orange note out of my pocket and held it out to him. I pretended it was a carrot. A proper carrot with green leaves coming out the top. He looked down at it and I could see tenderness in his eyes. He was a lonely surgeon. Only false teeth to talk to. He was becoming like them. Out of sympathy. Wouldn't do to be flashing perfect teeth in a hospital full of sick ones.

—Ten shillings is fine.

He wrapped Da's teeth in grease-proof paper and put

them in a brown paper bag with his name, address and telephone number stamped in red ink on the front. Going down the stairs, Andy rattled his drumstick along the banisters and I jumped the last eight steps to the ground. Outside, I showed Andy the other ten shilling note I'd kept under wraps in my pocket.

—My Da will be delighted.

Never produce money before you negotiate the price. It was a cardinal rule. It had paid off handsomely. What were his other money rules? Never jingle silver in your pockets. Always look like you haven't enough. Never give the impression you're getting a bargain. Always look for faults with the goods. Don't be misled by appearances. Fools and their money are easily parted. Learn the poor mouth young and practise it all your life.

Andy grabbed me by the arm and pulled me close. He couldn't believe I was going to tell Da about the half-crown I'd saved him. He tapped the drumstick against my forehead and asked me had I sawdust for a brain.

—You'll never be a millionaire. It's yours and you're giving it away.

Andy was right. By Da's own rules it was mine. I'd earned it. How could I be so dense? Running home to hand it over. To show how great a messenger I was. That was the role I'd been given by Da. I'd been called after him, named for him, and he expected me to live up to some idea he had of me. He was always organizing boxing matches between me and Shea. If I got the right-hand glove, Shea would get the left-hand one. We fought in the kitchen until one of us cried. It wasn't fair because Shea was three years older than me. There wasn't much in height between us but Shea hit harder than me. It was usually me who cried, but I tried hard not to because Da took it out on Shea if he made my tears flow. In the boxing matches I represented Da and Shea represented Ma. It was a terrible position to be in.

I had a lot of power over Da's moods. I could send him into a rage but I did my best to avoid that. I didn't like him when he raged. I didn't like being called a jinx when his horses lost. I liked going to the bookies' when his horses won and bringing home the winnings. I liked it when he brought home a large bottle of lemonade from the pub. I loved it best of all when he sang 'Frankie and Johnny' without being asked. Sometimes I could make everything come right by wishing for it. Sometimes I could do it by going on a really special message. I had to forget myself to make it happen. The half-crown would make him happy. But Andy was correct. It was mine by rights. I was never going to be a millionaire. I couldn't get it out of my head all the way down Talbot Street. Andy knew so much about money and he had a pair of drumsticks to prove it. Every lamp-post we came to he beat out a rhythm. I knew what it was saying.

—Mil – yon – air – no. Mil – yon – air – no.

I felt like a part of me had died. The millionaire part. Johnny Forty Coats was selling his shoe laces and holy medals under the railway bridge. He stood there with his half-open red eyes that looked like they were bleeding. Some people said he had been a millionaire once. I consoled myself that not all millionaires turned out so well. We walked down the boundary wall to Sheriff Street and straight into the shrine of The Little Flower. I told Andy he'd turn into a saint if he kept going on the way he was. He told me it wasn't for himself he was doing it. It was a promise he'd made to Catherine, his sister. If he escaped in her clothes, he had to pray every day to Saint Teresa.

—I told you she was holy.

In Christy Dooley's vegetable shop, Andy got him to empty out two orange boxes. He spilled them in on top of the cooking apples and gave Andy the empty crates.

—There y'are, Mary.

110

Andy was making a drum kit. He was going to cover the crates with rubber to get a nice sound. His Auntie Kathleen had two metal pots he could use for cymbals. Until he got the money to buy proper ones. Or found the money. Money, money, money. You could do nothing without it. It was the root of all evil. Andy headed into Phil Shanahan with the boxes and I headed into Mattie's with the ten shilling note. I changed it for four half-crowns. I ran home and put the teeth on the table and beside the teeth I put three half-crowns in a pile, one on top of the other, and stared at them. All the time I looked at them I thought only of the one in my pocket. Andy was wrong about me. I'd taken my first step on the road to becoming a millionaire.

Da made a big ceremony of trying out the teeth. We watched him lift up the gigot chop and plunge his teeth into the meat. He tore at it like a dog. When he finally yanked the meat off, he chewed it for ages before swallowing. He munched it at the front of his mouth like a rabbit. With his tongue in a curl, he hoovered all around his mouth for stray bits of flesh. He took the dentures out and checked the roof of his mouth to see if food had got through the crack or not. He replaced them in his mouth with a satisfied suck.

—They're perfect.

Everyone went back to eating their tea.

—You give proper instructions, you have no problems in life.

Da sucked his chop. Shea, Ita and Johnny cut their rissoles into tiny squares. I looked at my plate and felt miserable to my stomach. Every time I thought of the half-crown my stomach made to come out through my mouth. I loved rissoles and couldn't eat. I thought about handing it over but how would I explain? I tried to put it out of my mind and it came into my mind even more. Life as a millionaire was off to a very bad start.

Andy practised the drums morning, noon and night. Every

song that came on Radio Luxembourg had live drumming from Andy. He stopped going to the shops for his Auntie Kathleen and stayed in the house twenty-four hours a day. He practised so much the rubber on the orange boxes wore away. The neighbours on both sides were up in arms over the racket. Then things got better for a while. Andy covered the boxes with blankets. He got very frustrated. A drummer has to feel the vibrations. It goes through from the drum to the stick to the arm to the chest to the heart. After he got the sticks, Andy started to talk strange. He told me you had to be in rhythm with your heart to play the drums. He played a heartbeat for me on the orange box. He did it again. And again. I could have listened to it all day. It was my first lesson in music. He asked me what my heart was like after I'd run the whole length of the pitch and scored a goal. I told him. He did it for me. Faster and faster. Louder and louder. The walls shook. Louder and louder they shook. I could hear my heart. It was pounding the walls. The next-door neighbour was banging his fists. Andy stopped.

—If you don't stop those effin' drums, I'll tear your heart out.

Auntie Kathleen was spending a lot more time in the Ball Alley. The neighbours had no one to complain to. It got too much and someone called the police. Unheard of in Sheriff Street. The funny thing was we were as quiet as mice when the Gardai came to investigate the complaint. We'd just been up town where I'd spent the last of the lousy half-crown on two goldfish for the bowl beside the radio. We were watching them swim around when the knock came. It didn't take the Gardai long to figure out who Mary Griffin was. The Brothers were sent for. I was questioned and let go. Andy was sent into the bedroom to change out of Catherine's clothes. He got out of the first floor window, jumped onto the grass verge below and hurt his ankle. I was walking down Oriel Street when I saw him making his way along the boundary wall. I soon caught up with him. When we got to Amiens Street he walked straight out in front of the traffic. As he did, the black car with Turkey Head in it came into view. The car screeched to a halt. I ran across the main road with Andy behind me dragging his leg. We passed by the posh entrance to the Elec. When we got to the entrance for the wooders, Andy ducked straight in and crept under the pay hatch. I followed him. When the attendant in the blue and gold suit asked for our tickets, Andy told him we'd escaped from Artane. He let us in and shone his torch to a free space right in the middle of the wooders.

On the screen, Jack Lemmon and Tony Curtis were watching a gangland massacre. I couldn't concentrate on it, thinking about Andy's leg. Was it broken or not? Andy was right down in the seat as far as he could go. I bent down to him.

—Are you all right?

There were whistles in the cinema. I couldn't hear him. He shouted at me to get back in my seat. I sat upright. Marilyn Monroe was walking along a platform wriggling her arse. The film broke down. It often broke down in the Elec. The lights came on. There was more whistling. Turkey Head and two Gardai came in and started to walk along the side. They looked down every row of seats as they went. The whistling was deafening. Up on the balcony a man's voice rang out.

—Here, Brother O'Byrne, catch that.

I turned and saw a man pissing from the balcony, pissing down on Turkey Head. He was joined by others. Those who weren't pissing threw popcorn, ice-pop sticks and crumpled cigarette packs. Thick green spits flew at them. They tried to shield themselves with their hands. They were pelted out of it. It was the final nail. They withdrew from the cinema. There were huge cheers, quickly followed by a slow hand clap. It continued until the lights went out and Marilyn Monroe appeared in a black nightdress lying across a sleeper

113

bed in a train. Andy and I stayed on the floor. When it was over we split up. I followed the crowd out of the narrow entrance into Talbot Street, where four Gardai stood side by side staring at the faces coming out. Their eyes darted from left to right and right to left. I turned away from them in the opposite direction to home. I felt a hand on my shoulder.

—You're in serious trouble.

It was the Garda from Auntie Kathleen's who'd told me to go home. He put me standing by the entrance and warned me not to move. I could feel the build-up of diarrhoea in my stomach. I was going to gaol. I knew it. I should never have stolen the half-crown, that's when it started. I never wanted to be a millionaire in the first place. It was all Andy Griffin's fault. The drums, the half-crown, everything. I wanted to stay poor and happy for the rest of my life, only I didn't have a life any more. The only life I had was behind bars. Helping someone to escape was a serious crime. I'd be joining Andy in Artane, if I was lucky. Knowing my luck, I'd get Mountjoy.

The cinema emptied and no sign of Andy. They went in and searched it. They came out scratching their heads. They were in serious discussions with Turkey Head. There was lots of arm waving and pointing. First towards me, then towards Sheriff Street, then towards the docks. All of a sudden, Turkey Head was back in his black Ford, the Gardai were in three squad cars and they moved in convoy up Talbot Street. I stood where I was and held the cheeks of my arse tight. A queue started to form for the next picture. I could have made a run for it, but didn't. One step and I wasn't sure what would happen. I started to relax the cheeks of my arse a tiny bit. My stomach relaxed in tandem. Finally, I let it all go and there was no evacuation. I had a good look around for Gardai. Had they forgotten me? Or were they waiting for me to lead them to Andy? They had me under surveillance but I didn't know where they were watching me from. I heard Mikey Grey's voice from the queue.

—Have you seen it, Shero?

—Yeah.

—What's it like?

—I don't know.

—You don't know?

—I know nothing. Absolutely nothing. There's no point in asking me.

—Jesus, I only asked.

I looked up at the canopy over the posh entrance. *Some Like It Hot*. It was a good title.

I walked away and headed for home. I stopped and checked I wasn't being tailed. At the Ball Alley I ducked in and went to the toilet. I knew the Gardai wouldn't follow me in there. It was a rough pub. Noel Dargan was there. Ma didn't approve of the lodgers getting too friendly with the locals. Da was always afraid of information being leaked that could find its way to the tax man. Noel Dargan offered me a lemonade but I refused. I had to get home and lie low. I had to get home and pray that the Gardai didn't raid our house in the middle of the night and take me away. Andy was on the boat by now, I knew that. They'd never catch him. He'd had too much freedom to let it go now.

They caught him the next day in the casualty department of Temple Street Hospital with his foot in a cast. He'd had no chance of making a run for it. His Auntie Kathleen was with him when they found him so they weren't too rough with him. It was a sad end to his days on the run, though.

Andy had drumsticks on his person at the time of his arrest. The Gardai wanted to charge him with carrying an offensive weapon but for some unknown reason, or maybe it was the intervention of Saint Teresa, he was allowed to keep them and the charges were dropped. He was back in Artane where he would have plenty of time for listening to the beating of his heart.

6

1963

Frankie stopped being the baby the day Ma came home from the hospital with Gerard. We hadn't had a new baby in the house for six years. Everyone crowded around the Moses basket to make faces at the new arrival. I loved having a new brother but I got embarrassed when I thought about how he came to be there. Did Da not know Ma had enough to do without making new babies? When I put that out of my mind I enjoyed the smell of talcum powder. Seeing Ma shake it on the new baby reminded me of the night the aerial went up. Now everyone had aerials. Not everyone had a new baby. I loved the gripe water bottle with the picture of the baby on the front. I thought for years it was me. The ringlets were the same as mine. I was very upset when I found out it was someone else. I took a huge gulp out of the bottle. Soon as I did it brought me right back. I was in the blue cot again with the picture of the lamb. The taste of hot milk and giving in to sleep and Da's knee at the table. Being the baby in our house meant the privilege of Da's knee at all meals. Sucking the crust of his bread and drinking the dregs of his tea. Mashing his potatoes with a fork and sucking the marrow from the bones on his plate. I made way on Da's knee for Johnny. Johnny made way for Frankie. We all thought Frankie would stay king of the castle for ever, but his race was run. It was Gerard's turn to sit on the throne.

Frankie was all lovey dovey with Gerard. He wanted him all to himself. He'd soak his soother in gripe water and put it in his mouth. He wouldn't let anyone come near him. I was fascinated. Brotherly love. I'd never seen it like this before. Frankie talked baby talk to him. I stayed watching them for ages. Then it dawned on me that Frankie wanted him all to himself because he wanted to kill him. He pushed the soother further and further into Gerard's mouth. He pushed it so far he was choking him. I saw him convulsing, ran over and pulled it from his mouth. Ma knew exactly what was going on. She took Frankie on her knee and held him tight while she told him off for what he'd done. Ma's voice was harsh but Frankie looked like he was in Heaven. The more Ma gave out to him, the more he turned his face into her breasts. It was a kind of triumph for him. It was the opposite two weeks later at the christening party. Da changed his favourite song to 'Frankie and Gerard' and made up new words as he went along.

—*Frankie and Gerard were brothers,*
  oh Lordy, how they did love . . .
  Frankie went down to the shops,
  to buy his little brother some sweets . . .

Frankie lay down on the kitchen floor, bicycle-kicked his feet in the air and tried to scream the house down. Da was in no mood to humour him. He ignored the tantrum. In the middle of the song, Da balanced a full bottle of stout on the top of his head, did a ballet dance around the floor and sang more tales of the brothers Frankie and Gerard. Not even Ma's lap could console Frankie and he ended up being put to bed early, where he cried for another half an hour before his sobbing turned to snores.

It was the best party ever in our house. Da let us all try the bottle on the head trick. Six full bottles smashed on the floor. Every one that went down caused more laughter than the one before. Ma tried it, which is saying something. Uncle

Paddy nearly tried it but he was laughing so much he couldn't get the bottle on his head. He ended up lying on the floor with the bottle on his forehead pretending he was a happy corpse. We laughed until five o'clock in the morning.

The next day Sharkey's sent Da a copy of the receipt. In my hurry out of the shop I'd left it behind me. He opened the letter and asked me how much the teeth cost. When I told him twelve shillings and sixpence, he clattered me across the face and told me to go to my room. I crawled under my bed and waited for his footsteps on the stairs. I left the light off for protection. I deserved more than a clatter, I knew that. I expected he'd come up with his belt and give it to me on the legs and back. He'd only ever used the belt on me once. I'd gotten up to play on the railway line. It was strictly forbidden. I couldn't have been more than three. I deserved it then. I deserved it now. I'd betrayed every principle he stood for. He'd taught me how to wrangle. How to get a good price. I was throwing it back in his face. I deserved six lashes. Maybe ten. I wasn't afraid to take my medicine – I just hoped he'd come soon. Waiting was the worst part. Maybe he'd send one of the others up and get me to come down. Most likely Frankie. He was beginning to train him in. Small messages. The corner shop for razor blades. Up the stairs for me. I'd come down and lie across a chair. Pull my trousers down. The others would watch. Or maybe it would be a private lashing. I didn't mind either way. Waiting to be hit. It hurt more than the lash. I counted the holes in the wire mattress spring. I got fed up at a hundred. I heard soft footsteps on the stairs. The light switch outside the bathroom flicked on. More footsteps. The door opened.

—You're wanted.

It was Frankie. His head came in the door but his body stayed outside.

—Da wants you.

I didn't answer. I stayed still where I was under the bed. I saw his feet come into the room.

—I know you're in there.

I could tell he was scared. He came as far as the wardrobe. The door was slightly ajar. He started to pull it.

—I know you're in there.

As he opened it he jumped back at the same time. He looked ridiculous. Pretending not to be afraid when you're shit scared is the silliest thing in the world. I'd have laughed out loud only I was facing the belt myself. Frankie looked under the bed and saw me.

—I knew you were there.

I couldn't be bothered answering the little twirp. He was still a snotty-nosed little soother sucker as far as I was concerned, capable of murder. The smiling face didn't fool me. I knew it was the smile of the hangman.

Soon as Da asked me where the money went I knew I was in for the Sermon on the Mount rather than a lashing with his belt. The theme of the sermon would be the evils of stealing. I desperately wanted a lash of the belt so I could go out and play with my friends. I didn't need to go over the history of the half-crown, penny by spent penny. It was torture. There was only so much guilt you could muster over sweets that were eaten, chewing gum that was chewed, lucky lumps that were sucked and liquorice that was licked. I had a pain in my face trying to look sorry.

He started on about the loaves and fishes. It was a story much misunderstood, according to him. The miracle wasn't that the loaves and the fishes multiplied. The real miracle was that Jesus taught the crowd to share bread with each other. When man shares his resources, meagre though they be, there's sufficient for the world. Jesus taught us the meaning of true charity. To share what we have. The story of the loaves and fishes was the story of socialism. Jesus

119

himself was the first socialist. That was the gospel according to Da.

I couldn't think about the loaves and fishes. All I could think about was the five a side starting up in the playground. Macker would be there with his whistle. If Da didn't hurry I'd miss the start of the game. I put on the saddest face I could manage. Thought of Andy in his dormitory in Artane. Nearly brought tears to my eyes. I looked up so he'd definitely see how sorry I was. I wiped away tears with the back of my hand. He was still on about the food in the desert. It was a theory, you see, and when Da had a theory he could stretch it out to kingdom come. He moved from the loaves to the fishes to the half a crown. I hadn't stolen Da's money, I'd stolen the family's money. Every penny I'd spent, I'd taken out of their pockets. I'd taken food from the dinner table and stuffed my own mouth full of sugar. I didn't need to think of Andy any more. I'd never felt so guilty in all my life. I recalled every trip to Mattie's for lucky lumps that felt like the unluckiest lumps in the world. I thought of the goldfish in the bowl beside the radio. Maybe I could claim them back from Andy's Auntie Kathleen. Put them in a bowl on our table so everyone could get a look at them. Turn them into sardines even, and share them out like Jesus in the desert. Maybe everyone would feel full and prove Da's theory correct.

Then came the bombshell. Da wasn't going to give me his belt. He was sending me to my bedroom where I was to stay for the next three days. No visitors. No friends. No shouting out of the window. I was to be deprived of all human contact, having sinned against humanity.

I sat on the bed and I cursed Da. I cursed him for being the coward he was. I cursed him for sending me on messages he wouldn't do himself. I cursed him for his notes which were the written proof of his own cowardice. I tried to imagine him in Sharkey's laboratory. I couldn't. He was full of hot air. Overflowing with advice he'd never follow himself. To whom it may concern, I am a yellow bastard. Please punish the bearer for my inadequacies and oblige. My reference, one only cowardly bastard, supplied and fitted.

I looked in the wardrobe mirror. I could see no resemblance of any kind between him and me. I tried to see into the future. I stared into the mirror, for ages and ages. I was sure my reflection was looking back at me. Like it had separated from me. I was afraid to look away in case it wasn't there when I looked back. I moved on the bed and my image moved, too. Reassured, I slid down to the foot of the bed and leaned in close. My nose almost touched the glass. I looked straight into my eyes. In my eyes, I could see the reflection of me looking in the mirror. It was like a crystal ball. I stood back from the mirror and tried to look mean. I curled my lip and let it quiver. I pointed at the mirror. My reflection pointed back. I pointed at myself. The words came from deep down in my gut.

—I'm Elvis Presley.

I pointed at my reflection again.

—You're not Elvis Presley.

I repeated it over and over again. The more I repeated, the more I was transformed. I knew what I had to do. I slipped quietly downstairs to the kitchen. Frankie was in the armchair by the fire watching television. *The Black and White Minstrel Show.* On our telly, even the black bits were white. Ma was in the scullery with Gerard on her shoulder heating up a bottle.

—Where's Da?

—Gone to the dogs.

Ma gave me the lecture about staying in the bedroom. I went back up the first flight of stairs, slipped out of the hall door and put the lock on the snip. I went around to our back door in Emerald Street. I pulled myself up and looked over the top. Ma was still in the scullery. I waited 'til she was gone. I sneaked into the garage and took a sheet of leftover cardboard from the twin tub. It had been months on its perch on the wall. I rooted out Da's wallpaper scissors from a biscuit tin on the shelf and stuffed them in my back pocket. I made my way back to the hall door, closed it without a sound and tip-toed my way back to the bedroom and safety. I laid the cardboard on the floor and drew the outline of a guitar on it. I cut it out carefully with the scissors, took it in my arms like a baby and stood in front of the mirror for examination. It looked ridiculous. I looked ridiculous. It was tiny. A disaster. A complete disaster. I didn't look like Elvis Presley at all. The only thing I looked like was a fool.

I went back down to the garage and stole the remaining cardboard sheets. I stood in front of the mirror with the cardboard rectangle and imagined where the various bits of the guitar should be. I marked them with X's. The neck. The body. The hole where the sound comes out. I held it in my arms and checked the marks. Measure twice and cut once. One of Da's cardinal rules. I cursed it when it came into my head. Da knew nothing about music apart from the words to 'Frankie and Johnny', and for all I knew he made them up just like the night of the christening when it was Frankie and Gerard. Me and my guitar had nothing to do with him. To get him out of my head, I concentrated on my Elvis lip.

The second guitar was the perfect shape and size but still looked like leftover cardboard from a washing machine. I got some colouring pencils from my school bag and started to give it some life. I discovered that black was best at covering over faults. It blocked out words like spin dry and automatic. I decided on gold for the edges. It looked great against the black. I did the strings in red but they disappeared against the black so I changed them to white. The only bit that looked wrong was the sound hole because it wasn't a hole at all. It was a gold spot and it looked like a gold spot. I stood in front of the mirror and it looked perfect apart from the gold spot. I did my Elvis actions, I curled my lip halfway up my face, but my eyes kept going to the hole that wasn't a hole. I lost my temper. I got the scissors, plunged them into the guitar and cut out a proper hole. When I held it in front of the mirror my heart sank. In making the hole, I'd cut the strings in half. I deserved to be stoned to death with balls of my own shite. I'd made a proper pig's mickey of it.

I blamed Da for it turning out wrong. I sat on the floor and cried onto my wrecked guitar. I wiped my tears away and saw everything twice. Two school bags, two pencil cases, two wardrobes, two guitars. It gave me an idea. I put the guitar on the cardboard and drew an outline of it. I cut it out and held it behind the guitar. For the first time the hole looked like a hole. I glued them together with Bostik. The very same tube that failed with the coward's teeth. It worked perfectly on the cardboard. I drew white lines to connect the strings again. It looked like a real guitar only skinnier. I cut out more outlines to fatten it up. I stood in front of the mirror. It looked like a real guitar. It felt like a real guitar. The only thing it didn't do was make real music but make-believe was just as good.

—I'm Elvis Presley, you're not Elvis Presley.

I wasn't afraid of me. I was alone with my guitar. I was who I wanted to be. I was Elvis.

—I'm Presley, Presley, Presley. Elvis, Elvis, Elvis.

My reflection knew who was boss. It knew the real Elvis. It was me, me, me. The bedroom door flew open and Frankie stood there pointing at me.

—You're not Elvis Presley.

He pointed to himself.

—I'm Elvis Presley.

He doubled up with the laughter. I threw my guitar on the bed and made a run for him. He jumped the eight steps

123

to the bathroom landing. He jumped the ten steps to the hall door landing. He was about to jump the four steps to the kitchen landing when I caught him by the scruff of the neck and pushed him against the banisters. I threatened him on pain of death not to divulge what he had seen. He started to answer me back. I told him I'd make him drink piss the way I'd done with Johnny once. I'd disguised it in a lemonade bottle and he'd slugged it down before he'd realized. Johnny cried then and Frankie cried now just like the baby he was. I gave him an insurance thump on the arm and I went back upstairs to practise on my guitar.

*

On the Thursday night, my gaol sentence finished and Da announced all-out war on the water pressure. He was going to dig up all the pipes coming into our house until he found where the blockage was. When the work was completed, we would have one hundred per cent water pressure and Ma's twin tub would leak no more. He announced the commencement of hostilities for the coming Saturday.

—We'll have it over and won in a week.

The 'we' was ominous for me. He would wield the pickaxe, he always did, and I would scoop the dirt. A back-breaking job, scooping out with a long-tailed shovel. Always having to be in the right place when the axe went up and when the axe came down. Protecting eyes from the concrete shrapnel. I'd worked as his trench boy when he dug the foundation for the scullery wall. I watched the sweat run down his naked back and belly. As well as working the trench, I handed him his towel from time to time. Like him, it was a ball of sweat by lunch-time and not worth a curse. But he persisted with it, as always, to the bitter end.

Da took a crumpled piece of paper from his inside pocket and opened it out on the table. It looked like a note from *Treasure Island* – symbols and letters that contained the

124

mystery of something buried underground. It was a map, once deciphered, that unlocked the mystery of the hidden pipes. It looked like it had been rescued from a fire. It was the nearest thing to disintegrated you could get. Da decided to copy it onto a more durable material and sent me out to the garage to fetch the leftover cardboard from the twin tub.

—What cardboard, Da?

—The cardboard on the garage wall.

I went out to the garage and looked in the space where the cardboard used to be. I thought it might still be there. I had a good look around. I looked three or four times in places I knew it couldn't be. Just like when you lose money. You look in stupid places for it. You search your pockets twenty times. You look up at the ceiling and under saucers for it. Under the sugar bowl and the table cloth. That was me in the garage. How could I be so stupid? He never threw anything out. I was really angry with him because he never threw anything out, and went back in.

—The cardboard's not there.

—Of course it's there.

—It's in my bedroom.

—What's it doing in your bedroom?

—I made a guitar out of it.

I looked straight at him. He wasn't as angry as I was.

—That was a stupid thing to do, wasn't it?

—No, it wasn't stupid.

He stood up. For a moment I thought he was going to strike out at me.

—Well, I'm telling you it was stupid.

He went over to a shelf where he kept his bookies' paper and rooted out a giant-sized Christmas card he'd won in the Liverpool Bar raffle. He'd never sent it to anyone. But he'd kept it, of course. As he opened it out on the table he asked me why I'd made a guitar.

—I'm going to learn to play it. I'm going to take lessons.

—You won't get much music from a cardboard guitar.

Everyone burst out laughing. I didn't mind. I'd stood up to him. I'd served my gaol sentence and I wasn't going to take any more punishment from him. I was going to learn the guitar. I'd staked my right to guitar lessons. Nothing he could do would stop me.

Da got very serious about the water pressure. He took a week's sick leave from the booking office to do the work. His record before that was one day absent in twenty years and that was only because he had to take a chest X-ray for a medical. Ma said he wasn't normal. She said he should take more sick leave because normal people got sick at least once a year. Now they'd think he was really sick. Really, really sick. Cancer or heart trouble. The bosses never gave promotion to people they thought were really sick. They only promoted people who got sick at least once a year. This row over Da's promotion prospects went on all the time. It was an argument he never won. The only way he could win it was if he became boss of the whole train station. Ma knew how to stick the knife in. She told him it was all a question of who you knew, not what you knew. On all fronts it was an argument designed to make Da feel inferior. This morning it felt like a continuation of something from the night before. Maybe he wanted more babies and Ma didn't. I was waiting for him to put on his hat and coat and leave. Instead he ordered me out to the garage to assemble his tools. I expected to hear raised voices but there weren't any. In a few minutes he followed me out.

—You and your guitar lessons.

That was typical of him. He was fighting with Ma so he turned on me. Ma must have said something about my guitar lessons. It was a good sign.

We opened the garage doors and pushed the two cars out onto the street. He let me steer. We put the giant-sized

Christmas card on the floor with the new map. Da drew chalk lines on the floor representing the pipes below.

He took up the pickaxe and split the concrete along the chalk lines. I dragged the broken bits into a pile at the side, making sure not to stand in the path of his swing. Da got into a rhythm. He whistled 'Old Man River'. He hummed it. He la la'd it. He tapped it with his foot. At the end of each line of the song he paused, and followed it with a big crash of the metal axe on stone. The entire garage moved. He switched songs to 'Mack the Knife'. It didn't last long. In no time he was back to 'Old Man River'. It seemed inevitable.

The trench quickly took shape. I stood in it. It was an easier angle to get the shovel under the dirt. As I scooped I kept an eye out for money. I'd found some when we did the scullery wall. It would be difficult today. Not difficult finding it. Difficult picking it up and putting it in my pocket after the events surrounding the half a crown. I decided not to look for money. If I saw some I'd just leave it there. It was as difficult not looking for money as looking for it. It was difficult with Da's mood. There was no conversation. Nothing but the sad notes of 'Old Man River'.

He worked to a depth of two feet. There was no sign of pipes. He went into the kitchen and came back with the poker. He pushed it into the soil. He tapped it down with a wooden mallet and listened for the sound of metal on metal. He thought he heard something. It wasn't clear. He took up the pickaxe and went at it with renewed vigour. We were down to three feet. I was starting to disappear. There was so much soil the garage looked like France in the First World War. Da couldn't accept he might be digging in the wrong place. Just a few more inches and we'd be there. A dud map was a perversion of history. We were down very far. His rhythm slowed to a standstill. He stood out of the trench

127

and kicked a load of soil back in with his foot. It was the gesture of a defeated man.

—The guitar is only a mongrel, you know that?

I had no idea what he was talking about.

—Why can't you take up a proper instrument like the clarinet?

When he heard the clarinet on the radio he pointed it out, every time. In the middle of a song, he'd say, there's the clarinet. When the Black and White Minstrels appeared on the television he never tired of pointing out the wind section of the orchestra. After that he focused in on the clarinet. The thoroughbred of the orchestra.

—The guitar is a proper instrument.

—Where is its place in the orchestra?

I couldn't think of an answer. I could only think of Lonnie Donegan and Joe Brown and Hank Marvin. And Elvis Presley, of course. They didn't play in orchestras. They were their own orchestras. They were groups. Guitars, drums and a singer.

—The guitar doesn't need an orchestra.

He went from a temper to a rage in one second flat.

—I was going to offer you clarinet lessons but you can sing for them now.

He started on a second trench to the right of the chalk marks while I filled in the first one at double speed. Every stroke of the pickaxe was a confirmation of my ingratitude. The tune changed to 'Rawhide' and he kept up a ridiculous tempo that had me flat to the boards to stay with him. It turned out to be another dry well. He ordered me to fill it in while he started on a third trench to the left of the chalk marks. Four feet down he stopped in mid-swing and started to cry. Father, father, why have you forsaken me? The tears turned to curses. He cursed God first and then the Irish Government. Dublin Corporation and the 1916 leaders. He cursed the men who laid the water pipes. He cursed the perverted cripple with a hunchbacked father who made the map. He wished nothing else for him but every form of pox, gout and the dropsy. Shiny Suit got a lashing – the man with the weasel words. The guitar got another going over – bastard offspring of a Spanish gypsy. Ma came in for special mention. The Jonah of all Jonahs. The sinker of ships. The destroyer of men. She and her twin tub had brought him to a sorry end. How had he ended up a foul wretch with nothing to show for his life's labours only four dry wells? He marched into the kitchen for his tea. Ma was full of hope.

—How did you get on?

—Bad.

She knew not to pursue the line of enquiry. She knew her old man of the sea. The wrong word and we could end up with a hunger strike. Ma never wanted that. Nothing good ever came of his hunger strikes. Good dinners thrown in the bin. Silences that stretched out for days. The wrong word and it could take root. Jonah. I could see the word sitting on his lip like a torpedo. The wrong word from Ma and she was sunk. I willed her to keep her mouth shut. She poured his tea. I willed her with my mind.

Don't light the fuse. Stay out of the no-man's land between the trenches. One wrong swish of your dress and the whole thing will explode. She went out to the scullery to make more tea. She uttered not a word. The danger passed. I had won the day with my mind but I didn't like having to do it.

After tea, Ma switched on the Black and White Minstrels for him. George Chisolm came on. He did comedy with a trombone. He wore a red nose and made funny sounds. Da always laughed at men who wore red noses. At the circus he laughed the loudest at the clowns. George Chisolm blew a long note on the trombone and pretended he'd farted.

—Isn't that marvellous what you can do with a trombone?

He laughed out loud. It was a laugh full of the wonder

of something. For the moment the dry wells were forgotten. Ma looked over at me from where she was feeding Gerard. She hadn't had much time for me since Da adopted me as his messenger. The way she smiled over at me I felt closer to her than I'd done for ages. She knew what I was going through in the garage. I knew what she was going through with Da at night. She looked composed with Gerard in her lap. She was in control. Of the house. Of Da. Of us. She was at the wheel, steering the ship. Da was still laughing at the television, but inside he was seething with anger. Ma was more excited about the guitar lessons than I was myself.

—Go on, ya boy ya!

She clenched her fists and marched around the kitchen like she was playing the drums at the head of a marching band. It was typical Ma. You wouldn't want your friends to see her and at the same time she didn't care if the whole world was looking at her, which made it all right for anyone to see her. Something about the guitar connected to her. It wasn't the music, it was the rebellion. Ma loved underdogs. Outsiders. Rebels. She'd lived through the pogroms in Belfast in the thirties and had seen Catholics burned out of their homes. She knew what it was to be treated second class. The world was the haves and the have nots and Ma was with the have nots. It only took a spark to light her passion. She jerked around the kitchen by way of letting me know she approved of the guitar.

*

I found the ad under musical instruments. Guitar lessons. Beginners welcome. Evenings only. I phoned the number and got the address. It was five shillings a lesson with a deposit of a pound on the first night. Ma wouldn't let me go on the bike because Harold's Cross was too far. Specially coming home in the dark. Da was disappointed. I'm not sure if it was with Ma or me. He only made one comment. When Ma took the money from her purse and handed it to me, he looked over the top of the racing page and said to me:

—Make sure you get a receipt for that.

I hopped on the back of a horse and cart in Seville Place. It almost took me to Dorset Street where I got on a number 16 bus bound for Harold's Cross. I asked the conductor to let me off at Leinster Avenue. I sat in the television seat and looked at all the passengers. How many of them knew I was about to become a guitarist? How many of them knew my mother mimed the guitar like she was playing a drum? How many of them had bought tickets from my Da in the train station on their way to the beach? I played lots of games like that because it was a long way to Harold's Cross on the bus. I was glad I hadn't taken the bike. It looked like we were going all the way out to the Dublin mountains. The bus pulled up beside an open green patch in a housing estate. The conductor shouted from the back platform.

—Last stop, folks.

I assumed this was Leinster Avenue. I asked the conductor as I got off.

—You missed your stop, son.

I could feel the blood drain from my face.

—I called out Leinster Avenue miles back.

I started to panic.

—I didn't hear you, mister.

He pointed to the back seat.

—Sit down there and don't panic. We'll see what we can do.

He got off and went around to the front to talk to the driver. He hopped up on the bonnet and changed the scroll at the front of the bus. It read SPECIAL. He got on and banged the bell four times – that meant emergency, no stops. All the lights in the bus went off. I'd never travelled in a darkened bus before. It was spooky. People at bus stops put their hands out but we whizzed past. When we got to Leinster

Avenue the bus turned right off the main road and headed for Rathmines. The driver stopped the bus outside a red brick house with steps up to it. The conductor brought me up and knocked on the door. A young woman with a baby came out and told us it was the basement. The conductor slipped a sixpence into my hand and got back on his bus. I waved to him and the driver and went in the door under the stone steps.

There were lots of people sitting on chairs. I thought there would only be me. Me and the teacher. I was surprised there were other people in the room. They were looking at sheets of paper with diagrams on them and talking to each other. I was glad they ignored me. I sat on a chair near the door. I picked up some sheets and held them in my hand. I felt safer that way. The people were very old. There was no one under twenty. I counted them. Ten men and one woman. The teacher burst into the room and apologized for being late. He went straight to the top of the room and took his guitar from its case. It had a thick leather strap. He put it over his head without taking off his hat or his overcoat and he let it rest on his shoulders. He took the cigarette butt from his mouth and stuck it between two of the strings near the top of the guitar. He spread out his music pages on the desk beside him. He was the palest person I'd ever seen in my life. His skin was grey like the ash on his cigarette. He must have been at least thirty but it looked like he'd never shaved. He had a newspaper sticking out of each of his overcoat pockets. He put his hand in one of the pockets and rooted around. He took out a packet of Players Please and removed a cigarette from the pack. He lit it with the butt from his guitar and replaced one with the other. Then he looked up and around the class for the first time.

—Hello, hello.

—Hello.

He stopped at me.

—What are you doing here?

I didn't want to answer, it seemed such a stupid question.

—Me?

—Yes, you son.

—I'm here to learn the guitar.

He let out a short, frantic laugh. The others laughed in harmony.

—Who sent you here?

—My Ma.

—Your Ma?

—And my Da.

—Why did they send you?

—To learn the guitar.

—It's just that you don't have a guitar, son.

I looked around the room and for the first time I saw that everyone there had a guitar across their knee. All I wanted to do was run out of the room. To disappear. To turn into smoke. To run home and plunge the pickaxe in Da's skull. To bury Ma alive in the garage. I crumpled up the diagrams in my hand and squeezed them tight.

—I have a guitar at home.

—Why didn't you bring it?

I saw my reflection in the window behind him. It was laughing at me. You're a fucking eegit, I'm not a fucking eegit. I looked away and saw them all staring at me.

—The strings on it are broken.

It was the best I could do. I couldn't tell them it was made out of cardboard.

—Buy a set of strings and bring it next week.

I got up to go, when a man came over to me and handed me his guitar.

—We can share it.

I'd felt one in Walton's but it was the first time I'd handled the real thing. I was surprised the neck was so round and the body so big. It felt like reaching over a mountain to get my right hand on the strings. Worse still was trying to put the fingers of my left hand in the places represented by dots on the diagram sheets. My first finger was on the first string and my second finger was on the fifth string two miles away. Trying to get my third finger onto the sixth string was impossible. The chord was called G7. Whoever invented it had a sense of humour, that was for sure. After twenty-five attempts I managed to put my fingers in the right places. I struck the six strings with my right hand and made a sound that was definitely real music. When I finished G7 I was supposed to move my fingers to another chord but my hand was stuck to the guitar in a spasm. I couldn't move any of my fingers in any direction. I asked the man who owned it to pull my fingers off, which he did.

The marks left by the guitar strings were really sore. It looked like somebody had tried to saw the tops of my fingers off. I was hoping they'd last all the way home. I abandoned the 16 bus in O'Connell Street and ran down Talbot Street. When I pushed in the back door, Da was in the scullery washing his neck. He was obsessed with washing his neck. He had worked on in the garage but still hadn't found any water pipes. Ita was feeding Gerard his bottle but Shea and Johnny were in bed. There wasn't a sign of a lodger. Ma had gone down to the Liverpool to get Da a half-dozen stout. That indicated a serious foul mood. He came in from the scullery with the towel around his neck and asked me about the guitar lessons. I felt the tips of my fingers with my thumb but I said nothing. The only thing I wanted to say to him was how foolish I'd looked turning up with no guitar, but how could I? I knew what he'd say to that. That's what you get for turning your nose up at the clarinet.

I went upstairs. Johnny was fast asleep. If sleep made you grow, which Ma claimed it did, he was going to be a giant. I showed my fingers to Shea. He was only a little bit impressed. I took out my cardboard guitar and put my fingers in the shape of G7. It was simple. It didn't hurt and in my imagination it sounded great. Still, I wanted more than anything to play the real thing. I got into bed, put my arms around my guitar and held it tight like a person. I thought of Andy practising his drum in Artane. It was so much easier to play the drums. I wondered if Andy slept with his drumsticks. Under his pillow or up his sleeves? Or right beside him staring at him through the night? I wondered was he thinking of me? I told him the whole story of my first guitar lesson. I left nothing out. I filled in every detail right up until I played G7 by myself.

*

We were a whole week digging up the garage without success. Twenty-seven holes and two tons of dirt. I was beginning to think there were no pipes when Da struck water with the first dig on Saturday morning. It was nowhere near the chalk marks he'd drawn on the concrete. It was the complete opposite in fact. Whereas Da had drawn the lines two feet in from the outside wall, the pipes were two feet in from the inside wall. He was going through the litany of curses for the map maker when I pointed it out to him. He took out the crumpled map and looked at it. He turned the map around in his hand and I could tell from his face that he'd made a mistake. Except, of course, that he never made a mistake.

—Did you distract me when I was studying that map?

I didn't give it the dignity of a reply.

—I think you're becoming a bit of a jinx.

I had always been his lucky mascot. At the races. Going to the bookies'. I was the lucky one. The special one. I had the gift of bringing home the right thing. A stone of Jeffare's hard wall plaster. Two stone of fine sand with a little lime to mix. A four-stone bag of Drogheda cement. On the back of the bike. The front of the bike. On the shoulder or

135

dragged. By wheelbarrow, by trolley (funeral or otherwise), by boxcar (borrowed, begged or stolen), by Shanks's mare, my mission was to get things home. I carried his notes, I explained them, I turned them into English, I hid them, I burned them, I threw them away. I placed his bets, I collected his winnings. I was never a jinx. Everyone else but me. If I was a jinx, there was no future. Only last Christmas Eve I did Superman for him. Left our house at five to six to pick up a fort for Frankie's Christmas present in a shop in Capel Street. Pedalled so fast the wheels left the ground. Got there in ten minutes, a world record, and the shop was closed.

Checked every pub in Capel Street until I found the owner in Slattery's Pub and got him to open up his shop again. Carried the fort home balanced between my knees and the handlebars. The best Santa present Frankie ever got. Was I a jinx then? Or had he forgotten? I was going to remind him but I let it go. He was angry about the clarinet. I was angry about the guitar. At some stage I'd have to tell him I couldn't continue lessons without one.

Da dug out a two-foot channel around the pipe. He went out to the little shore on the street, lifted up the metal tongue, pushed the stopcock onto the square nipple and turned the water off. He came back into the garage and started to hacksaw at the lead pipes. He was only a quarter of an inch through when Mrs Scally and Mrs Hogan were at the back door wondering was there a problem with the water. Da explained that it would be off for an hour. Mrs Scally was upset because she was about to step into her bath. Da told her she'd be scrubbing the back off herself in no time. Soon as she was gone he turned to me.

—She hasn't had a bath in months, that one.

He cut out a six-inch section of pipe. The water drained out. He asked me to go in the house and ask Ma for an old pair of her knickers. I hated doing it. I had no choice. It was ask her or face a court martial. She gave me a white pair and I brought them out to Da. He started to plug one end of the pipe with them. It was a small opening so the fine material in the calico was perfect for the job. When he had it stuffed tight, he sent me out to turn the water back on. I did it and returned to the garage. Da was in the sniper position with his hand held fast against the knickers as the water did its best to push itself out. You could hear the pressure of the water hissing inside the pipe. It started to rattle. I lay down beside him and pressed my hand against his to keep the knickers in. Then he pulled the knickers away and thick gunge poured out of the pipe followed by a torrent of water. He was ecstatic.

—There's the silt, there she is, come on you bastard.

A pint of treacly shit emptied itself out. Da turned off the main, came back in and stood victoriously over the hole.

—No wonder we'd no pressure.

We took a well deserved tea break. Da studied form. He felt his luck was in. We were halfway to solving the mystery of the water pressure and the bookies were waiting to be relieved of their cash. It was a Saturday they were going to remember. He had six winners picked. He wrote out the bet in his usual free-flowing style and took a copy of it at the top of the racing page. Fifteen one shilling doubles, twenty one shilling trebles, fifteen one shilling four timers, six one shilling five timers and a two shilling six timer for luck. Total stake, fifty-eight shillings. Two bob short of three pounds. I put the money and the docket in my pocket and got on the bike. I took the docket back out of my pocket and kissed it. I cycled down to Bet with Security. With every turn of the pedal I repeated in my head:

—This is my guitar . . . this is my guitar . . . this is my guitar.

The number on the docket was 946. Added together they made 19 and S for Shero was the nineteenth letter of the alphabet. It was a very good sign. When I handed the docket to Da he wrote Toby Jug on the back in his best handwriting. It was his lucky name.

Da had a piece of white plastic pipe to connect the lead pipe back together. The problem was he couldn't get the lead pipe inside the white plastic. He took down one of his biscuit tins and rooted out an old Christmas candle. A red one. He lit the candle and held the plastic over it for several minutes until it softened. He brought the hot plastic to the lead and it slid onto it like a hand going in to a leather glove. He brought the candle into the hole and repeated the operation at the other end. When the plastic cooled the whole thing was a tight fit. He pulled at the join but there wasn't a budge. This was Da at his best. Cool, calm and not a smidgeen of anger to be seen.

—We might need a jubilee clip each end for insurance, what do you think?

Jubilee clips were Da's answer to everything. They'd been invented by the Greeks who discovered every worthwhile law in the universe. The first time I saw one was when he connected an unwilling hose to a tap. The panacea to all our ills, he said. I had to look it up in the dictionary afterwards. It meant solution. I looked in the hole and saw what I thought was a solution. I shrugged my shoulders.

—It looks fine to me.

We went in to the scullery for the big test. They were just off in the first race, so we waited. It was difficult to make out the horses with the snow. Not for Da, though. He knew by instinct where his horses were. They went by the post. His horse wasn't in the shake-up. He cursed the trainer, the jockey and the BBC. His horse finished last, which seemed to satisfy him in a perverse sort of way.

—What did I tell you? Last! I wouldn't mind only the winner was my first choice. Don't ever desert your first choice. Every time I do, I pay the price.

We went out to the scullery. Ma turned on the tap. There was a splutter and the water came. Ma watched it for ages and from every angle, near and far.

—I think it's a bit better, Da.

There was a look. A bit better? Twenty-seven water holes and a week off work for a bit better? Was she a mad woman? A bit better? He told me to fill in the hole in the garage. There was a second water pipe in the yard and this was now the focus of Da's attentions. He took up the pickaxe and began to smash the concrete in the yard. Mrs Scally and Mrs Hogan appeared at the back door saying it was nice to have the water back but the pressure wasn't as good as before. Da's rhythm increased considerably. Most of the yard went flying through the air in a concrete fireworks display. The women beat a hasty retreat. I'd never cleared a trench so fast in all my life. In no time, Da was hacksawing through his second lead pipe of the day. He repeated the trick with the knickers and another pint of silt spilled out its guts. There could be no excuse now for the water. It had a silt-free run from the street to the house. He wouldn't turn on the tap himself. He thought it might be bad luck. Ma was feeding Gerard. I could have volunteered but I suspected it might be a suicide mission. Ma put Gerard in the pram with a soother and came out to the scullery. She turned on the tap and it dribbled out as before. She knew not to say anything. He walked into the kitchen and sat down at the table with his head in his hands. He was inconsolable. A race came on the television. His horse was in a photo finish with another one. He knew it was second.

—Turn that miserable thing off.

I waited for a moment. I was sure I'd misheard him. He never turned the racing off. Usually it was the television and the radio on at the same time covering different races. Maybe he'd asked me to turn it up. The result came. He was right.

—Turn that miserable fucking thing off.

He was out the kitchen door before the click went. As I followed I heard his screams coming from the garage. When I got there I saw water seeping up through the hole. It had covered a good portion of the garage floor, leaving muck in its path. Da was standing there like a man whose house had been razed to the ground.

—What did I say about jubilee clips? Tell me what I said about jubilee clips?

—You said we needed them.

—You're the Jonah. I thought it was your mother but it turns out it's you.

He looked at me like he'd had a horrible vision of hell.

—I'm not a Jonah.

—What are you if you're not a Jonah?

—I'm not a Jonah.

—Don't answer me back or I'll break your mouth for you.

He was daring me to hit him. I wasn't afraid. Not any more. Not like when I was a kid and his voice would have me shitting in my pants. He wasn't a giant to me any more. I didn't have to look far up into his face. Not far at all. I wanted to kill him but not hurt him. The idea of my fist on his flesh seemed wrong. He was looking for someone to blame, as always. I wasn't going to be bullied, not this time.

—I'm not a Jonah. I'm not a jinx. And neither is Ma.

I could see he was surprised. My heart was racing but I wasn't afraid.

—I'm your father and if I tell you you're a Jonah, then you are a Jonah.

He picked the shovel up off the ground and handed it to me.

—Dig that hole.

I let it fall where I was standing and it bounced off the ground.

—Dig it yourself!

140

I walked out of the garage and into the kitchen. He didn't call after me. I went straight to my room and took out my cardboard guitar. If I'd had a real guitar that bit into the tops of my fingers I might have been able to forget him. I knew he was in a mess. I was determined not to give in to him. If I did, I'd be a Jonah for the rest of my life. Sit tight and do nothing. That was the only thing to do. Let it pass. I felt grown up when I thought about it like that. On the other hand, my chances of a guitar were gone for ever. I could never ask him now, not ever. I could ask Ma, of course, but she was paying for the guitar lessons as it was. I made the chords of G7, C Major and F Major. I couldn't stop thinking of him on his own in the garage. Maybe if I went down he'd apologize for calling me a Jonah. I had nothing to gain by sitting in my bedroom. He'd never come up to apologize. I started down the stairs and diverted into the bathroom. I went to the toilet and washed my hands after. Pure time wasting. I looked in the mirror. I put on a sheepish face. I pointed.

—You're the one who's sorry, I'm not the one who's sorry.

I wasn't convincing. I went back up the stairs to Ita's room. Her window looked down on the yard. The small door to the garage was open. I could see the soles and the heels of his shoes in the orange glow from the naked light bulb. He was kneeling. Just like he was praying by a grave. He was leaning into a hole, putting on a jubilee clip. I bet his knees were sore.

—I'm the one who's sorry, you're not the one who's sorry.

I ran down the stairs before I changed my mind. In the kitchen I gathered up a bundle of newspapers for his knees. In the garage he was tightening the screw on the jubilee clip as I suspected. A few feet away, Frankie was standing with the shovel in his hand.

—I brought you these.

I threw them down beside him. He didn't look up.

7

1965

There's no hurt that time won't heal. It was a great saying of Ma's. She said it at funerals and she said it when she cleaned our cut knees. When she daubed the iodine that made skin turn purple, you could be guaranteed she'd come out with it. It was small comfort when I came home covered from head to toe in nettle stings but she said it anyway. That was the past. I hadn't cut myself in years. When I told her about Frankie taking my place it was the first thing she said. No hurt that time won't heal. I felt like I was six years old. Usually I hated feeling like a kid but this was nice. In standing up to Da I'd stood up for Ma. I didn't tell her what happened but it was like she understood. She suffered his rejection the most. I remember one time at the Phoenix Park races. A summer's day. Ma sent me off with a kettle. There was a woman who sold hot water. I gave her sixpence. When I brought it back Ma had a picnic spread out on the grass. Banana sandwiches and coconut slices. She took a packet of tea and a silver spoon from her handbag. She made tea in our beautiful, battered teapot and covered it with a cosy to draw. She wouldn't let anyone pour it until Da came back from the grandstand after the race. I lay on the grass and listened to the horses hooves go by and felt the sun on my face. The cheers rose up to the sky and just as quickly fell down to the ground. Da came over to our picnic. He'd backed a loser. You always knew when he'd backed a loser. Ma poured his tea and handed it to him. He took one sip.

—That tastes like piss water.

He threw it on the ground and went off. I ran up to the stands after him to get him to come back down. There were thousands of people there. I found him by his shoes. I grabbed his arm and pulled myself up. From the stand I could see Ma. She was packing the picnic stuff away. I felt like our whole family was breaking up, right there and then. I pleaded with him to come down for the picnic. I pleaded with him not to let Ma go home on her own. I pulled at his sleeve. He pushed my hand away.

—Your mother's a Jonah. She's never brought me a day's luck.

Ma lived from one rejection to the next and was used to it. This was my first time to be cut adrift. I didn't know what to expect. I didn't cook his meals so he could hardly threaten me with hungers strikes. He could give me the silent treatment, I supposed. He did that with Ma. He would talk to her through one of us. Tell your mother to boil a kettle, I need a shave. Maybe that's how he would communicate with me. It didn't seem very likely. He couldn't replace Ma but he could replace me. He'd train Frankie in, the way he'd trained me. The hard way. Up on the bike to the bookies' and go like the hammers of hell before they're off in the five furlong sprint and wait to collect the winnings while you're there. He'd develop great thigh muscles. Just like me. Hardest shot in Sheriff Street. The peno king. I could retire as Da's messenger. Retirement without pension. I'd never get the ladders out again. Never climb onto the roof with the repair kit – stay wires, coaxial cable, pliers, vaseline, flashing, linseed oil and zambuck. My life was a clean slate from this out. I could fill it as I pleased. I was standing at the edge of freedom and I was afraid – I didn't know what the future held or what my role in it was. For the moment I was lost at sea and drifting.

144

I thought about Ma. No hurt that time won't heal. She was right. I felt better thinking about it. How did she feel? In between rejections, she had us. She had Gerard for when Da withdrew his love. She could throw herself into the deep end of nappies and talcum powder while she waited for her hurt to heal and the silence to end. I saw her marking out its time. Like slow music. Her face etched in pain. Every breath a sigh. Sometimes I thought there was a hurt that would never heal. A hurt buried deep down inside her. At those times I willed Da in my mind to put his arms around her and hold her close, but he only ever asked for another cup of tea. It was better than the silence and Ma lived on its comfort. At times she seemed happy. Almost. She laughed at his jokes and didn't bring up the subject of his promotion. She humoured him and stayed out of his way when he studied the racing form. She did everything to keep the bandwagon rolling smoothly along. She agreed with everything he said. When he cursed jockeys, she cursed them with him. Bad bastards. When he raged against the Government, she fanned the flames. Thieving swines. Sometimes she got in first. When it turned into a volcanic eruption, she backed away. I watched her playing her part. Watched her control his moods. At all times being careful. Being less than who she was. I watched her do all this because it wasn't safe for her to do anything else.

*

Ita wanted a sister but it was another boy Ma brought home from the Rotunda. Paul made it six brothers for her and no sister. She deserved to have someone to share her room with. The rest of us were in dormitories but Ita was alone. The rest of us shared in a way that brought us together. We weren't like any other family on the road. 44 changed everyone. It was like a new family evolved there. Mahony became a son to Da and Mossie became a father to me. We were planets moving around each other. I had moved out of

Da's orbit and Frankie had moved in. Shea orbited on his own, but affected everyone around him. Da was the sun that sat at the head of the table and presided over the galaxy. Ma was the moon that changed the tides and brought everyone back together. Ita was Ita, fragile and alone, and everyone's favourite sister.

Mahony had lost his job with Sten Oil and was working full-time for Da. His office was the dining room where he spent his days recording racing results into a giant ledger. Da had worked out a new system. He gave horses points for speed, taking into account weight carried. Each horse then came out with a rating. The horses with the highest ratings were guaranteed winners. Or as near guaranteed as you could get. That was if the system worked. There were several ifs and only time would tell. Mahony recorded every day with great care. He was as committed as the monks who created the first Bibles. If it worked out as well as he and Da hoped, it would be more useful and more valuable than the Book of Kells.

Shortly after Mahony began work on the ledger, Noel Dargan had a conversion. He came home from work one evening and placed a set of spectacle frames in front of Mahony. They were new frames. Identical to the old ones but without a blemish.

What had caused this change of heart? Only a miracle could explain it. When Mahony came to us he had just one break in the glasses. Within months, nothing of the original frame remained. The glasses were Sellotape through and through, including the lenses which Noel Dargan smashed one night at cards. Mahony didn't have the temperament for poker. Once he and Noel Dargan were at the table the only thing certain was a row. They'd start off polite. Compliment one another.

—Well played.

—I held on to the king.

—That was smart.

—I bought in three more kings for a poker.

—Your luck is in.

—Nothing to do with luck, it's craft.

—What would you know about craft?

—Enough to win the pot, that's how much I know.

—You know fuck all.

—I must know something.

—You know how a dig feels, afuckingmen.

That's how it went. If Noel Dargan was losing there always came a point where you knew the violence would start. Mahony would start to sweat. That meant he had a good hand. If his hand started to shake, it was a very good hand. Noel Dargan would accuse him of cheating.

—As God's me judge I didn't cheat.

—I threw down the four and you picked it up.

The glasses were always first to go. That immobilized Mahony and Noel Dargan could do with him as he pleased. That's how it was, until the conversion. Overnight he spoke softly to Mahony and treated card games like they were a contagious disease. He went to bed early every night. Spent less and less time in the Ball Alley. If his brother Liam was to be believed, he was turning his life over to prayer. Spending hours on his knees by his bed. He was on his way to sainthood.

No one had an explanation for it. Mahony said it was the house. There was something magical in it. We'd all been chosen to be there. All been touched by some spirit. We were modern-day apostles. Mahony wanted to start a new religion. He wanted me to be the leader of it.

—Me?

—I want you to be my God. I want to serve you, Allah Sheridan.

He got down on his knees in front of me and repeated it several times. Then he let out a squeal like a trapped rat. I thought he'd swallowed a razor blade. It was, in fact, an hysterical laugh. Mahony's sense of humour was unique.

Da loved checking the ledger. He'd sit with Mahony late into the night and pour over it for hours. They checked and cross-checked it. Every loophole was looked at. Every glitch was worked on. Mahony's new glasses were as good as a microscope. Da could barely conceal his excitement. It was the first time he'd had full-time help in creating a winning system. It was scientific. Logical. Exact. With the help of his full-time secretary, Da was on the way to becoming a millionaire. In return for his services, Mahony stayed rent free. Since Ma was in charge of the lodgers, Mahony, strictly speaking, was working for Ma. She was at the loss of the rent, not Da. Indeed, since the lodgers' money paid for our education, and there were three of us now needing brown envelopes to be filled, our futures depended on the success or otherwise of Da's system. It was a complicated situation. For that reason, when I said my night prayers, I included its success under special intentions.

Mossie was the quietest of the lodgers and the best. He was a great poker player but never got into a game if Mahony and Noel Dargan were playing. One or the other, yes, but never the two together. He never made a fuss. He'd just slip away from the table politely.

—Excuse me, gentlemen.

He had the biggest hands of any human being I'd ever seen. One blow from him and he'd break Noel Dargan in half. I couldn't imagine him raising his hands in anger. They were fat and gentle like a teddy bear's. One time after he finished shaving I felt his face. He took my hand and put it to his skin. Warm and safe. He brushed against his chin with the tips of my fingers. It felt like cut grass. The bristles tickled but I didn't pull away. Why would I?

—What do you think, little fella?

Da never stopped seeking Mossie's approval for his

system. Mossie was polite. He'd nod his head and say encouraging things but I could tell he wasn't sure. Mossie only laid his money down when he had inside information. Even with that, they sometimes lost. After the initial success with Tullow Lady, there was a string of losers. Da got so burned he started to question the quality of the information. The phone calls from Mossie's sister continued, but Mossie didn't share it with Da any more. That was how it was until Mossie got a call about Queen of Spades. A black mare entered at the Killarney Festival of Racing. She'd been got ready with this one race in mind. There was no question of defeat. Defeat was not being entertained. It was a racing certainty, to all intents and purposes. The only question was how far would she win by. Mossie simply could not keep it to himself and passed the information to Da.

Mossie insisted on taking me to the races with him. Ma said I'd be too much trouble. Da said I didn't deserve it. Johnny said it wasn't fair. Shea said he didn't care. Ita said it was a form of torture. Frankie said he wouldn't go, even if he was allowed. I said I didn't care what anyone thought, I was going. In the end, Da withdrew his objections and organized a free return ticket on the train. He was entitled to two a year. Ma helped me pack and made sure I'd plenty of vests and socks even though we were only going for two days. Da went to the bank and took out a loan. I heard him arguing with Ma about it. She'd already given him the lodgers' money for that week. Da was only following his own rules. Beg, borrow and steal when you have genuine information. Before we left for the station, Da gave me a brown paper bag. I asked him what it was for.

—To take home the winnings.

*

I couldn't take my eyes off the fields. They flew past the window and seemed to get greener as we went. Cows and hay sheds and barns. Rivers and hills. Golf courses and football fields. Ireland was a beautiful country. My grandfather had fought for it. In 1916 he'd taken up a gun and occupied the Four Courts with his IRA batallion. Was he thinking then of the green fields that passed our window, I wondered. Mossie returned from the buffet bar. He had sandwiches and currant buns. He put them in front of me and told me to pick. He pulled a bottle of red lemonade from his pocket and popped the cap off with his fat thumb. Then he pulled four tiny bottles of Paddy whiskey from various places and lined them up in front of him. Leprechaun bottles, he called them. He screwed the caps off and drank them one after the other. When he finished, he took his wallet from his inside jacket pocket. He took a crispy brown five pound note and pushed it across to me. I figured he was sending me to the buffet bar for more whiskey. Did he not know they wouldn't serve me? Maybe he'd write a note. Please supply the bearer with four only leprechauns and oblige. I didn't mind going for him. So far this was the best trip of my life. I picked up the five pound note.

—What do you want?

He looked at me and told me to sit down. I thought it was a strange request.

—That's for you.

I looked at the five pound note. I'd never owned one before. Not even nearly.

—I want you to hold on to it.

I was holding on to it. I was holding on to a piece of brown paper. Crisp and light and signed by the governor of the Bank of Ireland.

—You're not to spend it, you're to keep it!

I had it spent already. I was standing in Walton's picking out my own guitar. Steel string acoustic. The fret board studded with white enamel diamonds. My fingers formed chords with magical ease.

—Put it somewhere safe.

I folded it in two and put it in my right trouser pocket. I felt it every three minutes to make sure it was still there. It was hard for me to accept that I was sitting in a train going to Killarney with a five pound note in my trouser pocket and a bottle of red lemonade in front of me. I convinced myself I'd made a horrible mistake. I ran out to the toilet, locked myself in and slowly pulled it from its resting place. So slowly it almost didn't move. I closed my eyes, pulled it out and held it in front of me. I opened my eyes. A fraction at a time. Finally, I beheld it in all its brown glory. I returned to my seat and dreamt about guitars all the way to Killarney.

After we booked into the Ross Hotel, Mossie took me by jaunting car around the lakes. I hated the country. I was a city kid, through and through. All the things that country people hated about the city, I loved. The dirt and the grime. The fumes and the smog. The tar and the oil. The grey walls and tenement halls. I raced through dirty Dublin on my bike, delirious. Now, with every crack of the jarvey's whip, I was feeling as I felt about the city. I was undergoing a conversion, just as surely as Noel Dargan was, back in Dublin. We visited Muckross House, Ross Castle, Kate Kearney's Cottage and the Gap of Dunloe. It was so beautiful I went twenty whole minutes without feeling for my five pound note. No wonder it was called the Kingdom. No wonder Grandad Sheridan and the IRA had to fight to get it back.

We headed for the races after the jaunt. I'd never seen so many culchies all in the one place before. Red faces, peak caps and coloured waistcoats. Mossie spoke with a country accent in Dublin. Two minutes after we arrived in Killarney he was completely unintelligible. He introduced me to his sister but I'd no idea what he said. She was even fatter than he was. I hoped she wasn't riding Queen of Spades. The mare was running in the last race on the card. A two-mile bumper, whatever a bumper was. Mossie was engaged in whispered conspiracies among his friends. There was a strut in his gait as he moved from group to group. He imparted information as he went.

—The mare will win the last.

—You fancy her, so?

—She won't be beat.

—She must be a flying machine.

—My sister's never had one like her.

—It's your sister's mare?

—Don't say I didn't give it to you.

I could see the bulge in Mossie's pocket, put there by the wad of notes he was carrying. I felt for my own. Still there. I headed off to the roulette table and watched the white ball make its journey through the colours. I studied it for a pattern. Red. Red. Black. Red. Black. Black. Must be red next. It was. Red. The spin of the ball. First clockwise. Then anti-clockwise. It was hard to figure it out. I abandoned the roulette table and headed off.

Mossie was prowling the betting ring with money in his fist. Da's money. The lodgers' money. The bank's money. His own money. He was waiting for the bookies to mark up a price. Frankie O'Donoghue took chalk from his pocket. He put numbers beside the names. All fifteen runners got a price. When he'd finished writing he looked out to the crowd and shouted:

—I lay four to one the field, eight to one bar one.

Queen of Spades was eight to one. A good price. Forty pounds to my five. Mossie walked down the line. Most of the bookies followed Frankie O'Donoghue's lead. Terry Rogers, a bookie who wore flamboyant clothes, licked his fingers and rubbed out the eight to one. He put up ten to one against Queen of Spades. Mossie walked confidently over and handed Terry Rogers the wad of money. The bookie almost fell off his box trying to rub out the price. There was a great flurry of activity as Terry Rogers tried to lay off Mossie's bet. The word went flying around the ring. There was a stampede to back the horse. Women and children were knocked down in the scramble. It was frightening. Bookies were shouting at the tops of their voices, tic-tac men were waving their arms in the air like helicopters, punters were charging like bulls to get money on the mare. There was only one horse being backed in the race. Her odds tumbled all the way from ten to one to two to one. Some bookies had no price at all against her. It was any price you like bar the mare. Just before the off there was another avalanche of money. When the tape went up and the horses jumped off I heard Frankie O'Donoghue shout:

—I lay six to four Queen of Spades, twelve to one bar one.

You couldn't miss her, she was jet black. She cantered at the back of the field for the first mile or so. When they turned at the far end of the course with five furlongs to race, the mare pulled to the outside to deliver her challenge. At the three furlong pole the jockey was hard at work. At the two furlong pole she was going nowhere. The jockey's hands were turning windmill fashion. The distress signals were met in the stands with a huge groan. Terry Rogers threw his hat in the air and let out a victory cheer. I looked at Mossie. He was in great pain. Before the race was over he took his ticket from his top pocket, tore it in half and threw it on the ground. I watched the mare going backwards in the final furlong. In the end, she finished second last. Mossie made only one comment:

—Someone got to her. Some bastard got to her.

There was a change in Mossie after the horse was beaten. He turned in on himself. I could see him physically close off, shrivel up, like the sun had stopped shining for him. Whereas Da raged against the world, Mossie raged against himself.

We travelled back to the hotel in silence. We sat in the dining room and looked at the menu. He ordered steak for me and a large whiskey for himself. I read the menu twenty times before the steak came. I'd never had steak in a restaurant before. It was the size of a small cow. At home, Ma would feed all of us on this. If only they could see me now. My gums hurt from the chewing. It was only half eaten but I felt full to my Adam's apple. I struggled on because of the price. I knew I'd never forget this sirloin steak. Ten ounces of cow flesh. Prime Irish beef. Pity about the horse flesh. Queen of Spades. A perfect day if only she'd won.

—I don't have the money for the hotel, little fella.

I was delighted he was talking to me. The first communication for hours. I stopped reading the menu.

—That's all right, Mossie.

I didn't know what to say to him. I knew he needed comforting. He hadn't eaten his dinner. He'd lost all his money. Now he needed to talk.

—Do you still have the five pounds I gave you?

What did he imagine, that I'd lost it on the horse? That I'd staked it on roulette? There was a look of desperation on his face.

—You didn't spend any of it, did you?

The penny dropped. He wanted the five pound note. The crispy brown passport to my first guitar.

—I'm cleaned out, little fella.

I could say I lost it. I could sit straight up in my chair and tell him the money was mine. I won it. It's mine. You can't have it. It's in the bank. Can't get my hands on it. It's spoken for. I owe it. I posted it home. I'm giving it to charity. I've only a pound left. Don't pay the hotel. We can do a bunk. You shouldn't have backed the horse. Not all your money. It doesn't grow on trees. Or out of the ground. I'm not God. We're not in the Garden of Eden. I don't have it to give.

I was thirteen years old but suddenly felt like fifty. I didn't like the feeling. None of the adult words would come out. Mossie was in trouble and I had to help him out. I was his only way out. Why else was he turning to me?

—You'll get it back, it's only a loan.

That clinched it. I took the five pound note from my pocket and pushed it across the table to Mossie. He took my face in his hands and kissed me on the forehead.

—If I had a son, I'd want him to be you.

I went to bed feeling good that I'd bailed Mossie out of serious trouble. In the middle of the night I was awoken by a dull thumping on the wall. It was coming from Mossie's room. I went out to the corridor and looked through his keyhole. He was sitting up in bed with all his clothes on. He was banging the back of his head against the wall.

—Fuck racing. Fuck Queen of Spades. Fuck Killarney. Fuck my sister and her husband. Fuck Ireland and the Aga Khan. Fuck the Epsom Derby. The French Derby. And the Irish Derby. Fuck all of them. Fuck all racing. And fuck me. Especially fuck me.

I went back to my room and listened to the thumps. I wondered was Da doing the same thing at home. Maybe Ma was. I went down through the menu in my mind. The thumps got less and I fell asleep and dreamt of sirloin steak.

The countryside didn't seem as pretty on the way home. Mossie was tanked up from the night before. He was working his way through a half bottle of whiskey he'd bought in Killarney that morning. On the way down it had all been leprechauns and the promise of a pot of gold. Now it was the stale smell of defeat. Mossie's unshaven face matched the mood. I got up to go to the toilet.

—Are you going to the bar?

—No, I'm going to the toilet.

I stood in the aisle. The carriage went dark. We were in a tunnel. Seconds later it was bright again.

—Wait for me. I'll join you.

There were two toilets. One was occupied. I pushed open the other door and Mossie crowded in behind me. We had to squeeze into the corner to get the door closed. Mossie pulled the bolt across. I put my hands against the wall and leaned over the pan. It wouldn't come at first. I was conscious of Mossie behind me. I looked down at my limp penis and willed it to pee. I looked at the silver pedal on the floor. Press to flush. I stood on it. The toilet flushed and the wee came. It was a great relief. I shook out the drops and did up my fly. When I turned around Mossie was peeing in the sink. He turned on the tap and started to wash his hands. He took the baby soap in his hands, cupped them and let the water flow through his fingers. Pee the colour of whiskey flowed endlessly into the sink. It came to a stop.

—Shake that out for me, little fella.

He nodded towards his penis.

—Shake out the drops.

I'd never touched a penis that wasn't mine before. I reached out and took it in my hand. I shook it a few times into the sink.

—Squeeze it. Get all them bad drops out of there.

It turned into a stick in my hand. Like Moses in the film *The Ten Commandments* when he turned the snake into a rod before the Pharaoh. I ran my hand along the stick. It grew even stiffer.

—Tighter, tighter. Squeeze them all out.

He sounded like he was in pain. Why did he want me to do something that caused him pain? I relaxed my grip. He put his soapy hands on mine and held it tight. I didn't want to be there any more. I wanted to be asleep in my own house. A room of my own. A bed of my own. No lodgers. No brothers. No sister. Just Ma. Sitting on the end of the bed watching me sleep. Clean white sheets tucked under my chin. Soft pillows nestling my head. No moaning. No sound except birds singing. And beautiful dreams. Ma's hand on my face and beautiful dreams. I couldn't stay where I was. Knew I couldn't stay where I was. I reached up to the lock. It was jammed. I banged it with my fist. No move. I looked at the skylight. It was the only way out. I floated up to it and looked back down. I could see myself pulling at the lock. I was pulling it closed. I went on out through the skylight and made my way back to my seat. I was sitting there when I came back from the toilet with Mossie following behind. My hair was matted at the front. I was pumping sweat, too. I felt sorry for me that I looked so haggard. The ticket collector worked his way through the carriage. He stopped at me.

—You all right, son?

I looked at me looking at Mossie. I looked at me looking at the ticket collector.

—I got locked in the toilet.

—Are you all right?

—I'm fine.

Of course I was fine. Anyone could get locked in a toilet and panic. It was over. Over and finished with. Over and finished with for good. I was going home to 44. Going home with an empty bag. The atmosphere would be worse than the morgue. The post-mortem on what happened in Killarney would go on for weeks. Or months. Or for ever.

*

I couldn't look at Da. He'd passed me on to Mossie. When he passed me over for Frankie he cut me loose. He sent me out with no instructions. He'd spent his life sending me on messages with his notes. When it really mattered, when I needed his guidance the most, he'd left me defenceless and alone. I couldn't look at him because I hated him. I only needed to be told, that was all. I'd gone out into the world and brought him home messages from the four corners of Dublin, never failed, always brought the message home. Chimneys, hard wall plaster, copper pipe, false teeth. He could tell the people of Saint Laurence O'Toole's parish where the mystery train went. He knew all the destinations – Howth, Skerries, Mosney, Bray, Greystones and Arklow. He knew about the train to Killarney, too. He knew more than their destinations. He knew what happened along the way. He knew all this and never told me. I couldn't look at him I was so angry. I couldn't look at him because it was too late now to talk. I couldn't look at him because I never wanted to talk to him again. I avoided Mossie by going to bed early. I had Johnny there as protection. By the time he came up I was usually asleep. If I was still awake, I'd always hear him say:

—Good night, little fella.

There was a sadness between us. We were out of tune, like the music in church. He never brought up Killarney, the train journey or the five pound note. It was as if by ignoring it, it might fade. Some of it did seem unreal. Not the five pound note, of course. My biggest mistake was in giving it back. The moment I handed it to him I betrayed my innocence. If I'd refused to give it back, nothing might ever have happened. Nothing would happen in the future. I knew that. I knew Mossie. The shame was that I'd let it happen at all. I didn't blame Mossie. I put the responsibility for it squarely on Da's shoulders, where it belonged.

*

Catherine Griffin was in the Legion of Mary. That was one good reason for joining it. It also had something to do with prostitutes. That was a second good reason. A third reason was to get me out of the house. As a result of Queen of Spades, the atmosphere was worse than hell of a Monday morning. The fourth reason was my dreams. They were all snakes. Warm and slimy, they slid up from the end of the bed and made straight for my back passage. To keep them out, I had to squeeze the cheeks of my bum together, real tight. It was hard work. As soon as I relaxed, one of the bastards would slip in and work his way up inside me. Forcing them out was the hardest thing of all. Some nights I just don't know how I did it. If joining the Legion of Mary could enlist the Blessed Virgin's help, then I wasn't going to refuse. I preferred Mary to Jesus when it came to asking for something. It was like Ma and Da. You could approach Ma any time. You had to choose your moment with Da. He was prone to tempers, like Jesus. In fact, when Jesus lost his rag with Mary and told her he must be about his father's business, it was pure Da. Da would have put it better, that's all. So it was Mary I turned to in my hour of need with the snakes.

Catherine was a year older than me and had a woman's shape. She went in at the waist and out at the chest. Her hair was jet-black and her eyes were dark, dark brown which made her look like an Indian squaw, especially when she got annoyed. I knew she was physically more mature than me but at least I was two inches taller than her and that gave me some confidence. She had a mole under her chin with four or five hairs growing out of it, thicker than ordinary hair. It was her only blemish and I'd learned to look away as soon as I found myself staring at it.

I went around to the Griffins' to make enquiries of Catherine. Mrs Griffin made a terrible fuss. She forced Mr Griffin out of his chair and gave it to me. One of the kids was sent to Sheriff Street for Kimberley biscuits. The silences were awful. I filled them as best I could. Mr Griffin asked me eight times where the mystery train was going. Mrs Griffin answered for me that I didn't know. They argued over every last thing. They agreed on one thing only. Da had the best job in Dublin – deciding where the mystery train went on Sundays. I finally got around to asking Catherine about the Legion of Mary and was I eligible to join. As soon as I did, Mr and Mrs Griffin left us alone in the room. It felt like confession. Bless me Catherine for I have sinned, I'm joining the Legion because I lust after you. I was embarrassed but I didn't care. I'd made a pact with Mary, the mother of us all. I'd serve her if I could have Catherine. Mary made it all right. I was going to have her no matter what. Catherine explained the Legion's mission – to do Mary's work in the world. She explained how it was organized along the same lines as the Roman Army. Each group was called a praesidium. Each praesidium fought a battle. Lots of praesidia were a curia. The curia fought the war. All the curias together were the Legion and the Legion was invincible. I wanted to sign up straight away. I wanted to swear an oath and be in a praesidium before nightfall. I wanted to take up arms for Mary. A shield. A spear. A sword. I'd been touched with the lust for battle. Catherine had to restrain me. She quietly explained how Mary worked through prayer. I blessed myself on the spot. Catherine thought I was making fun of her and accused me of blasphemy. I pleaded my innocence but Catherine told me to go home and pray.

I went to bed early. I lashed out in my sleep with such force that Johnny took a ferocious kick in the back. My legs were jerking about all over the place, just like they belonged to someone else.

Ma wanted to know what it was all about. I told her there were snakes trying to get into me. I was trying to kick them off when I got Johnny. Da said everyone had those kind of dreams and told me to go back to sleep. Ma wasn't happy with the snakes. They were worse than rats, she said. Dreaming of snakes every night wasn't healthy. Something must have brought it on. They were bad luck, too. Ma asked me had anything happened I hadn't told her about. A cold shadow ran over my body from my head down to my toes. I couldn't answer her question. I could float up and away, I knew that, but I didn't want to.

—I got locked in the toilet on the way to Killarney.

—What did you do?

—I banged on the door. Banged and banged and banged. No one heard me and I panicked.

—Where was Mossie?

Ma looked straight at me. I was sure she knew. Just like she always knew if you were really sick. You couldn't fool Ma with lies. The future of the lodgers depended on my answer. How could I bring the house down? Reduce it to rubble? The truth from me and there would be no more money to fill the brown envelopes that we brought to school. No more late-night arguments with Da at the head of the table. No wrestling, no bottles on the head, no sing-songs, no Frankie and Johnny, no ledger writing. I had the power to end all these things or to hold it all together. I could act grown-up or I could act like a kid.

—Why didn't Mossie come for you?

—I'm not a child, Ma. He was having a drink in the bar.

I knew in that moment I could never share my secret with a living soul. It was a small price to pay for entry into the adult world.

*

My life as a legionary started badly. The praesidium meetings were held in rooms at the back of the church. I followed Catherine, only to be stopped at the door by a cross-looking woman in a green cardigan who pointed to a door across the hall.

—That's the boys' meeting over there.

The Legion of Mary had been founded in the Monto. The Monto was a famous red light district in Dublin, known throughout Europe. The Legion organized a crusade from the Pro-Cathedral Church and marched on the brothels. They splashed holy water at the entrance to every house of sin. It was all over in one night and the Monto closed for ever. It was terribly disappointing to find myself an enlisted member of an army that had gotten rid of brothels in Dublin.

I tried to get something for my endeavours. I prayed to Mary for peaceful dreams and an end to the snakes. I always prayed the night before a match and I always prayed before I took a penalty. I looked up to the top of the room and saw the Legion insignia staring back at me. Every army has an insignia. Mary the mother of God was ours. Above her head was an eagle and at her feet was a globe. In between the world and her bare feet, was the tortured body of a dying snake. She was crushing it to death. It was a grip as tight as the cheeks of my arse. Mary was smiling at her victory over it. I knew exactly how she felt and I knew exactly what the snake represented. I knew why I'd been brought here. I had to abandon myself to Mary to taste victory over the snakes. I had found my vocation. I was to be a soldier in a secret army. Not the IRA, but an army based on prayer. I was to be a foot soldier for Mary, the crusher of snakes.

I became a model legionary. The main work of our praesidium was delivering Catholic newspapers – the *Universe*, *Catholic Standard* and *Catholic Herald*. We had four deliveries that covered the parish. Within weeks, I knew every house in the four sections. I spent time at the hall doors spreading the work of the Legion. I was so enthusiastic, many of the elderly customers started to give me tips. The praesidium elected me treasurer, which meant I was in charge of the money. I paid Veritas House, who supplied us with the papers, and I presented income and expenditure accounts to the meeting.

At night I prayed to Mary. I pictured her foot on the snake and thought of putty. Or slime. That's how it was until one night the snake started to go hard. I woke up with my penis like a stick. The only thing that saved me was Catherine. When I thought of her I went hard but didn't feel so guilty, because she was a girl and not the mother of God. I wasn't sure what would happen if I kissed her for real. Or felt her breasts against my chest. If my hand touched the black stockings she wore to the Kylemore Bakery. If I fell under her charms would I be saved? Would I fare better than I had with Our Blessed Lady?

I had joined the Legion to get close to Catherine, only to end up separated more. When I went to Veritas House to settle the account, I always called by the shop, stuck my head in the door and said hello. One day after a bad night with the snakes, I called in to see her. My pocket was bulging with money and I had paper returns under my arm. I was determined to ask her out. I went straight to the counter and waited while she served a customer. She came over to me and said hello. I took a deep breath and opened my mouth. Nothing came out. She asked me what I wanted.

—A cream donut.

I put my hand in my pocket and took out sixpence. I took the cream donut and backed out as quickly as I could. It wasn't until I got to Veritas House I realized I'd paid for it out of the paper money. When it came to settling the account I lied about the number of returns. The little lie had earned me a free cake. It became part of my weekly routine. I was standing in the shop sinking my teeth into a fruit slice when Catherine told me about the talent competition. I choked on the news and Catherine had to come out from behind the counter and bang my back with her fist. It was the closest I'd ever got to rubbing up against her. I drank three glasses of water to wash down what wasn't there.

I left the Kylemore Bakery with a mushroom in my brain that was forming into a plan. I walked to Veritas House but my feet would not go in the door. I looked at the Bibles in the window and felt the bulge of money in my pocket. I turned away and started to run. I turned right into O'Connell Street and ran the length of it to Parnell Square, then up the hill and straight into Walton's, where I counted out four pounds and ten shillings before I pointed to the guitar with the white enamel diamonds on the fret board. The assistant took it down and handed it to me. It was mine. The miracle I'd been waiting for. My guitar. I had no other thought than to get practising. 'She'll Be Coming Round The Mountain', the only song I could play. I had to have it perfect for the competition. If I won it, Catherine would be mine. She couldn't refuse to go out with me if I turned out to be the most talented legionary in Mary's army.

I practised until my fingers bled. Ma came into the bedroom and asked me where I got it.

—Walton's.

—Who paid for it?

—The Legion of Mary.

—Oh. That's good.

Ma was entirely satisfied. If I'd tried to lie I would have tripped myself up. I told the truth and she didn't bat an eyelid. The guitar was the property of the Legion of Mary. I would sell it and return the money after the contest. Unless I came up with a better plan in the meantime.

I stood in front of the mirror.

—I'm Elvis Presley, you're not Elvis Presley.

I looked good. I hit the strings full force. The plectrum fell into the hole. I spent fifteen minutes trying to get it out, wasting good rehearsal time. I sat on the edge of the bed and practised the chords without looking, beginning to get the swing of it. It was all rhythm. Left right co-ordination. I remembered Andy's advice. Listen to your heartbeat. I was throwing myself into all this because of his sister. If I won the talent contest and married her, Andy would become my brother-in-law. It felt like the perfect ending.

—*oy, oy, yippy, yippy, oy*

Singing, oy, oy, yippy, yippy, oy.

I was starting to hate the words. What did they mean? They sounded like a horse's hooves but they made no sense. She'll be coming round the mountain when she comes. It was stating the obvious. It was childish, and I didn't know the chords to any other song. I bashed it out once more. A down stroke followed by an up stroke. I held the plectrum tight. In the middle of the second verse, Noel Dargan knocked on the door and came into the room. He was dressed in his pyjamas. I could see his pubic hairs through the pyjama slit. I averted my eyes.

—Are you going to play that song again?

—No.

He scratched his head and wiped his eyes. I noticed his hair was all tossed. I'd woken him up.

—I can't say my prayers with you playing that.

—I'm finished practising.

I picked it up and headed downstairs. The house was at perfect peace with itself. Liam Dargan and Mahony were playing cards in the dining room. Mossie was listening to old 78 records in the front room. Shea, Ita, Johnny and Frankie were watching television in the kitchen. They all wanted a go of my guitar. Frankie tried to take it off me. I pushed him away.

—It belongs to the legend of Mary, it doesn't even belong to you.

I knew what the little twirp meant. I didn't bother answering him, just stuck out my tongue as far as I could. I headed out to the garage, got the key of Father Ivers' car from the nail over the door, and practised sitting in the passenger seat of the shiny black Volkswagen. I practised till she came around the mountain thirty-six times.

165

I dreamt of white horses. They kept the snakes away from me. They did it with gentle kicks. Light spasms. I woke up. My legs were flicking out, but gentler than before. I hadn't woken Johnny up. Shea was asleep in Mahony's old bed, and Mahony now slept on his own in the front room downstairs. Mossie was in the corner bed, snoring as usual. It was light outside. I decided to get up and practise in the garage. I threw on my clothes and grabbed my guitar. I headed out the door and down the stairs. As I did, I heard Noel Dargan's bedroom door open. I stopped on the stairs where I was. A few seconds passed before a woman, followed by Noel Dargan, passed in front of me. The woman put her hand to her mouth when she saw me.

—Jesus, Mary and Joseph.

It was Mrs Power. She was married to Christy Power. The man with the golden dick. She was with Noel Dargan. The man with the thirty-inch scar. They were standing on the landing outside our bathroom, looking guilty. She elbowed him. He put his hand in his pocket and pulled out a half-crown. He handed it to me. I declined. He grabbed my hand and pushed it into my palm. They tip-toed down the stairs ahead of me. He opened the hall door without a sound and let her out.

—Say nothing to no one.

I continued out to the garage. I sat in the front of the Volkswagen. I couldn't take my mind off what had just happened. Noel Dargan had a woman from the flats in our house. A married woman. Her kids played in the playground. Her husband sang medleys in the Liverpool Bar. He called on Da to sing sometimes. His wife was sleeping under our roof. She kneeled beside Ma in the church. She took holy communion. Why was she in Noel Dargan's bedroom? He went to bed early most nights since his conversion. I pictured him kneeling at the side of the bed saying the rosary. Mrs Power kneeling opposite him making the responses. It didn't fit. He didn't bring her there to help him with his prayers. He wouldn't have given me a half a crown unless he was doing something he shouldn't be. I pictured them on top of the bed. It fitted straight away. It was an awful picture. I tried to tune my guitar. I couldn't listen to the notes, thinking of them. I suddenly thought of Liam Dargan. What did he do when his brother and Mrs Power were on top of the bed? Did he turn into the wall? Hide under the covers? Watch what they were doing from a mirror in his hand? Surely he didn't have his way with her, too? There was no way Noel Dargan shared Mrs Power with his skinny little brother. Brothers didn't share things like that. I didn't share my guitar. It was mine. If only I could play it. Something other than 'She'll be Coming Round the Mountain'. It seemed so banal in the light of events. I packed in rehearsals and headed for Mahony's room. He was staring at me as soon as I stepped into the room. I told him what I'd just seen. He held up the glasses Noel Dargan had bought him.

—The price of my silence.

I showed him the half a crown.

—The price of mine.

Mahony chuckled. He told me that Noel Dargan and Mrs Power were married. Not married in the eyes of the Church, but married under maritime law. They'd taken a boat from the docks headed for Liverpool. In the middle of the Irish Sea the captain, a friend of Noel Dargan's from his army days, married them as a captain is allowed to do. They were entitled to live as man and wife as a result. They had to consummate their marriage in secret knowing that Ma and Da would not approve. Their secret life, it seemed, couldn't stay a secret much longer.

*

The talent competition was held in a hall at the back of a large house with a Roman name over the door – Regina

Coeli. Praesidia from all over Dublin were seated at two long tables on either side of the hall. Everything was Marian blue. Cups, saucers, plates, tablecloths and balloons. At the top of the room was a platform that wasn't a stage but aspired to being one. On it was an enormous statue of Our Lady trampling to death the ugliest-looking snake I'd ever seen. In front of the statue was a table covered with a white cloth. On the front of it in blue letters were the words – Legio Mariae. In the centre of the table was a silver cup flanked by two smaller ones. It wasn't as big as the FA Cup but it was shinier. At the bottom of the cup there was a silver strip. I could see my name clearly spelt out on it. I looked around the hall to see where the competition would come from. I couldn't see any.

Catherine was making her way along the table pouring out tea. Everyone knew her. Everyone liked her. Especially the boys. Most of them wanted her. But they weren't going to get her. Today she was going to be mine after I lifted the silverware. I held out my cup for more tea.

—Brother Savage wants to see you in the house.

He was in charge of our praesidium. Despite his name, he was a kind, gentle man who blushed if a woman came into his company. His right eyebrow was twitching at the speed of knots. It twitched when he was upset. When I stood in front of him I could see it was dancing a jig.

—I've had a communication from Veritas House.

He took a letter out of his inside pocket. He read it to me. Our account was in serious arrears and didn't tally with my treasurer's report at the praesidium meeting. He wanted to know how we were five pounds in arrears.

—I forgot to pay it. I have the money at home.

His eyebrow almost left his face.

—You had better give me the money and I'll pay it.

—You don't trust me? Is that it?

He hated confrontation. Brother Savage's solution to

every problem in the world was prayer. Prayer wasn't going to pay the bill. He knew that and so did I.

—I was going to bar you from the talent show if it was true.

If Brother Savage had been in charge of the Garden of Eden, Adam and Eve would have got off with a caution. I had joined the Legion in the hope of meeting a prostitute. Brother Savage had joined to avoid that. I'd learned how to carry secrets. He was never going to get the truth from me. Nothing was going to stop me going for the cup. Nothing human.

There were three recitations, two Irish dancers, a magician who kept dropping things and a comedian who mixed up all his punch lines. I got a clap when I stood on the stage. I sat on a chair and checked the tuning. People started to talk. When I was tuned up I hit a C chord and everyone went quiet. I got the note into my head and started to sing. All the chord changes in the first verse were perfect. As soon as I got to the chorus, all the adults in the audience started to clap and sing along. They were all clapping in different times. Did they not know how hard it was for me to keep rhythm? It threw me. I lost the right hand completely. I kept going somehow and got to the start of the second verse. Down the back of the hall, Brother Savage was clapping his hands and singing:

—*Oy, oy, yippy, yippy, oy . . .*

I had to wait for him to finish before I could start again. It took me a while to get the second verse going.

—*She'll be riding six white horses when she comes . . .*

Soon as I got to the chorus, the hall erupted into a bedlam of singing and clapping. I couldn't even hear myself play. I struggled on to the finale. When it was over I stood up and bowed. They cheered and stamped their feet. I was so relieved I forgot to look and see where Catherine was. The MC in charge, Brother Rickard, asked the crowd would they like an encore from the young man with the guitar? I was mortified. I only had one song.

—We want more . . . we want more . . .

I retreated to the back of the hall and hid. They were still chanting for more when a group of lads in sleeveless red T-shirts entered the hall. They had beach scenes from California painted all over them. Two of them carried electric guitars, one had a microphone and the fourth carried a drum and a stand. They wore identical trousers and matching shoes. They were unquestionably a group. Everything matched. Their skins were golden-brown. Arms, neck and face the colour of the sun. It was the richest tan I'd ever seen. They looked like they were from Hawaii. They were actually from a praesidium in Castleknock. They were a mime group called The Blue Tones of Mary. They looked professional. Soon as they stepped onto the platform, they each knew their positions. The drummer put on the record and the lead singer struck a pose at the microphone. From the first second his lips were in perfect time with the record.

—*It was a moonlit night in old Mexico. I walked alone between some old adobe haciendas. When suddenly, I heard the plaintive cry of a young Mexican maid.*

The drummer jumped up from his seat, put a scarf around his head and howled to the sky like a Mexican maid.

—*La la la la . . .*

The other three held out their hands towards him for effect. He howled again.

—*La la la la la la la la . . .*
La la la la la la la la . . .
La la la la la la la la . . .

They jumped in the air together and landed on the first beat of the song.

—*You'd better come home Speedy Gonzales*
Away from Tannery Road.

Stop all of your drinking,
With that floozy named Flo.

It was perfect ... Every move, every shuffle, every harmony, every curl of the lip, every beat of the drum, every note, every chord, every tap, every word, every frown, every Mexican grin.

—*Hey Rosita, I have to go shopping down town for my mother. She needs some tortillas and chilli peppers.*

I knew I would never play my song again. My repertoire was down to nil. Speedy Gonzales. Pat Boone. This was real music. Jumping and jiving. The hall was hopping. I saw two girls twirl around each other like spinning tops. I saw another girl slide between a boy's legs and come out the other side. The Blue Tones of Mary had unleashed something and they seemed intoxicated by whatever it was they'd unleashed. The song seemed to get faster and the volume to increase.

The Blue Tones of Mary did four encores. It got better each time. I'd been reborn in the Legion hall. That mattered much more than winning the cup. Anyway, it wasn't as big as the FA Cup. And to be truthful, it wasn't as shiny either. I'd been fooling myself.

Catherine kept asking for a look all the way home on the bus. I took the cup out of my pocket and showed it to her. She was full of praise for my second place finish. I told her to keep it. She wouldn't hear of it. I told her it reminded me of dead music. She asked me to explain. I tried but couldn't. She said I was jealous.

—Are you jealous of their tans?

My brain was too confused to take it in.

—I'm not jealous of their tans.

—It's only Tanfastic, straight from a bottle, that's all it is.

It was after eleven when we got to 44. I stopped at the railings and said good night to her.

—Are you not going to walk me around?

There was an appealing look in her eyes. It took me by surprise.

—Let me throw my guitar inside.

I rang the bell and Mahony answered.

—Did you win?

—Second.

—Bastards. What do they know?

I walked Catherine to the flats. She stopped at the bottom of her steps. I felt awkward. My hands felt the worst. She said something about the talent competition. My only thought was what move to make. It was win or lose. No room for rehearsal here. I leaned with my back to the wall for support. I raised my leg so that my knee stuck out. I thanked Catherine for introducing me to the Legion of Mary. I knew instantly I'd said the wrong thing. I tried to think of something else. The only thing I could think of was the Kylemore Bakery.

—Do you like your uniform?

—It's all right.

—What about the black stockings?

—What about them?

—Do you like them?

—They're all right.

—Would you prefer any other colour?

—I'm going to have to go in.

—Yeah. Good night so.

—Do you want to give me a good-night kiss?

It seemed to take a long time for me to get my lips on hers. When I got there, I didn't know what to do with my hands. I put them on her hips. They felt too far apart. I slid them around to the hollow of her back. I wasn't sure how long to keep my lips on hers. I looked at her. She looked beautiful. Sometimes when I looked at her in the Kylemore, she looked ugly. Pale skin stained with sweat. Tonight she had make-up and perfume on. I loved make-up. Lipstick and powder and eye shadow. Powder puffs against the skin. Like a baby's hair. Under the nose and along the top lip.

Her lipstick was pink. I could feel it on my lips. Slightly sticky. I loved its slight stickiness. Lips glued together. I leaned in and put my lips on hers again. I tried to nudge them apart. I slid my right hand down and pulled her towards me. My penis stiffened. She took my hand and put it back where it came from. She took her lips away and said good night again. I let my hands go and she ran up the stairs away from me. I watched her until she disappeared. I wasn't sure if my penis had frightened her. It thrilled me. The way it stood up. Stood to attention like a good soldier. A soldier in Catherine's army. Obedient to her command. All the way home I felt for her lipstick with my tongue. I took it back into my mouth and swallowed deep. Her taste went all the way down inside me. I hobbled home, slid into bed and fell into a charmed sleep.

*

Mossie was sitting at the kitchen table with his heavy brown overcoat on. He put three spoons of sugar in his tea and stirred it into a whirlpool. He leaned down and blew on the brown liquid. Then he lifted it up, slurped it into his mouth and swallowed it. It was noisier than the twin tub.

Ma was in the scullery making his sandwiches. She'd been crying. Mossie was her favourite and now he was heading off to England on the boat. It was sudden and unexpected. I wondered was he leaving because of me? Maybe he regretted what had happened in the train? Maybe he was afraid it might happen again? He hadn't pushed himself on me since Killarney. There was one small incident. Going up the stairs when he was coming down. He stopped to let me pass. My tummy rubbed against his. I felt his weight for a moment. He took a breath in and heaved against me but I slipped through. I wondered what went through his mind at

173

night as he lay in the corner within easy reach of me. Did he have to restrain himself? What would happen if he found me on my own with no Johnny to protect me? Or was it that he just wanted everything to return to how it was before the train? What digs would he find in England? Would there be someone to replace me? Would the someone be stronger than me? I would likely never meet the someone yet I knew how he would feel. I shook Mossie's hand outside the front door. I remembered the night he had stood there with the other lost souls. How they'd all got in 'cos Ma couldn't say no. I felt sad for my part in Mossie's going. He was still my favourite. He might never have had to leave only I was too young to know what to do. My stupidity had made the whole thing happen. It left me with a secret to carry as heavy and real as the suitcase in Mossie's hand. I would never get to live it down.

That night, under my pillow, I found a white envelope with my name on it. Inside was a card. When I opened the card to read it, a crisp brown five pound note floated from it onto the bed. The card simply read:

—Good luck, little fella, from Mossie.

8

1966

When Ma discovered the second place cup among the smelly socks in the bottom of the wardrobe, she gave me a clip behind the ear. She loved trophies. Prizes, medals and especially cups. Any silverware that came into the house found its way onto the china cabinet in the dining room. Above the china cabinet on the wall was a plaque studded with hooks. Da had cut it out himself. It was a bit irregular because the saw he used was blunt. He got it in a carpentry set when he was a kid and he still had it. For delicate carpentry work. It was made of soft metal and it bent when cutting hardwoods. I'd brought it to Shaw's Saw Sharpening Service in Talbot Street but they refused to take it in. Shaw himself told me to bring it over to the National Museum in Kildare Street, that it might be from the Bronze Age. When I brought it home Da asked who served me. I told him it was Shaw himself. He threw his eyes to Heaven.

—That fella eats, pisses, shits and barely exists.

Forever after that it became Shaw's Shit Sharpening Service.

Da cut out the plaque with it regardless. Irregular but artistic. Across the top he painted 'Medals 1st 2nd 3rd and others' in green and then varnished the whole thing. The plaque was dripping with medals. Soccer, school exams, religion, Irish dancing, summer leagues, boxing, yo yo competitions, elocution and swimming. They were all there.

The achievements of Ma's children, treasured equally, hung for posterity. Cups were far scarcer than medals and went on the china cabinet. Ita's one for swimming, the biggest even though she was the smallest competitor in Ireland. Ma put the Legion one in front of it. I put it behind when she wasn't looking. Every time I went into the dining room it was back in front. I gave up and just left it there.

Shea started to change towards me. It wasn't the cup. He had a medal for the harmonica on the plaque. It was more to do with *Top Of The Pops* than the Legion of Mary. One evening he asked me up to the bedroom. He handed me the guitar and asked me to play it. Play what, I said.

—The song that won you the cup.

—It's a crap song.

—I know, just play it.

I hit the C chord. Perfect. Shea was very impressed. I knew because he wasn't telling me what to do. I played the first verse and chorus. Shea put his hand across the strings.

—You could play other songs using the same . . .

—Chords.

—Chords.

You could only I didn't know any other songs. I knew 'Speedy Gonzales'. I knew it could be mimed. I told Shea.

—Forget Pat Boone. He's a drip.

I was shocked at the character assassination. He hadn't been in Regina Coeli House the night of the competition. I told Shea he didn't know his arse from his elbow and to come back to me when he could play 'Speedy Gonzales' on the guitar. He told me that Pat Boone pulled out of a picture with Marilyn Monroe because it required him to kiss her and he couldn't because he was a married man.

—He's a drip.

—'Speedy Gonzales' is still a good song.

—Not as good as this. Listen.

Shea cleared his throat and put on his aggressive face. He pointed his finger and screamed into my face.

—*I'm gonna tell you how it's gonna be*
You're gonna give your love to me.

I thought he was picking a row with me. He bashed the strings of my guitar like he meant to break them. I took my hands off it in fright. He took it up and stood with it on the floor.

—*Love can last more than one day*
Love a love not fade away.

He bashed the strings four times. One of them broke and hit him in the face. He flinched like it was his eye. He put his hand up and held it.

—Is it your eye?

—Fuck me eye. What did you think of the song?

—I didn't know it was a song, I thought you were giving out to me.

—It's a song. I wrote it.

I was more proud of that song than Ma was of all the cups and medals. My older brother had written a song. He was only eighteen. I got him to sing it another twenty times and I tried to put my three chords to it. By the end of the night we were a duo. A duo with their own song. 'Not Fade Away'. We never would.

*

Father Paul Cobb had film star looks and smelt of Old Spice aftershave. All the girls in Laurence O'Toole's parish flocked to his Mass on Sunday. We called him Father Paul rather than Father Cobb, which didn't seem disrespectful because he had long locks and wore Brylcreem in his hair. His father was a solicitor over near Fitzwilliam Square with a brass plate, Cobb and Son, in the centre of a Georgian door. Father Paul was an only child and wouldn't be joining his father's practice so the 'and Son' was superfluous. Catherine Griffin thought he was a double for Gregory Peck. Mahony said he was the spit of Gary Cooper. Whoever he was like, he was top of the bill in our church. All the posh weddings wanted Father Paul and he performed them like he was the star attraction, which he was, in a way. Most of the women he married wanted to marry him. He did nothing to disguise his delight at the attention but he did it in a removed way, he was honoured, yes, but he was above it all. Like Jesus, he was dismissive of women. Combined with his unavailability, it made him irresistible. He never set foot in the flats but kept strictly to the posh houses on the far side of Seville Place. He had his Sunday dinner and his Sunday tea there. I would see him sometimes in the early hours of Monday morning making his way back across the street to the Presbytery where he lived but didn't spend a lot of time.

We were in the middle of tea when the ring came to the door. Perry Mason was on the television. The ring went on for ages and was followed by a knock.

—That's a policeman's knock.

Ma was looking at Da who didn't take his eyes off the attorney at law. I answered the door. Father Paul was standing there. He'd never been in our house. He waited until I had the door fully open before he stepped into the hall and removed his hat.

—Your Mammy.

I hopped down the four steps and burst into the kitchen.

—Father Paul for you, Ma.

Da reached out to the volume control. Before he had it turned down Ma was looking into a compact mirror powdering her face. She spread perfume on her fingers and dabbed it behind her ears. Up in the hall she pleaded with him to have a cup of tea in his hand. His refusal was firm but polite. He was on a mercy mission. A young boy coming out of an orphanage. Immature sixteen-year-old. Looking for a family situation. A secure foundation. Genuine Catholic home. Somewhere the boy wouldn't feel out of place. There was no question of charity. He was starting a job and would pay his way. It was important he paid his way. He knew there were many mouths to feed. Nothing was free. We were firmly in the modern world. Pope Paul and the Vatican Council in Rome. Father Paul and the laity in Seville Place. Arms and legs working hand in hand.

Ita made up Mossie's bed for the new lodger and Da turned up the television. He wasn't happy. Worse still, he wasn't saying why he wasn't happy. Ma asked him was he unhappy because it was an orphan.

—No.

Ma was as persistent as Perry Mason. She prodded and goaded but he wouldn't reveal the truth. I thought he was going to plead the fifth amendment. Ma switched her line of enquiry.

—This has nothing to do with the orphan.

Da finished the dregs of his tea. Pushed his cup and saucer away. He fished between his teeth for tea leaves that had slipped the strainer. Ma closed in on him.

—This is about Father Paul.

Da. His Majesty the Baby. Ma put the words in his mouth like the teat of a bottle. Suck, suck, suck. Guzzle, guzzle, guzzle until it was all gone, then pat and stroke his back 'til he burped up the wind that gave him a pain in his tummy. Once he got it all up and out he was happy babbies again.

—What did Father Paul do on you?

Da sat dumb. Perry Mason answered Ma.

—He drove you insanely jealous, isn't that the truth?

The witness started to crack.

—The green-eyed monster devoured you. Isn't that the truth?

—Yes ... yes ... yes ...

The gallery gasped and the witness broke down in tears. Not so Da. Calm as you like he switched off the television.

179

Ma cleared the courtroom. There were half-hearted protests. I slunk into the dining room and rearranged the medals. I heard every word spoken in the kitchen.

It was about Noel Dargan. He had left our house shortly after I found him on the stairs. He went to live with Mrs Power in the flats. Her husband, Christy, the MC, confronted Noel Dargan in the Ball Alley and a row erupted. It spread onto the street and ended up outside the Presbytery where Noel Dargan left the MC for dead on the granite steps. Father Paul was coming home from his nightly in the posh houses when he stumbled across the badly beaten husband. The next day Father Paul stopped Da on his way home from the station and asked him did he know about the scandal concerning the lodger. How he was living an adulterous life and was obstructing the God-given rights of a husband and father. The following Sunday, Father Paul preached a sermon on scandal-givers. Da felt publicly humiliated. Here now was the self-same priest looking for a favour because he was in a fix.

—We're not responsible for Noel Dargan and what he does.

Ma was emphatic. She hadn't done wrong. Da hadn't done wrong. Let others answer for their own sins. She'd answer for hers. That was Ma. She was much tougher than Da. Much tougher at dealing with the world. She could cut through to the heart of a problem while Da dilly-dallied at the edge. Ma was like Perry Mason, which was Da's favourite television programme.

—We don't have to take the orphan, Da.

Ma was serious. Da's happiness was more important than any lodger. Ma was prepared to say no even if it meant disappointing Father Paul and the church. All it required from Da was a nod, a word, he didn't have to do a thing.

—Sure, aren't they all orphans, the lodgers.

He was kicking for touch. He didn't want to confront Father Paul. Even if it was Ma doing it for him.

—It's your decision, Da.

In the silence, I moved the cups back to their original positions and knew what the decision would be.

When John Charles Gallagher arrived at 44 he cried non-stop for three days. He cried so much he couldn't eat. Ma didn't force it. She just left his plate on his mat and took it away again without comment. She treated him just like she treated Da or any other grown-up baby. She cajoled, she encouraged, she rewarded. On the third day, John Charles ate his first forkful. Ma left a cigarette and a box of matches on his side plate as a reward. He pretended it wasn't there. He put four spoons of sugar in his tea and stirred it vigorously. He looked over at me and smiled. I could see the stain of cigarette smoke on his teeth. I looked down and saw the brown colour I loved on his finger tips. I smiled back at him and asked him how many a day he smoked.

—I don't smoke.

He fingered the cigarette. He picked it up and examined it.

—How do you do it?

He put the cigarette in his mouth and lit it. He pulled on it and swallowed the smoke. He blew it from his lungs like a professional.

—Do I look good?

He held it out to me. I couldn't take a drag on his cigarette. I didn't know him. It was a very personal thing putting someone else's cigarette in your mouth. Their lips on your lips. Their mouth in yours. I did it with Ma's butts. The sweet taste of her lipstick mixed with smoke. John Charles Gallagher sucked his way down the white tube. With each pull he took more of the room in. For two days he'd sat staring at the floor. Now his eyes darted all over the room from behind the safety of cigarette smoke. They came to rest on the trophies.

—You're all very intelligent, aren't yous?

I couldn't tell him the trophies had nothing to do with intelligence. If I did he'd feel stupid. I kept my mouth firmly shut.

—Who won the most medals, you or your big brother?

—Me, I'd say.

—You must have brains to burn.

—Not really.

—You have the high forehead. It's a sure sign.

He stubbed out the cigarette and got up from the table. He beckoned me to follow him.

—I've something to show you.

I followed him up the stairs to the bedroom. Once inside, he took his only jacket from the wardrobe and slid his hand into one of the pockets. He took out a silver box and pointed to the engraved initials in the top right-hand corner. J.C.G.

—Do you know what they stand for?

—Your initials, John Charles Gallagher.

He smirked and shook his head.

—Jesus Christ is God.

He waited for my reaction. I felt I should look amazed.

—JCG, wow!

—You'll have to give me some of your brains. I'll need them if I'm going to be a priest.

He had too many freckles to be a priest. In Dublin, anyway. He'd have to have his teeth cleaned. Professionally. I supposed the Christian Brothers would take him. Deformities didn't matter as much with the Brothers. His lack of brains wouldn't be against him either.

He opened the cigarette case and offered me one. I took it and put it in my pocket. I should have taken a light but I wanted to get away from him. I was glad he'd stopped crying and was settling in, but I didn't want him to get any wrong ideas about our friendship. I didn't want that above all else.

*

I was furious with Shea and even more furious with myself. 'Not Fade Away', it turned out, wasn't his song at all. He hadn't written it. Not the words. Not the music. Nothing. He'd stolen it from The Rolling Stones. Shea had assumed I knew all this because it was number three in the hit parade. I was a fool for not knowing. I learned the truth from Gerry Green. He was in Shea's class at school. He knew everything about music. Every group, every label, who were good, who were bad, who were going to make it, who weren't. There was nothing Gerry Green didn't know about pop music, soul music, rhythm and blues, blues, gospel, rock, country, folk, traditional and Indian music. Music was his life's study. He knew everything including the fact that The Rolling Stones had a hit with 'Not Fade Away'. And even though he did know everything, the only instrument he could play was the maracas. He had a bass guitar which he couldn't play but which he loaned to Shea. I wanted to break the bass guitar over his head. I'd gone around in a permanent state of singing 'Not Fade Away'. It got better every time I sang it. I was so proud I had a brother who'd written a song.

—*I'm gonna tell you how it's gonna be*
   You're gonna give your love to me.

It said precisely what I wanted to say to Catherine Griffin but couldn't. I didn't know what to say, I didn't know what to do. I didn't know where to put my hands, my tongue, my body. If I knew what to do she would pour her love out to me. If she did, the awkwardness would disappear. Shea had written and now not written a song that described my deepest pain, the thoughts that swirled around my brain in the moments before I fell asleep.

—You stole it, Shea!

183

—Genius steals, mime groups borrow.

He always had an answer. I didn't care that he was clever. I had stupidly believed him. I'd turned him into a genius. I had been looking forward to his next song. It was all ashes now.

—You stole it.

—The Rolling Stones stole it from Buddy Holly.

It was Gerry Green dropped the bombshell into the conversation. Shea looked at me and shrugged his shoulders.

—See what I mean, everyone steals.

Buddy Holly was American. The Rolling Stones were British. We were Irish. Irish and nameless. No groups came from Ireland except ceili bands. I suggested we call ourselves The Robbers. It went down like a fart in a space suit. Gerry Green had an idea for a name. It was a brilliant idea. It was so brilliant he couldn't say it.

—I can't say it. I can't fucking say it.

He became hysterical. So did Shea. It happened a lot when Gerry Green and he got together. They got hysterical by telepathy. I'd never been part of their circle. Not until I learned the guitar. I watched them to see if I could learn. They looked at each other and just got hysterical. The only way to do it, it seemed, was to jump in. It was difficult to become hysterical out of nothing. If you thought about it at all, it was impossible. I waited until my mind was fairly blank before I chanced it. I became hysterical at Gerry Green first. He looked at me in horror for just a split second before he left for planet hysteria completely. Shea was in orbit, too. My hysteria fuelled theirs. For the first time I was part of it, I saw how it worked. It was brilliant. Mass hysteria. When we returned to Earth, Gerry Green still couldn't talk. None of us could. We were worn out. I picked up my guitar and hit the A chord. I'd been practising it all week. A, E and D. Six chords now in my repertoire. Gerry Green shook his maracas. Shea plucked a note on the bass. It was hard to hear the electric bass without an amplifier. He played it again. It was the wrong note. I slid his hand along the fret board until the note made the A sound. We started to belt out 'Not Fade Away'.

—*I'm gonna tell you how it's gonna be*
  You're gonna give your love to me.

Shea's vocals were fine, the playing was awful. We were all in different times. Ma knocked at the wall in perfect four four time. I repeated it with my foot on the floor. We went at it again. Ma knocked at us again, in double speed. It was time to stop. Shea said starting a group was like starting a religion. We had to believe we were God to create followers. We had to give them something to believe in. Fans would come and worship at our altar. We shouldn't be afraid of that. We were the gods of our own religion. We could start off with other people's material but eventually we'd have to create our own. I suggested we learn how to play first. Shea thought that was bollix.

—The fact that we can't play is an advantage.

—How is it an advantage?

—Think about it.

I couldn't figure it out. How could we stand up in front of an audience and not play? I asked Gerry Green what he thought.

—It's so brilliant I can't talk.

He threw his arms around Shea and kissed him. They were nearly three years older than me. It was a lot when you were fifteen. Maybe I would understand when I was their age. I didn't want to have to wait that long. I had one foot in their circle and I liked it there. I got my foothold because of the guitar but my knowing how to play it was a negative. It would take time for me to understand.

—Not knowing how to play means we're free of all influence.

Shea and Gerry Green were feeding off each other, they were revving up to leave the planet again.

—Stop talking, you're too brilliant.

They went into orbit. I needed to stay grounded for the

185

present. I picked up my guitar and went upstairs. John Charles Gallagher was lying stretched out on my bed. I walked up beside him.

—What are you doing?

—I'm filling my head.

—What are you filling it with?

—Brains.

—Oh.

I was sorry I'd asked. I felt I'd intruded.

—I can feel your brains in the pillow. I'll be a brainy bastard soon.

I left John Charles Frankenstein on the bed and headed downstairs. I felt like a nomad in my own house. Da and Mahony were in the dining room pouring over the ledger. In the kitchen Ita, Johnny and Frankie were watching television. Ma was in the scullery cursing the water pressure.

—You'll have to make that racket some place else, do you hear?

I went out to the garage for some peace and quiet. Even the garage was crowded now. Three cars. Da had bought a Ford Anglia. It wasn't much of a car. He measured the space in the garage before he bought it to make sure it would fit. He bought the skinniest car he could find. A car with wings like an angel. It was so close to the other car the door wouldn't open. To get the door open meant driving Father Ivers' car out first and then pushing Da's into the open space. Parking it was a nightmare. You had to get out of the car and close the door before pushing it gently into its bay. The garage wasn't built for three cars. It meant there were only two places left to sit down. Da's toilet or the Volkswagen. It wasn't a difficult choice to make.

*

Andy Griffin was released early from Artane Industrial School. A week before his sixteenth birthday he walked out the front gates with his brown suitcase. The world was smaller than when he went in. He'd grown up in Artane. He'd filled out despite the horrible food. It was the cream cakes Catherine brought on visits. I could have gone once or twice but didn't. I couldn't bear the thought of walking out the gates and leaving him there. On his walk down Seville Place to freedom, Andy rang at our front door and asked for me. Ma didn't recognize him. She thought he was a trainee priest. The lovely crease in his trousers. His shirt spick and span. His impeccable manners. He was a credit to Artane. Pity more weren't sent there. Everything Ma said was true. Andy was a new person. From the outside in. He looked like an insurance man. What startled me the most was his voice. It was gentle and soft with a lilt. It gave everything he said an air of respectfulness. An air of deference. Only I knew how Dublin Andy was, I'd have said he was a culchie from Carlow.

Andy wasn't interested in Artane. He'd done well by it. That was enough. He wanted to know what I was doing tomorrow. I told him I was going to school, the same as today. We sat on the wall of the naller across from the broken ship. I asked him had he ever dived off the very top. The question went right through him without a reply. I found it difficult to reconnect with him. There was so much we hadn't shared in the time he was away.

—You swopped me while I was in Artane.

—I beg your pardon?

—Me for Catherine.

She wasn't mine. That was the tragedy. I'd walked her home and she invited me to kiss her. It was a giant step forward. The next time I walked her home was after a Legion meeting. I had it in my mind to touch her breast because I knew her arse was off limits. As soon as we entered the flats I saw Billy Boy Brennan and Scissors Kane. They were up on top of the pram sheds drinking cider. As soon as they saw me they started screaming.

—Leave our women alone.

I pulled away from Catherine, unsure what to do. They smashed their bottles and jumped down on the ground. I looked at Catherine for protection. I knew she was safe. She was one of them. They were claiming her back. Without telling them, my feet started moving at the speed of wind. I could hear the mad dogs behind me all the way from the flats, by the back of the church, around the Presbytery corner and along Seville Place to the bell of 44 which I held pressed 'til the door opened and I fell inside past Mahony, their voices ringing in my ears . . .

—Leave our women alone.

I didn't know where I stood with Catherine. I had no experience of limbo but I was sure it felt like this. I looked at Andy and wondered did he know I was a coward. That I'd run away. I wanted to tell him but I couldn't. I was too vulnerable. Things had changed since he went away. I needed to take my time.

—I'm going to find a girl.

He said it matter of fact. He was going to find a girl. Just like he used to find money. He'd find a girl and put her in his pocket. Like catching a falling star. I believed him. Hundreds of rainy days in gloomy dormitories preparing for it.

—She's at home now putting on her make-up. She's looking in a mirror not knowing I'm going to pounce. Gas, isn't it?

Andy was going hunting to the hop in the Galway Arms.

*

Teresa Mannion was wrapped around Andy. He was wrapped around her. They were only going out three days and they could hardly walk down the road they were that

188

wrapped around one another. Her chest was rubbing up against him and his hand was firmly on the cheek of her arse. I walked beside Catherine and pretended not to notice. I took hold of her hand. It felt a bit pathetic beside the other two. I felt so uncomfortable I let Catherine's hand go. I didn't know if she wanted me to take hold of it again. I was racked with indecision but I smiled like I was having the best time of my life. We were going out as a foursome on a day trip to the seaside. Going up the steps of the station, Andy suggested the mystery train. They asked me where it was going and wouldn't believe me when I told them I didn't know.

Teresa Mannion had never heard of the Legion of Mary. It came up in the conversation when Catherine pointed out the statue of Our Lady that overlooked the bay from Dollymount pier. It had been put there by the dockers of Dublin out of their hard-earned money. You couldn't escape Our Lady in Dublin. I thought how much like her Catherine was. Teresa Mannion was more of a Mary Magdalene of whom there wasn't a single statue in Dublin. She sat on Andy's knee all the way out. As we approached the tunnel outside Killiney, Andy tapped me on the shin and nodded towards his sister. Moments later we were in darkness. When we re-emerged Teresa Mannion's face was stuck to Andy's. I could hear their tongues sucking. I looked out of the window and cursed the Bay that was supposed to be more beautiful than Naples. When they stopped kissing, Teresa Mannion put her fingers to her mouth, took out a big lump of chewing gum and flicked it out the window to the feet of Killiney Bay. The mystery train came to a final stop at Bray, much to the delight of all the passengers.

On the promenade we bought pink candy floss. Andy bought Teresa's. I noticed she didn't say thank you. Catherine insisted on paying for her own. She was working and I wasn't. Andy and Teresa's candy floss got tangled up together and they couldn't separate them. It ended up all over their hands and faces and made them sticky. They didn't seem to mind. I wished Catherine was more like her. We headed for the amusement arcade and queued for the ghost train. It was reaching crisis point with Catherine. I couldn't put off making a move much longer. I'd kissed her before for God's sake. It was time for initiative. If I didn't make a move, I'd never know. I had to grasp the broken bottle. There was no retreat.

As the two-seater carriage crashed through the double doors into darkness, I put my arm around Catherine's waist. A luminous red hand came down and stroked my hair. I started to panic. I could see only darkness. Not even a sky-light. I was trapped. Just like on the train to Killarney. I couldn't leave my body, there was nowhere to go. I had to make a run for it. I jumped out of the carriage and headed back the way I came. I saw some light and then the sparks of wheels on a track. The carriage almost hit me. I didn't care. I could see a pencil of light. Top to bottom. I made for the light. I got my fingers in the crack of light and pulled the doors open. The girls in a waiting carriage screamed at me. I ran past the queue of people and across the road to the promenade. I climbed over the blue railings and ran down the hill of large stones before coming to rest on a small bed of dried seaweed that looked like it might be friendly. I sat there crushing the seaweed into dust until the others found me. I heard Andy first.

—It wasn't that scary.

Catherine stood in front of me. I saw her flat shoes.

—Are you all right?

—I suffer from claustrophobia, that's all.

Teresa was standing near Andy with her hands on her hips.

—Is that contagious?

Catherine answered her sharply.

—No, it's not contagious.

Andy held out his hand to pull me up. I refused his help. He squatted down on his hunkers.

—Let's climb Bray Head.

—You and Teresa go. I'm not in the humour.

Catherine and I watched them march away like contestants in a three-legged race. We watched them in silence. What was there to say? We watched them go up the hill and cross under the cable cars until they looked the size of birds. Up there was the Eagle's Nest. We watched them until they looked like ants in a line of ants all the way to the summit where the cement cross stood.

—What would you like to do?

—I told my Ma I'd bring her home blackberries.

I don't know why I said it. It was a lie. Catherine knew, too. We got a brown paper bag from a shop and headed away from the sea towards fields at the far side of the town. We'd rented a house there when I was nine. I retraced the journey now. I remembered it so well. When we arrived at the field I climbed the gate first. I turned and helped Catherine. She used my hand to ballast herself.

—I'm going to jump.

She had a glint in her eye like a child. It was the best moment of the day so far. She took a breath, let go of my hand and leapt into the air. She landed and rolled over in the grass, several times, yelping as she went. I felt comfortable at last. Open air, country, freedom and Catherine yelping. By the time she came to a stop, the yelps had turned to cries directed at her ankles. I ran down to where she lay. From her calves to her toes she was covered in dung. She'd landed in a cow pat. Her feet were caked in it. It sat on her stockings and leaked into her shoes. She pulled up her dress to keep it from contamination.

—What am I going to do?

It was an awful situation but I was glad it wasn't me. I

looked around for inspiration. I took the brown paper bag and started to tear it into small squares. I laid out the squares on the grass. Catherine asked me what I was doing. I didn't know, I was working on instinct. She asked me again. I shrugged it off. I didn't want to drag Da and his arse-wiping techniques into the conversation. This was as close as I'd been to her all day. I picked up one of the squares and scraped a section of dung off her leg. I wiped the dung in the grass and re-used it till the paper got soggy. It wasn't very romantic. The smell especially. That apart, it was an improvement on the ghost train from my point of view. At least I was doing something for Catherine. Something other than running away.

—Why did you run out of the ghost train?

—You really want to know?

—Yes, I really want to know.

I told Catherine about getting stuck in the toilet. I made a story of it. Added lots of colour. Lots of detail. I enjoyed telling her. I compared it to a coffin. I surprised myself by thinking of it. The coffin gave me a whole new lease of life on the tale. The fear of being buried alive. A morbid fear. Air running out. Banging on the lid. Pulling at the lock my fingers started to bleed. I showed her my hands. I wanted her to take them in hers. Stroke them 'til there wasn't a blemish left. My poor hands. Her poor legs. I wanted to rub them smooth. I couldn't. I wanted to lie beside her and slide into her folds. Turn my mouth to hers and let her swallow my air. Forget the day. Forget Andy and Teresa and candy floss and stones. Forget ghost trains and seaweed and chewing gum and dung. I couldn't forget the dung. I showed Catherine my hands and told her my story, until a cow's hot breath told us it was time to go home.

I couldn't stop thinking of Mossie all the way to Dublin. I wished he were still there. He'd taken a part of me with him and I wanted to get it back. I still felt connected to him. Like he had a power over me. I'd have loved him to meet Catherine and give her the thumbs up. What he did was wrong but he'd done it because he'd loved me. I wanted to love Catherine as much as he'd loved me. I didn't know what was stopping me. I just wished he'd come back and make everything all right.

I woke up the next morning trying to kick myself in the balls. It was the first time I'd tried to do it. I deserved nothing less for suggesting picking blackberries. The cows out Bray way were laughing still. The gobshite Dublin boyo with the girl from Sheriff Street, the Good Knight holding her by the hand so she wouldn't miss the cow dung in waiting. The only consolation was it didn't rain cow pats. I kicked at my balls and finally got a left heel on target, sending my right testicle flying up into my belly. It liked where it landed because it didn't come back down. All day I felt for it but it stayed stuck where it was. I pretended I didn't care but in reality I was petrified it had gone for ever.

I couldn't keep my mind on the band practice. We were rehearsing in the garage. I'd invited Andy to join. He was the drummer, naturally. He had a snare given to him by his Auntie Kathleen. The snare and two orange boxes made up the set. Andy was the most professional in the group. He could have played with the Artane Boys' Band but never did on account of the fact that he wouldn't wear short trousers in public. Michael Maltese was the name of our band. For three days I tried to prise it out of Gerry Green. He knew it but wouldn't say.

—I can't fucking talk.

We decided to push Father Ivers' car out of the garage to make room for the drums. Shea went in to ask Ma, because she never refused him anything. I slipped into Da's toilet on the pretext of a pee. I was checking to see if my ball had come back down. It hadn't. I tried to push it down. I imagined it was one of the snakes. No good. I heard Shea coming back in.

—We can't move the car.

He was in a temper.

—Me oul' fella says it could get damaged outside.

Soon as I stepped back in from the toilet I could hear raised voices coming from the kitchen. Ma's voice was the loudest. Shea was a ball of rage. Da came into the garage. No one knew where to look. He took down the Volkswagen key and opened the double doors. He drove Father Ivers' car out at high speed, came back in and started to push the Anglia out of its bay. He jumped in and drove it out, then he drove Father Ivers' car back in and closed the double doors, by himself, without speaking a word, before he went back in and shouted at Ma:

—Satisfied?

They'd been rowing all week. It was over money. John Charles Gallagher had lost his first week's wages in the slot machines near where he worked. Ma took pity on him and put it down to him being an orphan. She told him not to do it again. Da wanted to kick the little fucker into the middle of next week until Ma pointed out that she'd had no money from Mahony for seven months. It was a haymaker. Da had no defence against it. He was out for the count and he didn't like it. Not one bit. When Shea walked into the kitchen Da turned on him as a way of getting at Ma. It was his favourite trick. It drove Shea mental. Humiliated in front of the band. We were doing our best to ignore it. It was all you could do with Da sometimes. Bottle your embarrassment. Andy broke the silence.

—There's something I want to ask. Do we have a rule about people coming to listen?

Shea was in a rage and said nothing. I was the baby. Gerry Green had picked the name from a cartoon on the television. He was the leader, I suppose. He shrugged his shoulders. Nobody expected the question. We weren't really a group yet. We didn't have rules. We didn't have a single song we could play all the way through. Andy had put us on the spot.

—Will we take a vote on it?

I'd never voted before in my life. Not on anything important. I knew about democracy. We'd studied the French Revolution in school. The storming of the Bastille. It was important in a distant sort of a way. This was much more real.

—Who's for?

Andy put his hand up.

Shea and Gerry Green kept their hands down by their sides. It was all up to me. I could tie the vote or make it three to one. Andy was my best friend. Before he went away to Artane I wouldn't have hesitated. It was different now. We had shared our secrets growing up. Now our secrets kept us apart. Andy had grown up in Artane. He had learned to survive in a dormitory of a hundred and fifty boys. He had only ever known fear in Laurence O'Toole's yet he had conquered his fear in a prison where Christian Brothers turned the key. He'd lost all his vulnerability. He never explained it. He lived only in tomorrow. I lived with at least one foot in the past. I shone a light in its dark corners for clues to myself. Sometimes I felt stuck there, the more so as I saw Andy steaming ahead. What did my academic progress count for compared to him? I didn't know how to get a girl. Andy knew it instinctively. On the way home from Bray when I wasn't thinking about Mossie, I reminded him of the day he took down his trousers and showed his arse to the class. He looked over at me and smiled.

—When was that?

He knew. We both knew. He was deciding not to remember. He had decided not to be a victim any more. He'd eradicated it from his history.

Andy still had his hand in the air. I kept mine in my pocket and nursed my single ball. It was very immature to kick yourself in the balls over a girl. I was jealous of him, of his maturity, of his way with girls. I couldn't vote for him in those circumstances.

—I'm against.

He accepted the decision with such good grace I felt he was glad. Still. It made him the outsider, no doubt about that.

Gerry Green was the brains of the group. He introduced us to the blues. The Rolling Stones and The Beatles owed everything to the blues and so would we. The blues were simple. Twelve bar and every song started the same way:

—*Woke up this morning* ...

Woke up this morning was followed by a litany of woe. The woe was usually woman trouble. She was gone. About to go. Had killed her man. Had kicked him out. Run off with another man. Withdrawn her love. Moved to parchment farm. The main thing was the man was in shit.

—*Woke up this morning*
  Only one ball in my sack.
  Yes, I woke up this morning
  With only one ball in my sack.

I sang it quietly to myself. A two-line song. Couldn't find a third line to go with it. Gerry Green taught us a song by Leadbelly. I loved his name. I wanted to adopt it. We were rehearsing a song by the ex-convict when Ma came in. She had more of the blues than Mr Leadbelly. A face on her to sink a thousand ships. Andy got the brunt of it.

—Please tell your girlfriend not to ring at my hall door. I'm not a maid.

Andy was frothing at the mouth with apologies. He ran out of the small door and met Teresa on the street. I could hear her as clear as the church bell.

—Who's that mad oul' wan?

Andy had to work hard to make the peace before he told her she couldn't come to rehearsals. The band had taken a vote.

—I don't want to come. Yous can't even play.

Andy came back in smiling. Not a hint of the blues. He knew how to treat his woman and she knew her place.

Michael Maltese before Andy was like a car without an engine. Andy was the motor. He drove the band. He beat out time with his sticks and we struggled to keep up. After twenty attempts it started to feel comfortable. We were starting to make music. We had discipline. Like a classroom with a good teacher. Order and chaos side by side. Andy was the fulcrum, the boiler man, the driver. I couldn't help thinking back to Denehy's class. The uncontrollable fear that made him say stupid things. Nine and a half commandments. The pool of piss. He was totally transformed from that time. A smiler. Relaxed and gentle. No hint of fear. And yet despite this, I felt a greater distance between us. As if we'd lost something in the years apart, an innocence that we both shared in which we'd never see again.

The rule excluding outsiders didn't last long. We were rehearsing the blues when there was a knock on the double doors. Shea spoke through the door.

—Who is it?

—I heard you playing. I'm looking for talent.

It was an English accent. We were all taken aback. I whispered to Shea.

—Let him in.

Shea looked to Gerry Green.

—Will I let him in?

—I can't talk. I can't fucking talk.

Shea turned back to the door.

—Are you a talent scout?

—I'm over from Liverpool. My name's Andy Epstein.

—Andy Epstein? Are you anything to Brian?

—He's my older brother.

—It's Brian Epstein's fucking brother.

Shea went out the small door to the street. Seconds later he came back in followed by Andy Epstein. Hair, glasses, complexion, all the same. A Brian Epstein lookalike, only it was Mahony our lodger. I thought he was going to be sick he laughed that much. We let him stay. He was followed in minutes later by John Charles Gallagher and Liam Dargan, the former insisted on singing out of tune and the latter imitated every movement of Andy's using a knife and fork. I had to tell them to stop. I expected that would end their attendance at rehearsals. It didn't. They came every night. Listened to every tortuous effort. Went in and brought out their supper so as not to miss a beat. They got to bringing out our tea and bread. It became a cavern for Michael Maltese and friends, the garage. Groupies. Worshippers. We were well on our way to starting a new religion.

Da wasn't pleased. No one to discourse with any more. No one except Ma and she was no match for him intellectually. So he thought. There was Frankie but at nine he was too young to shout at. The garage had ousted the kitchen. The academy of music had replaced the academy of thought. There was nothing to stop him sitting in on our rehearsals but he was too proud to do that. He hadn't invented Michael Maltese so why should he nourish him? The music we played was a corruption. He didn't say that to our faces, of course, but in a feeble gesture of defiance he bought Frankie a recorder and made an enormous song and dance of it.

Da bought a leather-bound copy of the *Complete Works of William Shakespeare* and started to read it. He started in the middle. One night I came in to get a plectrum and he was sitting at the table with the book open on page 475. He was reading Macbeth. *A knocking within. Enter a Porter.* He was bent close to the small print and was chuckling away quietly to himself. It was a real giveaway, because

198

everyone knew there are no jokes in Shakespeare. At least
no jokes that a normal person could understand. Maybe he
was thinking of Mahony when the Porter entered and that's
what made him laugh.

One result of the garage ousting the kitchen was that Da
started to take Ma out again. They went to the theatre,
mostly the Abbey, although Ma loved the variety shows in
the Theatre Royal. She loved the tenor, Josef Locke, but her
favourite was the comedian Mickser Reid, who was funnier
than Charlie Chaplin and smaller than Peter Pan. Ma always
tried to repeat his jokes for us but she laughed too much
and got convulsed with the phlegm from her chest caused by
smoking and she ended up deferring to Da for the punchlines.
He preferred what he called the real life dramas of the Abbey
stage. He'd tell the story of the play by acting out the parts,
sometimes performing it too well. More than once Frankie
ended up in floods of tears and Johnny refused to go to bed
because he didn't want to have nightmares.

Attendance at rehearsals was confined to residents of 44.
As the band improved, teenagers gathered outside the double
doors to listen. Teresa Mannion hung out with them, which
seemed to please Andy in a perverse sort of way. Some nights
they danced. Some nights they made more noise than we did
and it got out of hand. Some nights Mahony chased them
away. He was now our manager. Some nights we jumped
ship and abandoned rehearsals. Da was adamant we'd have
to find another place to practise. He knew there was nowhere
else.

—There's the Oriel Hall.

Ma made the suggestion. It was the parish hall where the
old folks played bingo and had their Christmas party. No
one but old folks were allowed inside the door. It had been
an IRA arms dump in the Black and Tan war. When we
got our independence and Ireland was divided up among
Irishmen, the Catholic Church got the Oriel Hall.

—Maybe it's time the young people got their chance.

Ma always stood up for youth, as she called it. I loved the way she attacked crabby old people. Crabby old folk were the crowning work of the devil, according to Ma. I loved the way she said it. Them and their bingo. Monsters.

—Get the keys off Father Paul and let them rehearse in the Oriel Hall.

Ma had unleashed a torpedo. I could see it sailing across the kitchen table straight for Da. He saw it too late. There was no escape.

—What would I be asking him anything for?

—They're your sons, that's why!

Ma had made her stand for youth and caused a quiet, beautiful explosion. For her children. For the future. She'd put it up to Da to make a stand. We all knew Father Paul owed us. It was time to call in the favour. I could see the terror on Da's face. Ma was asking him to commit to something. To action. Da was a brave talker. The bravest. This didn't require thought. It required Da cashing in a docket with Father Paul and claiming his just reward.

—Why can't you mime like The Beatles do?

No one understood what he was talking about. He didn't want to confront Father Paul, that was clear. But what was he saying about The Beatles? Why would they mime to their own songs? Maybe the words came out of his mouth wrong and he meant we should mime to The Beatles? Or maybe not? I asked him directly what he meant. He drank long and slow from the Guinness bottle before he addressed the assembled audience.

—The Beatles don't play their own instruments.

He was serious. Seriously mad. They didn't play their instruments? They held them but didn't play them? Who played them?

—It's all done with tape machines. It's illusion. Engineers

produce the sound. They just stand there and count the money.

He might as well have claimed he was the Son of God. The whole room turned on him. Gerry Green was so upset he couldn't get hysterical. He'd heard The Beatles play in the Adelphi Cinema.

—It's too insane. I can't talk.

The whole room was shouting him down. Andy turned to me and whispered through the shouts.

—Your Da's mad.

John Charles Gallagher did what he always did and swam with Da against the tide.

—Your father could be right.

It was so lick arse it was pathetic. Mahony was very annoyed, which was unusual. He depended on Da for his very existence.

—You're out of order there. Definitely out of order.

Da welcomed the abuse. The insults. He was delighted. He had everyone around the kitchen table again with him at the centre of the storm. He didn't mind being out on a limb. He probably didn't believe the nonsense he was coming out with. I knew the depths of his madness from my days as his messenger and it was possible he did believe it. The main thing was in putting down The Beatles he was putting us down. They were flawed, just like we were flawed. In exposing their failure and ours, he was covering up his own. He was afraid to confront Father Paul and he had carefully deflected the conversation away from that. We were talking about the Fab Four and we'd been hoodwinked by them. All of us had, except him. What a stupid world. Two billion fooled. And Da, not fooled. What was the failure in his own life that he had to be right all the time? We were Jonahs and jinxes and disasters. Most of the time we absorbed his negativity. Tonight Ma had reflected it back in his face and he was squirming like a worm to get out of the light. It almost made me sick.

I went out to the scullery and splashed my face with cold water. The pressure was as it always had been – disastrous. I dried my face and brought in the teapot. I offered it all round. Da pushed his cup two inches towards me. His usual signal. It annoyed me. I started to pour.

—Why don't you tell us what you're afraid of? We're not going to judge you.

I stopped pouring and put the teapot on the table.

—What is it you're afraid of that you can't stand up for us?

The next thing I felt was his knuckle on my chin and I disappeared onto the floor. I was aware of Shea putting his body between Da and me. Andy and Mahony lifted me onto the armchair by the fire but I tried to push them away.

—It's all right, I deserved it.

I was aware of Shea again. He had his hands out like he was on a cross. I thought he was a crucifix. He was shouting at Da and blocking his path.

—Look, no hands, no violence.

There were bodies restraining Da. Gerry Green and John Charles Gallagher.

—I'll kill him if I lay me hands on him.

—Kill me, look, no hands no violence. You won't touch him, d'ya hear?

Ma was putting some ice on my lip. She told Da to sit down.

—That's an end to the digging or I'll put my hat and coat on.

It changed the atmosphere in a second. The tension evaporated.

Everyone in 44 was sitting. Sitting in silence sipping tea. I thought they were doing it deliberately because they knew I wanted to write a song. I felt weird in my head. I wanted to hold out my hand to Da and say sorry. I started singing in my head. 'I Wanna Hold Your Hand'. I turned to tell Shea what was going on in my head and he was miming 'A Hard Day's Night'. It was all getting too weird. I couldn't keep my eyes open. I fell asleep where I sat, concussed to the world.

*

I don't know when it happened, it could have been when the blow was struck, or when I hit the floor, but the following morning my missing ball was back in its sack. My head hurt real bad but I smiled through the pain because of my testicle. I'd missed it more than I could have imagined. I'd worried that it had gone into space and would never return, in which case I would never have children. It was great to be back to normal.

Andy agreed to come with me to see Father Paul. I had my Sunday best on. Ma insisted. I looked at Andy. He now had two creases down the front of his trousers. Still, he looked neat. Father Paul eventually came out in his shirt sleeves. He had a white napkin in his hand and wiped his mouth with it the same way he wiped the chalice at Mass. I expected he'd take us inside but he held fast by the door.

—I'm in the middle of my tea.

I remembered the night he'd called to our door. Had he forgotten? I willed him to remember.

—What do you want?

—We have a band. We're looking to rehearse in the Oriel Hall.

He brushed his front with the napkin. I tried to put thoughts in his head. Good thoughts. We were an orphan band. I willed him to offer us a home. Everyone deserved one. We did. Father Paul stepped past us onto the granite step and looked up and down the street, like he was expecting someone to appear. Christ or the Angel Gabriel. He turned around and looked at the hall door. I could see his reflection in the brass plate that said PRESBYTERY. There was a thumb print on the surface. He took the napkin to it and started to wipe it.

—The Oriel Hall is for parish activities only. Did you know that?

I waited for him to finish. I didn't want to talk to his back. The mark was gone. He stepped back inside.

—I'm from the parish. You know where I live.

—You're a parishoner, yes, but your band is not a parish activity. I'm sorry.

The door was still open. He didn't want to close it. Not while I stood there. I stood a while longer. Enough for it to embarrass. I looked at him and thought of Judas. He looked at me and thought of his tea, I suppose. I couldn't let it pass. My face hurt too much simply to let it go.

—John Charles has settled in very well.

—Good. That's good.

He seemed happy with the news. On Sunday he'd stand up on the altar and preach the Christian message. The great promise of eternal life with God in his celestial home. All that mattered were the keys to the Oriel Hall. He had them and he wasn't giving them to us. There was nothing further to say. Nothing to add. I turned away from him and walked down the granite steps with Andy.

9

1967

Frankie started seeing the moon again. Like the night the aerial went up. He couldn't speak properly then. Tebibision. Just a baby. He was ten now. Sat with his puffed up face resting on his hands, trying to smile at the television.

—What's on the telly, Frankie?

—The moon.

—I don't see the moon. How can you see it?

—I saw it a million times once.

It made us laugh. We saw *The Fugitive* run from place to place across America, Frankie saw the moon dancing. I asked him what it was.

—It's where I come from.

—Yes, but what is it?

—It's home.

It hurt him to talk. His face was still a black shade of blue from where it was dragged along the ground outside our house. We were rehearsing in the front room (our manager's bedroom), when Frankie and a gang of his friends got into the garden and started to make a racket outside the window. I went out to the front door and chased them away. They hopped over the garden railings and jumped on a horse and cart coming up empty from the docks. Frankie was slow in getting to it. He struggled to make a clean jump onto the cart. He could only hold on and run along. His friends tried to pull him up by his jacket. He left the ground but his body,

instead of going forward, flipped backwards. His head hit
the ground and he bounced along for a few yards before he
came to a stop. He jumped up, in shock, and started to run
after the cart again. Then he realized he was hurt. He stopped
and put his hand up to his head. I ran down to him. I
could see his forehead was badly grazed. A purple lump was
starting to appear. I brought him home and Ma inspected
the damage. She put him sitting in the armchair by the fire
and put ice on it. Surprisingly, he was hardly crying. It
lessened my guilt a good deal. I went up to the front room
and rejoined the band.

The following day his face was dark blue. More than
that, it was crumpled. There didn't seem to be any light in
his eyes. Frankie had the biggest eyes of any of us. I hadn't
noticed before. You couldn't not notice now. It made him
look sad and made me feel guilty. I told him I'd bring
him fishing in the naller. Or the Liffey if he'd prefer. He
didn't want to go fishing. I was glad I offered, but relieved
when he didn't want to go. Why would he want to do
anything with me? I only ever called him a little twirp and
now I'd helped bash his face in. Going fishing with me was
probably his idea of torture. He hated me, I'm sure. Hated
me with the same passion that he idolized Da. He looked
at me from behind his black sockets. It hurt his face to get
words out. He tried to talk but couldn't get his tongue
around the words. He mimed it. I should have known. It
was that time of year when every kid in Dublin wanted to
possess conker number one.

I skipped Wednesday afternoon sport and took Frankie
on the 24 bus to the Phoenix Park. We sat on the side seat.
People stared at him along the way. He looked ugly. I put
my arm across his back and held his shoulder. I couldn't
remember if I'd ever done it before. The bus hopped and
bounced its way across the cobblestones of the north quays.
I cushioned him against it as much as I could. It brought

back memories of the horse and cart. I cursed myself that I wasn't on the back of it to haul him up. I was ashamed. His face made my shame public. I embraced it. My shame felt like nothing compared to his dark suffering. I gave him an extra tight squeeze. I wanted everyone to know he was my brother.

I hadn't felt that way towards him since he was a baby. Outside the bus, there was a gale blowing. All along the river, pedestrians bent their heads and pushed against the wind. Men held onto their caps and women clutched their shopping bags. Only the very brave mounted the Ha'penny Bridge. I could see some people being blown backwards and others moving their legs but standing still. A trilby flew over the railings and almost landed on a seagull who was flapping his wings but going nowhere. The hat looked like it was heading for a watery grave when a gust of wind caught it and blew it over Merchant's Arch. It looked like it was heading for Dublin Castle when it disappeared from view. I was glad to have the shelter of the 24 bus.

The 24 stopped directly opposite the entrance to the Fifteen Acres. No one ever got off at the stop except football players and chestnut hunters. There were dozens of football pitches and acres of horse chestnut trees, much more than fifteen, which made a mockery of the name. On Saturday afternoons the Fifteen Acres looked like every schoolboy in Dublin had been ordered to run after a ball. When the wind blew, like it did today, it looked like blow football. As I held Frankie's hand and took him through the gate, the wind took charge of our clothes and turned us into human sails. It blew us back a few steps before it changed direction and swept us through the gate at high speed. We were greeted by a sign on the road – 'Beware of Fallen Trees'. What was there to beware of? Fallen trees were exactly what we wanted. Trees full of chestnuts face down on the ground.

Drunken trees on the seat of their pants spilling out their guts.

I couldn't believe the noise. The assault on the ears was constant. Nature could be impressive, no doubt about that. Elemental. I couldn't talk with the barrage. I climbed over the railings into a small copse. Frankie was small enough to slip between the bars. We were only a few yards in when it started to rain. They were large drops. Plopping down between the branches onto the ground covered with leaves. Frankie raised a scream to the heavens. He realized before I did. It was raining chestnuts. He held out his hands to catch the drops. One landed at my feet. It looked the size of a tennis ball. I picked it up and peeled back the green spiky skin. Inside it was thick with a soft white lining like a womb. The chestnut was a perfectly formed miracle. Shiny and hard with the thinnest layer of oil. I rubbed it against my face. It felt exquisite.

Frankie was in anarchy. His pockets were stuffed, his hands were full and he kept on finding yet bigger chestnuts and nowhere to put them. He ran from one discovery to another with complete abandon. It was biblical. Rain after drought. Harvest after famine. Conkers falling from the sky. And just us two. Not another soul anywhere to be seen. Frankie and me alone in the Fifteen Acres. Alone in a sea of plenty. Worlds of wanwood leafmeal lie. It was a line of poetry. Gerard Manley Hopkins. We'd read it in school. Poetry of the soul. I understood what it meant for the first time.

Goldengrove unleaving. The trees were dying but there was a light in Frankie's eyes for the first time in days. It was better than any poem. I'd brought him to relieve my guilt. Brought him out of pity. There was nothing pitiful about this scene. I felt a transformation in my relationship with Frankie. Seeing his abandonment and knowing that I'd made it happen. It gave me a pleasure I'd never felt before. I understood that I had a role as his older brother to protect him in a way I hadn't done up until now.

Back home we caused major excitement when we spilled out our pockets. Nobody had ever seen a collection of 'juicers' like it. They spread across the table from one side to the other. A sea of chestnuts. The table could take no more and yet more appeared. Da was the most excited of anyone. He'd had a conker sixty-eight as a kid but he could see a conker hundred among this lot. He graded them according to size first. Then he took them one by one in his hand and felt them between his fingers. If there was a gap between the skin and the core, he discarded it. It was a fatal flaw. He discarded all the ones that had a flat side, too. They made too large a target for enemy conkers. The ideal conker, he explained, was rugged. It should have a weather-beaten look, a pock-marked face. A barnacle more than a stone. Frankie's hand reached out and plucked one up.

—Like this?

Da looked at it. We all looked at it. We waited for his pronouncement.

—Not bad. Not bad. But not as good as this.

He put his hand in his pocket and took out the ugliest-looking chestnut I'd ever seen. It looked like it had a skin disease. He let it roll around the palm of his hand. He took Frankie's and put it beside it.

—Put them two fellas in the ring and that fella will beat the pants off that fella every day of the week.

Frankie, Johnny and Gerard started to sort them out according to Da's criteria. They inspected them one by one. Gold diggers looking for nuggets. Every so often a rush of blood to the head.

—I have it. Conker a hundred.

Da would look across.

—That could be the one, all right.

The excitement was intense. It transmitted from him to

them. He was infectious, a child in an adult's body. He was totally engrossed and at ease. Every day he worked and performed in the adult world. He was respected in it. Secretly he wanted to be with the under 12's. That's where he was most himself. Where he didn't have to pretend to be other than what he was.

The warrior chestnuts were finally chosen. Sixteen made it through. The next stage was toughening them up for battle. Hardening of the armouries. Da got into the fire grate, put his hand up the chimney and felt around for shelf space. Ma came in from the scullery and threatened to put her hat and coat on if he didn't change into his work clothes. It wasn't a serious threat. Da said he'd be careful. As he spoke the words, soot fell and exploded on the collar of his white shirt. It left a beautiful design. By the time he'd hidden the sixteen conkers, Ma was ironing a fresh shirt to get him out to the dogs on time. While Ma ironed, Da lathered his face in shaving foam and issued an edict. No one was to remove the chestnuts from their resting place. They'd been placed in purgatory and only Da could release them from their suffering. It was an edict that found immediate and total acceptance from all his subjects.

*

Ma was the first to notice the problem with Frankie's balance. It was a Friday at tea-time. Da and Frankie were out at the Anglia removing spark plugs and cleaning them for the hundredth time. John Charles Gallagher was in the dining room crying into his dinner. Ma sat down with him and put on her stern voice.

—You must tell me what's wrong, John Charles.

She gave him a hankerchief to wipe the snots from his nose.

—I told them in work I want to become a priest.

—You've no need to tell them any of your business.

The tears streamed down over his freckles making them look like little fish.

—Is it true you can't become a priest if you're an orphan?

—Someone in work said that to you?

He got so upset, Ma got upset. She reached out and put her arms around him. He snuggled into her shoulder.

—There, there.

You could never tell with him whether it was real or not. I felt sorry for him. Soon as I did, he stopped crying. He looked up at me and smiled from ear to ear. He put his thumb in his mouth and his nose in the air like a jester. Ma brought him into the kitchen to have his dinner with us. In doing it, she was breaking one of her golden rules. Then, unbelievably, she took out the maggot maker and put it on the table. The maggot maker was a silver potato masher that only ever saw use on Christmas day. It stayed firmly at the back of the press for the other 364 days of the year. Ma brought it to the table, poured the potatoes from the pot into it and turned them into five million maggots. Da and Frankie came in from the garage covered in grease and oil.

—Come and get your maggots, Frankie.

Frankie couldn't believe his eyes. He didn't wait to wash the oil off his hands either. He lifted up his fork to dive-bomb into the maggots. It never reached the plate. No one was sure what happened. He looked like he'd been pushed off his chair only nobody pushed him. He just collapsed to one side and ended up on the floor. Ma picked him up and put him back on his chair. People fell, slipped, were pushed and dragged off chairs all the time. We were all too busy dropping maggots into our mouths to pay much heed to Frankie.

—Is it your balance, son?

It was the first time I'd heard Ma use the word.

—Is there something the matter with your balance?

—I slipped.

211

—I don't like the look of you, you're very pasty.

I thought it very strange, the reference to his balance. Recently in school the teacher had asked us what happened to the soldier who'd had his ear sliced off by Saint Peter in the Garden of Gethsemane. No one knew. He fell over, the teacher informed us. He fell over because our ears control our balance. There was nothing the matter with Frankie's ears. Over the next few weeks, he had a few more slips. I was convinced he was doing it on purpose. Like a monkey in a zoo who has learned a new trick and just keeps on repeating it for the gallery. That was Frankie. Soon as he was down he bounced straight back up with a grin. Just as well Ma didn't see him. He'd be in big trouble. One night we were rehearsing in the front room and I told him to do it for the band. It wasn't the same. He was pretending. You could tell. When he did it in reality, he just crumpled. Shea got annoyed. At me, not at him. In getting Frankie to perform his falling trick I realized for the first time there really was something the matter with him. I wasn't sure what it was. I thought Shea knew. He wouldn't say. I asked him was it to do with his head. I didn't look at him but I felt the emotion in his reply.

—I think so.

The television reception continued to deteriorate to the point where there was no picture, only sound. We'd had it seven years. Da said it was good for another seven with a bit of luck. Sometimes the picture came back with a gentle tap to the panel at the side. We were listening to *The Fugitive* and waiting for Richard Kimble to be caught as surely he must be caught one day, when Frankie came in from the backyard. Da asked him to give the television a tap. Just as he reached it, he hit the floor. He bounced straight back up and sat at the table.

—My Jesus, are you all right?

Ma came in from the scullery.

—That's it, Da, I'm getting Doctor Wallis.

Ita turned off the television. No one objected. We all helped to clear off the table. Frankie sat impassively as if he'd been waiting for it to happen. Doctor Wallis had his surgery next door in 45 Seville Place. He came straight in behind Ma with his shirt sleeves rolled up and the black bag in his hand. He put it on the table and took out a pencil light. He shone it in Frankie's eye. First the right. Then the left. He was still looking into Frankie's eye when he spoke.

—Have you transport?

Yes, Da replied.

—Get him to the hospital.

The garage doors never opened faster. The wheels were still moving on their track when Da was reversing the Volkswagen out. We pushed the Anglia onto the street when Ma appeared with Frankie wrapped in a blanket. In seconds they were moving away from us towards Temple Street Children's Hospital. Inside the house, there was silence. An awful silence in which we imagined only the worst. Imagined but were afraid to put words to. The silence grew every minute we awaited their return. Would they have medicine to fix Frankie there and then? Or would they have to hold on to him and do tests before they could make him better? Could it be they would have no answers? A mystery illness where they just don't know? I tried not to think of chasing him from the garden. Try as I might, it was uppermost in my mind.

John Charles Gallagher came in brandishing his birth certificate. He now had a piece of paper that told him who he was. He had a mother and father and he had names for them. The certificate also showed he was three years older than he thought. He'd lost three years of his life and there was no getting them back. It was a bitter blow that in other times would have evoked sympathy but it seemed petty compared to Frankie's situation. It wasn't long before he was enveloped in the mood of the house. I was sorry the silence gripped him because his story was the only respite I'd had from seeing Frankie's head bouncing along the road at the back of the horse and cart.

Ma came in first. She put a bag of clothes on the table. I could see Frankie's jumper sitting on top. She went out and put on the kettle. Da hung up his coat when he came in. He didn't sit on his chair, though. He stood at the fireplace and leaned on it. Ma came in from the scullery and sat on Da's chair at the table. The lodgers filed in and joined us in the kitchen. It was a full house.

The news was there was no news. They couldn't say much until they did some tests. They could see something by looking in his eyes. Just as Doctor Wallis had seen something. Was it a case that his eyes were windows with the blinds down that prevented them seeing into his brain? Or did their light penetrate and show them something ugly inside? We had a right to know but they weren't saying. All we could do was pray. Pray it was something curable. All we wanted to do was ask questions and get answers. We didn't want to pray. We wanted action. We wanted Frankie fixed. We had a right, a divine right, to fight and make him better. John Charles Gallagher said it was in God's hands. He brought God into everything. It wasn't in God's hands, it was in our hands. There were too many unanswered questions to be talking about God yet.

Ma and Da didn't go to The Liverpool. We all sat around throwing out the same questions and giving ourselves the same answers. The bricks and cement heard us. Neighbours came in. They were all reassuring. He'll be fine, they told Ma. Possibly just concussion. More than likely it was concussion. Very little doubt but it was concussion. No question it was concussion. Concussion pure and simple. Kept him in for observation. It was a good line of enquiry. Tossed out this way and that. Up and down, out and about, backwards and forwards, in circles and straight lines, always coming back to the inevitable conclusion. Concussion. Everyone had a tale to tell of Frankie banging his head. The time the garage door fell on him and only for Johnny he'd have been killed. The time he came over the handlebars on his way to the bookies' and Bet With Security himself ran on to the street when he heard his skull hit the ground. Or the time of the horse and cart on Seville Place. That was a bad fall. I said a silent prayer. I prayed for concussion. I prayed to the one with compassion. Sitting on his arse right now. The right hand of the Father. I picked up the bag of clothes and held them on my lap. They seemed lonely, sitting on the table. Untouched. Untouchable. I held the bag because I wanted to say sorry. I didn't know if I'd get the chance again.

Tomorrow would be a normal day, Da decided. It was past midnight. It felt like the most abnormal day of my life. We would all go to school. The hospital would carry out tests. In the evening we'd visit Frankie in the ward and see how he was. No, we'd see him in the ward and tell him how great he was. We had to keep his spirits up, no matter what. That meant keeping our own spirits up. We had to pull together as a family, we had to do it for Frankie. Frankie was all that mattered. Frankie. I pictured every letter of his name as liquid gold. Turning solid. I stood up and wished everyone good night. Ma asked me what I was doing with Frankie's clothes.

—I'll mind them until you need them.

I put them in the wardrobe next to my guitar. I got into bed and lay awake. I worried that the clothes were afraid of the dark. I knew it was silly. I also knew I couldn't leave them there. I took them out and put them on the floor beside the bed. I started worrying about the guitar. I hoped it didn't feel left out. Guitars had feelings. Personalities. Anyone who played knew that. I took the guitar out and put it on the armchair. I draped the clothes loosely around it. The neck and the body. I stared at them until my eyes hurt. I don't

215

know if I was awake or asleep when I heard Shea getting up off his knees and into his bed. I turned around and looked at him.

—That's nice, what you did there.

I was glad I'd done it. They looked well together.

—I don't think he'll be needing them again.

There was a tremor in his voice. It was shocking. It put Frankie in a hole in the ground. It was a thought we'd all had but were afraid to say. It was too painful to contemplate.

—It's in God's hands.

I found myself saying it. The words coming off my tongue. It wasn't in God's hands, I knew that. I said it to comfort Shea. It was still in our hands. I didn't know what action we had to take. We would know when the time came. Putting it in God's hands was the only way I knew to stop my brain hurting me from thinking too much. I needed to give my head a rest. Shea needed to rest, too. He needed to sleep. I willed him to sleep. I wondered what he was thinking about. Was he thinking the same thoughts as me? It was a relief not thinking about Frankie. I started thinking about him again. I thought about Shea with his eyes open. I thought about him with his eyes closed. I played open and shut with his eyes until I slept.

Frankie was sitting on another boy's bed doing a jigsaw. His name was Alan. They were large pieces. Alan was six. They knew each other a day. They were best friends. Frankie showed the younger ones how to play with the toys. He was the oldest in the ward. He bossed them around, just like Shea bossed me and I bossed Johnny. He showed Alan the jigsaw. There was a piece missing in the middle. He asked Alan where it was. Alan shook his head. Frankie asked to see his hands. Alan showed him a closed fist. Frankie forced it open and there was the missing piece. He finished the jigsaw and went off to colour in a picture with Vanessa in the pink pyjamas who was eight.

216

Frankie didn't look sick. He was too busy to be sick. As the senior patient in the ward, he had taken on the role as chief organizer with gusto. It was brilliant thinking on the part of the staff. By not having the time to be sick he was already on the way to recovery. We were sitting around Frankie's empty bed and smiling to ourselves. We watched him, mesmerized, as he powered his way from one bed to the next. Things had changed so much in a day. What medicine had they given him? I picked up his chart from a hook at the end of the bed. There were badly written numbers. I figured they were his temperature. There were more numbers. Blood pressure. They were illegible. At the bottom was a scrawl. Three words. 'For' was the middle one. The first one looked like 'prepare'. I wasn't sure. The last started with an S. Prepare for S. I couldn't ask Frankie because he didn't have time to talk. It was an opportunity I was delighted not to have.

Outside in the corridor we waited for Ma and Da. They were in an office talking to the Ward Sister. Further along was another ward. No sound came from it. It seemed shrouded in a brown light. I walked as far as the door. There was only one bed. A child lay motionless, just the slightest hint of movement from the breathing. This was the ward for really sick children. No doubt about that.

That first day in the hospital there was great hope. The next day the hope renewed. If Frankie was sick, he wasn't showing it. And when you were really sick, you showed it. You couldn't help it. Ma and Da looked worse than Frankie. They hadn't slept for days. They were going to the hospital alone. They were seeing the specialist for the results of the X-rays. They were quietly confident. Da especially. Concussion. The slips might have been a temporary aberration. A mental spasm. A glitch that had worked itself out of his system. It happened all the time, according to Da. A man who worked beside him in the booking office knew a farmer in Roscommon who had a child who suddenly started falling. On examination they discovered what was wrong with the child. He needed glasses. We laughed when Da told us the story. Laughed more than we should. I noticed Ma didn't laugh at all. Ma always prepared for the worst. This time she was wrong. Every positive thought could help the situation. Negative thoughts were a liability.

Da gave me the admission price for the match in Tolka Park. He gave me enough to sit in the stand. Me and Johnny. Stand seats and Bovril at half-time. I felt funny about going. I knew it was no children at the hospital but I'd've preferred to sit it out at home. Da insisted on no one sitting around moping. Everything was going to be fine. He wanted us out enjoying ourselves. Everything as normal. Everything as Frankie would want it.

Drumcondra were playing Dundalk. It was ironic. Da's team against Ma's team. Semi-final of the Leinster Senior Cup. 'Drums' versus 'the town'. I didn't care who won. I loved soccer. But right now I couldn't see the point of twenty-two men chasing a ball around a field trying to put it into a net. If they thought about it seriously they'd all get dressed and go home to their families. The only thing of any consequence was the Dundalk number 9. Jimmy Hasty. He had only one arm. Despite his one arm, he had great balance. He looked sharp. The home supporters were very sympathetic. Every time he touched the ball they applauded. In the space of three minutes before half-time he scored twice for Dundalk. The Drums supporters didn't like being two goals down to a centre forward with one arm. The sympathy turned to hostility.

—Tackle the bastard, he only has one arm.

Drums were awarded a corner kick. The ball came across the goal mouth and struck Hasty on the stump of his arm.

—Hand ball.

The cry went around the ground.

—Hand ball, ref.

Unbelievably, the referee pointed to the penalty spot. The Dundalk team surrounded him. They wanted to lynch him. It was the first time in the history of Irish soccer that a penalty had been awarded for hand ball against a player with only a stump. The Dundalk players were joined on the field by their mentors. Trainer, kit man, substitutes, all poured on. They were remonstrating with the referee. Finally, a man in a suit, the Dundalk manager, made his way onto the field and spoke to the referee. The manager stood with his head bowed and listened attentively. God, in his black suit, was laying down the law. In Temple Street Children's Hospital, the God with the X-rays held up Frankie's fate to the light. The crowd in Tolka Park had no idea what was happening less than a mile up the road. Their laughter seemed so out of place. Why was I sitting here a part of it? I'd been sent here with Johnny to maintain the appearance of normality. There was nothing normal about this. It was a circus. I'd been sent to watch the clowns while Ma and Da had an audience with God. I'd been sent here as a ploy, a distraction, to be out of the way when the news broke. I knew in that moment the news would be bad. I looked at Johnny and wondered did he know. I knew we wouldn't be sitting in the stand at Tolka Park if the news was good. I stood up and tapped Johnny on the shoulder. He followed me without protest, as if he knew. As we emerged from the stand onto Richmond Road, the howls told us that Drums had missed the spot kick. I didn't give a damn.

The news wasn't good. I knew by Da's hair. It had turned white. Nobody was saying anything but everyone noticed. It had turned from grey to white. The news wasn't good. The phrase passed around like a well-worn cliché. As constant as Ma's sandwiches. Ma, as ever, looking after people. Poured herself into it. As if life depended on everyone having a

219

sandwich. The news wasn't good. Not even Ma could hide it. The news wasn't good.

The news was disastrous. Frankie had a lump the size of a golf ball growing out of his brain. The professionals called it a tumour. It was a lump. An old-fashioned lump. Growing inside his head. There was no opinion, scientific or otherwise, that it would do anything but continue to grow. The news wasn't good. The news was disastrous. The lump had been there for some time. Lying there, quietly growing away by itself. Lying there for months, years maybe. Lying there before the accident with the horse and cart. Lying there and feeding itself into a life. The news was disastrous but I was glad the lump had been there a while. I hated myself for having the thought. I hated myself but couldn't stop feeling glad. Condemned and then reprieved. I'd stood on the gallows and walked away. Not so Da. There was no walking away for him. I felt sorry for him for the first time in a long time. It was now up to Da. The X-rays had spoken and now he had to decide what to do. He'd been a gambler all his life. No one understood odds better than he did. He ate, slept and drank odds. He'd never gambled before on anything like this. The life or death of his son. Our brother, Frankie. It was science versus religion. Heads or tails. Who would want to call it with the coin in the air? No one. Yet someone had to. In the end it would be Da. It was an unbearable burden for anyone to carry. Already it had turned his hair white. He knew what the choice was. It was the scissors versus the relic. Cut in and cut away. Or leave closed and rub with a relic. Ma would help him make it. They would make it together. A joint decision. But Da would call it at the end of the day. Da would call it because Da was Da.

Da plumped for science. He brought us all together and told us. We were delighted with the decision. We were living in the science age. An age of miracles. Medicine was at the forefront. Pushing back the boundaries. In South Africa, a man had been given another man's heart. He was eating, breathing and living. The gap between science and miracles was shrinking. It was Frankie's best chance. We couldn't deny him his best chance. The surgeons were going in.

—This just means we have to pray harder.

Ma was right. God could help, too. We weren't letting God off the hook. We needed his help. We would take help from wherever it came. We knelt down for the rosary. Ma offered it up for Frankie's intentions. As we worked our way through the mantra of Hail Marys, I imagined the surgeon cutting through into Frankie's brain. God's gentle hand guiding it where to go. A brain odyssey. A sea of blood. Stainless steel scissors floating through a cauliflower reef. Diving ever deeper into the black-red sea. A surprising light. No, not there, here. Snip, snip. Two cuts. Perfect incision. A floating floret. First sighting of the space ship parasite. Disguised as a gold ball. Malignant bastard. Attached itself to the mother ship with a web line. Anchored there for months. The web line now a tree trunk. Has taken over some functions of the mother ship. No point in a lateral attack. Won't diminish parasite capability. Only option to attack at the core. Cut through trunk and remove. Red alert. Watch out for cranial arteries. Parasite disguises them as her own web lines. Full-scale attack on parasite imminent. Stand by all stations. Oxygen. Blood. Emergency response unit. Light. Two. Prepare for immediate assault. One. Let's take her out of here. Hail Mary and God on your fat arse we need you. Cut, cut, snip, snip, cut. Strong parasite resistance. Revert to lateral attack also. Attack outer shell and remove all debris. The fruit of thy womb, pump more blood. Parasite has dual functions. Parasite is a chameleon also. Never seen this before. Ensure web lines attach to the alien. This is the mother and father of all parasites. Blessed art thou I'm losing contact with the holy Mary. I can't see mother of God, I'm lost, give me some light. Now and at the hour, cut, cut, cut,

cut, cut. I don't know what I'm cutting, pray for me, pray I'm cutting the right lines lost in outer space, now and at the hour of our here comes the parasite, just one more snip, I have it in my hand, stitch up the mother, now and at the hour of our death, amen.

Frankie looked pathetic with tracks running across his shaven head. He was in the room for really sick children. We sat and stood around the bed in a semicircle. We were all being nice to each other. Johnny offered me his chair because I'd been standing for a while. I declined. Da said I'd been standing for ages and should sit down. Johnny got up and I took his chair. When I sat down he squeezed me on the shoulder. It was the first time I'd ever felt such tenderness from him. I reached up and put my hand on his. It was strangely powerful.

Ita suggested a decade of the rosary. It seemed superfluous. God had done his work. Or not done his work. We were waiting for Frankie to open his eyes and talk to us. We were waiting for his testament. In the meantime, all words seemed redundant. No one spoke. No one needed to speak. Yet somehow we all ended up on our knees. Ita offered it up for the doctors and nurses. We were in the middle of it when the door opened and Alan, Frankie's pal, walked into the room. He had a jigsaw in his hand.

—When's Frankie coming back to play with me?

We tried to carry on. He wasn't going to be denied.

—What's wrong with Frankie?

Ita couldn't hold it. She broke into a laugh that was close to tears. Once she went, we all caved in. It wasn't unusual for the rosary to induce laughter. A fart or a belch often did the same thing at home. Here, in the hospital, it was total abandonment. The first time I'd ever seen it happen.

The following day Frankie opened his eyes and spoke to us. He didn't move much because his head hurt. His head looked like the garage after Da had dug it up. Yet, he knew who we all were. I tried to imagine how he felt. They had drilled into his skull. How painful it must be. Faces coming into his vision. Did it hurt telling one from the other? Did it hurt to move the lips and speak the names? His memory was intact. Did it hurt to call on it?

That night all pretence at normality was dispensed with. Forty-four turned into a house of tears. Operation parasite had been a failure. Despite his best efforts, the surgeon didn't get what he went in to take. In the end, he could do no more than stitch him up again. Science had let us down. It was a miracle now or nothing. It was all up to God. Da wasn't crying, he was howling. Every time Uncle Paddy tried to get the whiskey into him he threw back his head and let out another howl. As soon as that died away, a round of crying started somewhere else. Ma was grief-stricken. She'd cried herself out. Supported by Auntie Anne on one side and Mrs Hogan on the other, every breath was a sigh. In between every sigh, Mother of God. Mother of God. Holy Mother of God pray for us. In another corner Auntie Becky led a group of women in a continuous recital of the rosary. A genuine relic of Matt Talbot was promised. A piece of the holy man's coffin to rub on Frankie's poor head. It was known to have worked miracles. A woman in Dolphin's Barn. Cancer. Out in the scullery Auntie Lily and Auntie Sally made another plate of sandwiches that no one wanted.

Uncle John, Da's youngest brother, kept shaking my hand. Poor Frankie. Your poor brother. He shook my hand a hundred times. The only time he let it go was when he broke into tears and reached for his hanky to wipe them away. Uncle John had procured me a bottle of stout. It was the first time I drank one openly in front of my parents. Not that they noticed. They didn't. No one cared. It was a house full of people but it was the loneliest place on earth. I reached out and picked up a glass with whiskey in it. I took a gulp. It felt like getting a dig in the chest. I chased it down with a slug of stout. After a few minutes I felt a warm glow descend through my body. It was the first time the grief seemed bearable. I drank more whiskey to dispel the darkness further. It worked beautifully. I thanked God for whiskey. The water of life. There was one small problem. The room started to spin and wouldn't stop. Or maybe it was my head spinning. I wasn't sure. I tried to wrench my hand from Uncle John's grip. He wouldn't let go. Poor Frankie. Poor me. Could he not see it was poor me? I freed myself and made for the door holding on to the wall. I crawled up the stairs and into bed with my clothes on where I spun into a whirlpool that had me holding on for dear life.

Frankie was still conscious the next day. He looked better than I felt. As sick as a dog. My mouth was dry and I couldn't eat or drink. I vowed I would never drink whiskey again. At eleven o'clock Mrs Scally arrived with the piece of Matt Talbot's coffin. She and Ma stroked his head with it and said the prayer for his beatification. Later on, I picked up the relic and kissed it. It didn't do any good. I joined Shea in the corridor and we looked out of the window at the traffic streaming by. It was cruel the way life went on. People going to work. Hawkers shouting their wares. Kids climbing the railings of George's Church. The square was called George's Pocket. My favourite place name in Dublin. It didn't matter today. Twenty feet from us the life was draining out of Frankie. Minute by minute, his system was shutting down. Soon it would be second by second. We were taking it in turns to go in and see him. We were saying our goodbyes without admitting as much.

Johnny came out and I went in. I knew I couldn't get emotional. How could I? He was my kid brother. I had to put up a front. Didn't want him to know he was dying. I'd avoid saying 'goodbye'. That was most important. I'd keep it light.

—You look like you were in a fight.

He smiled. I couldn't believe he still had the energy to smile. His lips parted but I couldn't hear. I leaned in close. His lips touched my ear.

—You're Elvis Presley . . . I'm not Elvis Presley . . .

I collapsed in a heap on the bed, crying and crying and crying until I didn't know where the tears were coming from any more. I didn't want him to die. I didn't want to lose him. I realized I'd been playing games in my head because I didn't want to face this moment and hadn't allowed for his dying. I wanted him to stay. I didn't want him to go to Heaven. I didn't care how nice it was – I wanted him to stay and grow alongside me and do all the same things I did. I didn't want him going home to the moon. His home was 44. That's where he belonged. That's where I wanted him to be. The lovely little twirp. I didn't want him to leave me.

He died the following day in the early afternoon. He died in the room for really sick children. We were all there. Ma, Da, Shea, Ita, Johnny, Gerard, Paul and me. We were all there with Frankie when his lights went out. It was peaceful. Very peaceful. We took him in his little brown coffin to Laurence O'Toole's church. Outside the school in Seville Place, the boys from his class formed a guard of honour. All dressed in the green and white of O'Toole's. From the school we carried the coffin to the church. We paused for a minute opposite the hall door of 44.

The church was filled to overflowing. I thought about all the times I'd prayed for the souls in Purgatory. All Souls' Day. Were they looking down from Heaven at me now? I didn't blame them for anything. I blamed God for being the fat lazy bastard he was. We'd said a million rosaries and he still hadn't lifted a finger. Just sat on his arse and did nothing. He'd broken Ma's heart and turned Da's hair white. He'd turned his back on us and shut us out. I wouldn't forget because I'd never forget Frankie. I made a vow, kneeling there.

—I'll never forget you, Frankie. I'll remember you every day of my life.

Those who remembered were with us in the church. They filed up to shake our hands. School friends, neighbours, teachers, cousins, uncles, aunts, doctors, nurses, dockers, milk men, coal men, train drivers, ticket sellers, inspectors, bus conductors, shop keepers, bookies, gamblers, lodgers past and present, bank officials, politicians, old IRA men, *Cumann na mBan* women, nuns, brothers and assorted parishioners. Andy, Catherine and Teresa came up. Catherine gave me a hug and a Mass card. It was the only nice moment of the day. That night I drank more whiskey and felt its awesome power. The following morning we went to Glasnevin Cemetery and put Frankie to rest with Grandad Sheridan.

James. Dublin Brigade old IRA. Died aged 72 years. Underneath it would go *Francis. Died aged 10 years. Rest in peace.* As the coffin went down and the prayers rang out I repeated my vow.

—I will remember you every day of my life, Frankie.

10

It wasn't necessary to remember Frankie every day, it was impossible to forget him. He was there in every way. The armchair by the fire. The old green fort I'd raced up town to get him that Christmas Eve. His school bag that had been put on the shelf above the kitchen door. An old pair of wellingtons he wore when helping Da in the garage. They had once been mine. They now sat in an alcove by the back door and no one moved them.

Despite his presence, his name was seldom mentioned. Everyone had their own memory and carried it privately within. 'I will say their names to my own heart in the long nights.' Padhraig Pearse had written those words and put them into his mother's mouth. In 44 it was too painful to hear his name out loud. It was easier to grieve within. He looked down at us from his photograph above the fireplace and we looked back at him in silent acknowledgement. It was easier that way. I looked at his photograph a million times once. That was my way. That was how I kept my promise.

Gerard took to sitting across the back door sucking his thumb. He'd be there when I got home from school. The keeper at the gate. He'd stick his legs in the air to stop me getting in. I'd give him a sweet as a bribe. One day I asked him why he sat there every day. He kicked his shoes off and wouldn't talk to me. I bent down to him and he flailed me with his fists. I produced a penny and showed it to him. He tried to take it but I closed my fist. I told him I'd give it to him if he told me why he sat there every day.

—I'm waiting for Frankie.

I explained that he was in Heaven but Gerard still wanted to know when he was coming home. I was delighted he couldn't grasp eternity. I was delighted he spoke like Frankie was still alive and living with us. Most of all I was delighted he said his name. Frankie. It was good to hear the sound that had once been so familiar. A sound that struck such a sad note now with Ma and Da. We had all learned not to say it when they were around. Paul was too young to even know but Gerard blurted it out in his innocence now and then.

—Where's Frankie?

In those moments, you could see and feel the unbearable pain on Ma's and Da's faces. It was wrong to inflict it on them and we did our best not to. No one reprimanded Gerard. In the end he stopped saying it but still kept watch at the back gate sucking his thumb, waiting for someone who was never going to show.

Da took to the bed convinced he had a brain tumour. The pounding in his head was so bad we started to live with the curtains drawn, day and night. Doctor Wallis put Da on the strongest pain killers he had but they did nothing to relieve the pressure inside his head. The only thing that brought him relief was to lie on the bed, curtains drawn, with a cold face cloth on his forehead. At these times the rest of us tip-toed around the house in almost perfect silence. Da was sure it was hereditary. A genetic flaw. He'd given it to Frankie and now he was next for the surgeon's knife.

—It's in your head, Da.

Ma was at the end of her tether. She didn't care about the double meaning.

—All in your head, Da.

Ma soldiered on. She couldn't buckle. If Ma collapsed we all went under. I don't know what she drew on to keep going. We all muscled in to help her out. I took to making the beds. Top to bottom of the house. Johnny did the hoovering. Ita cooked at the weekend and Shea did nothing because he was working in the bank since he finished school. It was Ma who kept the show on the road and made sense of it all. The booking office in Amiens Street could operate without Da. So, too, the greyhound track and the mystery train, but 44 without Ma, it just wasn't possible. There were too many little things, small details that Ma carried uniquely in her head. How would we remember to soak the corned beef overnight in water if Ma didn't tell us? Not to mention the marrowfat peas and the jelly for the sherry trifle. How would we know how much to pay off the shop bill and what to give the butcher against the Christmas turkey? Not to mention the coal man, the milk man, the pools man, the insurance man, the slop man, the planned giving campaign for the church restoration, the Easter dues, the window cleaner and the Fianna Fáil national collection? Ma carried that information and dispensed it without having to think. Inside, in the silence that we'd all developed, she grieved for Frankie in her own way. Once or twice I walked into the scullery and she was standing over the cooker crying into the potatoes. Another day she sobbed her way along the North Strand after she saw the Dundalk bus pass her by.

One day she walked into the bedroom as I was straightening out the sheet on Gerard's bed. It had been Frankie's up until his death. I continued what I was doing but became self-conscious that she was standing there watching me. I fluffed the pillows and wiped my hand across the bedspread to finish it off. When I turned around to her, she half smiled at me.

—You were his favourite, you know that.

The truth was, I didn't. Ita and he were close. And of the boys, he looked up to Shea the most. I was surprised and delighted by what Ma said. It felt like a ray of sunshine through a dark cloud. To see her smile, or half smile, that was the best part. After she left the room, I lay down on the bed and felt like I was suspended in mid-air. It quickly became a habit. Some days just a few seconds. Other times a few minutes. I could hear the shouts from the street or listen to the sounds of the house. I could tune in to whatever I liked. Horses and carts, men digging the road, cattle bound for the boats, the sound of the hoover. Hall, stairs and landing. Johnny pushing the hose and sucking up dirt. My work finished, I tuned into the world and I tuned into Frankie who wasn't of this world any more. It was perfectly sad by being not too sad. One Friday afternoon, directly outside the bedroom door, I heard the hoover come spluttering to a stop. I heard Ma's voice and Ma's steps. She stopped on the landing outside.

—You were his favourite, you know that.

Her tone was exactly as she'd said it to me. I was shocked. I'd never taken Ma for a liar. I could picture her, half smiling into Johnny's face and lying. It couldn't be both of us. It was one of us. Or none of us. More likely none of us. More likely it was Ita. Or Shea. We'd both been lied to. I was happy for Johnny. He'd feel great. I didn't know how I felt towards Ma any more. I was glad any time she mentioned his name, or inferred it. It broke the silence. It let in air. And whatever her motives, it made us feel good.

*

Da had hardly missed a day at work in twenty years. Now there was hardly a day he went in. He spent the morning sleeping off his headache and got up for his breakfast about the time we came in for our dinner from school. He took his tablets – two for his head and two for his blood pressure – and washed them down with porridge drowned in milk. Before Frankie died he always ate his porridge with his face stuck in the racing page. All that was gone. He slurped at his porridge without pattern or conviction and the racing page was the one part of the newspaper he never opened under any circumstances. It was a too painful reminder, I suppose, of the only gamble that ever mattered and how it came unstuck. It also consigned the racing Book of Kells to a dusty drawer and robbed Mahony of his role in life. He went around to Busaras where Da knew the head man, Lenihan, and landed himself a cushy number as a porter. He didn't actually carry anything. He took in bags for storage and handed out tickets. When he wasn't doing that he sat on his arse all day and did nothing, as he said himself.

In the afternoons, Da tackled jobs he'd been putting off for years. Like whitewashing the walls of his toilet. Entirely non-essential but entirely reflective of his state of mind. I made up buckets of whitewash when we did the back of the house every spring. Frankie, too, had learned the art. Now he was back to doing it himself. Sitting at the table, he asked me how many shovels of lime it was to a bucket. He'd forgotten his own formula. There was a river of porridge running down his double chin towards his neck. He was unshaven and still wearing his pyjama top. He looked like he was straight out of a men's shelter.

—Is it two and a half shovels?

—It's five to a full bucket.

—Of course, of course.

It wasn't like he'd forgotten. It was like he was working at half power. Like half of him had gone away somewhere. I thought about offering to make up the mixture for him. I didn't want to make him feel any more inadequate than he looked. It was no big deal to make a bucket of whitewash. He'd do it with his eyes closed and his hands tied behind his back. It would have been Frankie's job if he were alive. I kept my mouth firmly shut and the thought to myself. The river of porridge had hardened into a thick white vein that made him look like a mental patient. It was the first time I thought about him dying. Da would one day die. He'd go in

231

on top of Frankie. I hoped it wouldn't be soon. We couldn't deal with another death in our family right now.

*

Andy asked me out to the pictures. We were still in official mourning. There were no set rules as to how long a family spent mourning, but we were still in it. It was like living in a capsule. There was no radio or television. No music and no singing. The house was insulated against the march of time. Da's headaches and the gloom of the ever drawn curtains made our official mourning feel like it would never end. Andy wanted to see *Helga*. As soon as he said it I felt helpless to do anything but accept. I knew all the reasons not to go and I knew I would go. I sneaked upstairs with the scissors and cut the threads that held the black rectangle on the sleeve of my jacket. I stuffed the piece of material in my pocket and knelt down and said a prayer asking God's forgiveness in advance. I met Ma on the stairs going down and she wanted to know where I was off to in such a hurry. I told her I was going to a Legion of Mary meeting. I slipped out the front door feeling like a weasel and blushing from the lie. I met Andy at the corner and we walked up town slowly in case I met anyone I knew and gave the game away.

There was a queue two hundred yards long outside the Irish Film Centre at O'Connell Bridge. I wasn't surprised. *Helga* was the first film in Ireland to show close ups of a woman's fanny, a woman's tits and a woman's arse. There had been letters to the papers and now there were protesters with placards proclaiming the sanctity of a woman's body. As luck would have it, I recognized one of the protesters. He was Speedy Gonzales, the drummer from the Blue Tones of Mary who'd beaten me in the talent competition. My head automatically withdrew into my jacket like a snail when I saw him. Speedy Gonzales and his friends launched into the hymn 'Hail Queen of Heaven'. Out of habit, I joined in on the chorus until a dig in the ribs from Andy brought my singing to a premature end.

It was a small cinema and we were lucky to get in. The front seats naturally were first to go so we ended up in the second last row. At the very back, standing just a few inches out from a wall dripping with sweat, were several St John's Ambulance men. It was the first time in my life I'd seen them on standby in a cinema. They had a look of expectancy as palpable as our own. So too had Helga and Max when we met them in the film and the doctor explained they were going to have a baby. Max squeezed Helga's hand and their faces beamed out at us with Swedish smiles. Helga was not an actress. The doctor explained to us that this was the real thing, a real baby and we would witness a real birth, if we were brave enough and kept our eyes open. Lots of detailed examinations followed with Helga's legs strapped in stirrups that made her look vulnerable and uncomfortable. Minute by minute, Helga's stomach got bigger and bigger until she could hardly walk without assistance. The smiles of earlier were gone and Max looked mightily worried at the size of his wife.

Helga was a line in the sand. Life before Helga was bathed in ignorance. Now life was awash with new concepts and new ideas, with life cycles and terms, with pre-natal and ante-natal, with uterus, cervix and placenta, words that sounded like planets from the outer reaches of the solar system, words that bombarded the brain but words that meant nothing compared to the life experience of Helga projected before us. When the head appeared at the mouth of Helga's vagina, the effect was more profound than the changing of bread and wine into the body and blood of Our Lord; it was the most profound educational moment of my entire life, and of everyone who sat in that cinema, for when the head appeared and tried to barge its way into the world, it was clear the vaginal opening was not big enough for the job. The doctor

233

asked for scissors and as he started to cut into Helga's genital flesh, six men collapsed onto the floor. The St John's Ambulance men sprung into action and administered first aid to the fallen. Helga panted, pushed and sweated her baby into the world in full view of a cinema that had turned into a field hospital. When the film was over and the lights came up, groups of people gathered around the injured and gawked. Curiously, Andy tugged at my sleeve to get out of there. He opened his fist and displayed a half a crown he'd found on the floor. It had rolled out of the pocket of one of Helga's victims.

We walked home from the pictures in thoughtful mood. The pictures had always been our favourite entertainment. Andy never liked sport so we never went to football or boxing together. It was always pictures. Pictures, pictures, pictures. From the time we were eight and I split my pocket money with him to go to the Saturday matinée, it was always pictures.

Stagecoach, Rio Bravo, The Alamo. On the way home we'd hide in every doorway shooting arrows and firing guns and fighting over who was a cowboy and who was an Indian and wrestling on the ground because we could never agree. Now we passed those doorways in darkness, having been to an adult film for which we were under age. We could get served in public houses, too, which is where we headed armed with Andy's half a crown.

The taste of the hops in Guinness when it hit the back of the throat was a sweet discovery. It tasted like liquid nectar – the food of the gods. Watching a pint settle and waiting for the darkness to conquer the cream was a delicious anticipation not felt since the days of the lucky lump from Mattie's shop. Unlike a lucky lump, however, the power of Guinness to transport to other realms was immediate and sublime. We touched glasses, took a giant swallow together, wiped away our creamy moustaches in tongue-like harmony, and waited for the black stuff to work its magic.

—What did you think of Max?

I could only think that Max felt as we all felt in the cinema – guilt at what he'd put Helga through. Guilt that a woman had to endure such pain to bring forth life. Guilt that all we could do was sit back and watch silently. Before I had time to answer, Andy added to the question.

—That's going to be me in a few months, what do you think?

He fancied himself. The Ringo Starr of Sheriff Street, rhythm machine of Michael Maltese, destined for stardom.

—You're very slow, I'm going to be a father.

I knew it was true. It explained Andy's mood. It explained *Helga*, the world, conception, everything. I was still a virgin and Andy was going to be a father. It was cruel as only the truth could be.

When I got home that night the television was on signalling the end of our official mourning. The reception was pure snow. The sound was turned down and the radio was on providing the music that filled the room. Da was sitting at the table with his decorator's scissors and an old telephone book. He was cutting neat squares for use in his toilet. Ma was sorting through some old clothes and separating them into hand-me-downs, of which Paul and Gerard would be the beneficaries, and hand-me-ons for which the rag man would be grateful. I could tell the atmosphere was frosty between them because Ma had that long face she wore when she was annoyed with him. They were sitting in silence so I decided to break the ice.

—Why is the television on?

—It's on for no good reason.

—It only requires a valve and it will be perfect again.

—It's a waste of electricity having it on.

—I don't want you to start rowing over it.

Some nights I wouldn't care, but I felt loving towards them, I really did. I hoped they noticed.

—Have you been drinking?

—Me? I don't drink.

—You're slurring your words.

Ma didn't look up from the table but her tone was acerbic. To lie or not to lie. We had started *Hamlet* in school. Discretion is the better part of valour. Hamlet was right. I bade them both adieu. They weren't impressed.

The following day, Da had a serious-looking valve on the table with a history of the television attached. It began with his customary salutation. 'Please supply the bearer with one only valve.' The note was intended for me but I ignored it. I was done with delivering strange missives from the king. Seeing that he had abdicated temporarily from his day job, I figured he could get it himself. When I came home from school at lunch-time, the note was still there with the valve on top. When Ma put my plate on the table she pointed it out to me like I had some responsibility towards it.

—Let him get up out of bed and get it himself.

—Your father's not in bed, he's out in the garage.

I went out to confront him. He had the Anglia jacked up and the front wheel was on the ground with him kneeling at it. He had a crow bar jammed inside the rim, between the steel and the rubber, and he was pulling at it with all his might. I asked him what he was doing.

—I'm repairing a puncture.

There were dozens of places that repaired punctures within walking distance of our house. Places that had the equipment for the job. He looked like a Stone Age man trying to find a spark while all around him the forest was on fire.

—You could send it to the garage. I'll bring it down for you.

—I'll manage.

—You'll break your back without the proper tools.

—And what are proper tools, tell me? What did the Greeks have? And the Romans? They didn't build the Acropolis or the Coliseum by sending down to the garage.

For a brief second they sounded like fighting words, someone coming out of the corner and standing centre ring with fists up, only with Da there was no one to fight, no opponent, only himself. He would spend the rest of the day inside his head where he would invent the wheel, the crow bar and rubber; where he would build ancient cities in Greece and Rome; where he would end up inventing the car jack, the wheel brace and the automobile itself. I hadn't the heart to say anything negative about the valve. I told him I'd go up the town after school and see if Clifford had it.

Clifford's was a small electrical repair shop in a lane off Talbot Street. Clifford always wore a long brown coat with several screwdrivers and phase testers sticking out of the lapel pocket. He always seemed to be repairing the same broken radio when you entered the shop and he always commenced a lecture on the magic of radio and the transistor pick up when he saw me coming in. Clifford knew the name, rank and serial number of the valve, the factory where it came from in Birmingham and the engineer who designed it. He told me I wouldn't get one in the city of Dublin. It was easier to replace the television. Indeed, the television without the valve was nothing more than a shell. The news would be received back on the Acropolis with dismay and disbelief.

There was great excitement back in 44. John Charles Gallagher was pouring champagne into cups, glasses, saucers or anything he could find. He'd been to see his mother, having tracked her down from his birth certificate. She lived in a rough part of the south side but already she wanted

John Charles to move in with her. Mahony proposed a toast to mother and son.

—To mother and son.

Da didn't join the celebrations. He stayed out in the garage re-inventing the wheel. He had the tube in a basin of water checking for the puncture. It had taken him five hours to separate the tyre from the rim. I watched as the bubbles came to the surface. It brought a faint smile to his face. He took out the tube, dried it off with a towel and marked the spot with white chalk. I broke the news about the valve when he looked to have the puncture under control.

—There has to be a spare valve somewhere in the city.

The holy grail. Saint Patrick's shillelagh. The lost chord. The Garden of Eden. Noah's Ark. The television valve. All part of the same quest. Treasure hunts for the mentally deranged. Maps and instructions from 44 Seville Place. Apply in person to the keeper of the garage.

—Fuck Clifford. Soon as I have this wheel back on we'll take a dander round the city.

The waves of nausea that flowed through my body threatened to drown me. I was a member of a rock'n'roll band. I drank pints of stout and had acquired a taste for whiskey. My friends were making girls pregnant. I couldn't spend any more of my youth combing the city for television valves. I couldn't do it. I'd made my contribution to the development of television. I'd turned the aerial towards England and brought pictures into our home. The sixties were slipping away and it was my turn to take something from the decade. It was my turn to be selfish. I'd given all I could.

There was relief that the mourning for Frankie was over. Ma let us turn on Radio Luxembourg for the hit parade and all the talk was about the television we might get now that the replacement valve could not be found. Allied to that was the excitement of John Charles Gallagher finding his mother. It would have been a perfect supper only Da was still in the garage repairing the punctured wheel. His cup was still in its place but Ma had given up calling him and poured the tea without him. It was getting on for midnight by the kitchen clock. I went out in a last attempt to get him to come in. He had the wheel back on the car and was pushing up and down on a foot pump slamming air into the tyre. I volunteered to take over but he wouldn't hear of it. I couldn't deny him his moment. The tyre looked full and strong and his rhythm slowed as it became harder and harder to force the air in. He gave it one last, slow, satisfied push. He disconnected the air line from the valve. As soon as he did, the hissing sound of leaking air could be heard. He turned away from it in disbelief. It was a venomous sound. I could see the wheel starting to deflate under the weight of the car. Da fell backwards onto the seat of his arse. He put his head in his hands and started to cry. The wheel he'd nursed back to health was turning on him.

—Help me, son.

—It's all right, Da, I'll get it fixed.

—Tell me where I went wrong, just tell me.

—Everything is going to be all right, I promise.

I put my two arms around him and pulled him into my chest. There was no resistance. I could feel him sobbing. I felt strangely comfortable with his big frame against me. I looked at his white hair and his emerging bald spot. He looked vulnerable, like a baby, and I felt like a father holding him, caressing him, absorbing his tears, his failures, absolving his sins, mending his broken pride, giving him back his spirit. It was something I'd never felt before, this feeling of continuity between us. It connected me to him and through him to his father, my grandfather, and all the grandfathers I never knew but who in that moment were part of me like never before in my life. As the car sat down and flattened the tyre and Da cried his eyes out, I felt invigorated and connected to the past in a whole new way.

The following morning I carried the wheel to Stafford's garage at the Five Lamps and left it in for repair. I collected it on my way home from school at lunch-time and brought it into our garage. Da was plunging the toilet. The plunger was homemade and consisted of a broken chair leg onto the end of which he'd nailed a piece of rubber cut from an old car tyre. He pulled the chain, replaced the handle as per his written instructions and went at the pan with his plunger. I put the wheel in position and hand-tightened the four nuts. Then I lowered the car with the jack and took up the wheel brace to finish home the nuts. Da came out of the toilet.

—Don't overtighten them!

—I know how to change a wheel.

There was a tone in my voice that I instantly regretted. It reminded me of him at the races when he lost. I was annoyed with myself. I didn't want to lose the closeness we'd achieved the previous day. It was a fragile state of grace, in jeopardy from the least thing.

—I had a very good teacher for this.

—For what?

I smiled and indicated the wheel. He smiled back in recognition of the compliment I'd paid him.

The following Saturday we set off in search of the lost valve. He wouldn't allow me to turn on the heater in the Anglia. He had a piece of tape over the switch. He insisted on driving with his window open to keep the front windscreen clear. It was arctic inside the car. Our maximum speed was twenty-five miles an hour because it was the perfect speed for minimum fuel consumption. He claimed it was deductible from Einstein's theory of relativity. Who was I to argue? A moderate speed meant we could keep our eyes peeled both sides for discarded television sets although I had never seen one in any of my travels anywhere in the city. He was living in fantasy land. I turned on the radio for amusement but he shut it down immediately claiming it ran the guts out of the battery. I asked him about the 'system', the dynamo and the fan belt by which the battery constantly recharged itself.

—What happens if your fan belt is loose? Or the brushes in your dynamo are worn? Your radio will destroy you then. Destroy you.

You couldn't remain neutral with Da for long. He had that ability to provoke a reaction when you swore on your life not to get involved. In one way, the search for the valve was him getting well. At least he wasn't lying in bed with blinding headaches or sitting in the garage crying at his punctured wheel. I was glad of that but I still wanted to kill him.

He drove straight out to the dump in Finglas. It was a ghastly place dominated by a terrible stench. Da came prepared. He gave me a handkerchief and we put them on and looked like cowboys about to hold up the stagecoach.

It was a wasteland. The debris of other people's lives lay all around. Mattresses, brown-stained with great patches of urine; grey tufts of pubic stuffing peeping out through slits everywhere; and over all this and dominant the repulsive odour of spent lives. We stood back to back before we headed off in opposite directions in search of discarded television sets. We were giving ourselves an hour before rendezvous. I was completely dispirited after fifteen minutes. Battered old radios by the dozen but not a television in sight. Lots of twin tub washing machines, too, which didn't surprise me. A rat ran across my path which made me dance on the spot where I was standing. It was ludicrous, knowing as I did that the place was infested with them. Then I saw a television set, not unlike the one at home. When I got to it I saw that it was divested of its insides. Still, I carried it back to the car and waited for Da.

He arrived back with spare parts for every machine in the house, bar the television. A new hose for the twin tub (Ma would be disappointed); a spare wheel for the junior bike (it was Gerard's now); a blade for his fret saw (Shaw could go shit himself); plus a toilet-roll holder, brand new paint brush, a box of masonry nails and a pumice stone. There was no valve, however, but he was delighted by my find and said it was an omen. Someone had got to it before us, that was all, a question of bad luck, we'd fare better next time. My find pointed clearly to a return visit and next time we'd make it early in the week so as to get there before the professional picaroonies and beat the bastards at their own game.

*

Officially, it was a party to celebrate the new Beatles LP. Unofficially, it was a stag party for Andy who was getting married the following morning. Andy and I had been to the presbytery to make the arrangements. Father Paul saw us initially but he passed us on to Father Bingham when he realized it was a flats' wedding. Father Bingham knew immediately it was a shotgun wedding so he arranged the wedding Mass for six thirty in the morning so as not to embarrass the bride. Andy and I were going straight to the church from the Beatles party.

We were anxiously waiting for Gerry Green when I heard Teresa's voice outside the front door.

—Is Andy Griffin in there?

Andy dived behind the couch.

—Tell her I'm not here.

I went out to the front steps. She looked fierce standing there with her bloated stomach, her overcoat that was too small for her and her beehive hairstyle that looked like it might unbalance her.

—Are there women in there?

Teresa leaned in past me and tried to look into the front
room.

—It's bad luck to see your bride the night before your
wedding.

I'd read it in a book I'd found under Da's pillow one
time.

—Have you the ring?

—Yeah.

—Tell him I'll see him in the morning. Don't be late.

—I'll get him there.

I watched her walk down the street. She seemed so desperately alone. I remembered the day we went to Bray when
Andy and her were like Siamese twins.

When Gerry Green eventually rang at the door we all
piled out into the hall. He held the LP in the air so we could
all see it. *Sgt Pepper's Lonely Hearts Club Band*. John, Paul,
George and Ringo in multicoloured uniforms with huge
shoulder pads. It was the most impressive LP cover I'd ever
seen by a million miles.

—What's it like, Gerry?

—I can't talk. I can't fucking talk.

Gerry Green wouldn't come in. He ran down the steps,
held onto the railings and refused to bring the LP into the
house.

—Don't make me listen to it, I'll go out of my fucking
mind.

Shea put his arm around Gerry and whispered something
in his ear. He let go the railings and started up the steps. We
parted like the Red Sea to let him through. We followed him
in and watched the record being ceremoniously placed on
the turntable. Gerry Green sat in the corner with his hands
over his ears.

—I can't listen to it. I can't fucking listen to it.

The needle hit the groove and made its way towards track
one, side one. It was straight into an urgent guitar solo and

vocals that felt like they'd always existed. Had we heard these words in another existence before we were born?

We sat on the floor with the cover open and followed the lyrics printed there. Gerry Green was right for once. This wasn't a record. It was an experience from another world.

The second track followed without a break. Just like a symphony. A continuous stream of music with everything related to what went before and what came after. This was better than a symphony. Better than Mozart, Beethoven and Brahms. Better than Handel and his *Messiah*. Ringo Starr was getting by with a little help from his friends. He was getting high with a little help from his friends. Who were these friends? Were they the other Beatles? The refrain kept coming.

It was a simple word, 'high', but in this context presented a whole new meaning. Shea suggested the song was about drugs. A homage to marijuana. Gerry Green put a hand on either side of Shea's face and kissed him full on the forehead. While that was happening, John Lennon took up vocals against a haunting instrument like a harpsichord or a zither.

We fell backwards into multicoloured pictures as Lennon painted oils with his voice. We were high. We were up in the sky with Lucy, or down on the ground fixing a hole for the benefit of Mr Kite while his daughter pined that she was leaving home. How would she feel when he was sixty-four, within him or without him? Would he love lovely Rita meter maid, would she crow for him in the early hours, good morning, good morning. *Sgt Pepper's*, a day in the life, I'd never forget you, just like I'd never forget Frankie, I'd never forget where I met you and heard you first. We played it over and over and it got better and better. Gerry Green took a small lump of turf from his pocket and placed it on the cover of the LP in the centre of the big bass drum. Mahony was intrigued by it.

—What is it?

—I can't say, I can't fucking say.

It looked distinctly like turf to me.

—Is it turf?

Shea smiled at me.

—It's what made the record possible.

Mahony put his hand up to his mouth and suppressed a laugh.

—Is it marijuana?

—I can't say. I can't fucking say.

Marijuana. I'd only heard the word, never seen it written down. Mahony picked it up between his fingers and sniffed it. He stood up, put it in his pocket and made for the door.

—I'll see yous.

He burst into his manic laugh, came straight back in and threw the marijuana at Gerry Green. He straight away started to disgorge a cigarette of its tobacco. He broke the marijuana into tiny pieces and mixed it with tobacco before he put the mixture back into the hollow tube. He lit the concoction, pulled on it hard several times and inhaled deeply before he passed it on to Shea. It went around the group of us. The effect of the marijuana was immediate and powerful. I looked at Andy and knew what he was thinking. I could actually hear his brain moving inside his head. Gerry Green put *Sgt Pepper's* on again and I could hear George Harrison's plectrum hitting against the strings of his guitar. I no sooner had the thought than Andy said it.

—You can hear the plectrum, listen.

I told him I knew he was going to say that. We both started laughing and couldn't stop. Other people were laughing about other things and I knew exactly what they were laughing at. I could switch in and out of everyone's mind at will. I looked at Shea who was looking at Gerry

Green who was looking at Mahony. I knew what Shea was going to say. I got in before him.

—He's our Brian Epstein.

Mahony was reading my mind as I was reading Shea's.

—I'm not your Brian Epstein, I'm your John Lennon.

Shea and Gerry Green fell over and rolled on the floor. There was a knock on the door and Da stuck his head in to say good night and to tell us to keep the music down a bit. He was glad to see us enjoying ourselves. I was glad he was glad and he was genuinely glad, you could see. There was music in the house again, even if they didn't play their own instruments. I wanted him to come in and listen to the genius of *Sgt Pepper's*. He was mad, of course, but he could appreciate good music if he let himself. He was a long time standing in the doorway, I realized that because I'd been looking at him for ages and he didn't move. I raised my hand, not that way, not in anger, I raised it in peace, I beckoned him with it.

—Come on in, Da, it's *Sgt Pepper's Lonely Hearts Club Band*.

—It sounds good.

—It's The Beatles and they play their own instruments.

George Harrison was good. He wasn't as good as Da. He wasn't as good a person. Da was a good person. He'd given the world seven children. Six left now. The one that died was destroying him. He couldn't see it. His own life ebbing away.

I looked at him framed in the doorway. He looked fragile. Maybe he had to die for us to live. Maybe that's all there was – procreation and death. You live on in your children but you die. You give them your strength but you give them your weaknesses, too. Like Frankie's genetic flaw. Passed down from Da. He knew it and he wanted it to kill him. Wanted to die by the same sword. If guilt could do it he wouldn't last 'til morning. He should listen to George Harrison. He should talk to him. That was the thing about this LP, you could talk to it.

—Good night all.

—Good night, Da. Good night, good night.

Gerry Green asked Shea to pile all his records in the middle of the floor. They were fakes and he wanted to destroy them for their own good. They weren't real records because *Sgt Pepper's* was the only real record. All other records were impostors and had to die. After an argument and a show of hands, it was decided to select one record and execute it on behalf of all the others. The choice was unanimous – Mario Lanza singing 'The Student Prince'. We trooped down to the scullery after Gerry Green where he found a good-sized potato pot. He put Mario Lanza into the pot, lit the gas and melted him into liquid. Then we went out to the backyard and quietly poured his remains down the shore. It was a beautiful funeral. We returned to the front room, played The Beatles and passed around another marijuana cigarette. By five o'clock we were starting to wilt. Johnny was sprawled out on the couch fast asleep. Shea, surprisingly, was out for the count in the armchair, his mouth wide open like a dead fish.

It was an hour and a half to the wedding. I suggested to Andy we go upstairs and lie on the bed. No getting under the covers. We couldn't afford to fall asleep and miss the church. We kicked off our shoes and lay side by side. Our shoulders were touching. The last time we'd been in this room together was the day I rubbed Sudocrem on his sore bum. Today I was his best man. Tomorrow he was going to be a father. Not literally, but soon. Procreation. It was the meaning of our existence. The feeling had stayed with me all night. Andy would experience fatherhood before me, he experienced everything before me, that was his nature, he was a natural. I was slow in relationships because I didn't know how to take the initiative. I froze with Catherine because I never wanted her to feel pressured, put upon, abused, a victim. All the things I felt with Mossie in the train. Lying beside Andy I wanted to hug him. I took his hand in mine and squeezed it. I was afraid his marriage would change everything.

—Don't let Teresa come between us.

He squeezed my hand in reply.

—I don't love her.

I had known that all along but I was surprised to hear him say it.

—Why are you marrying her?

—I'm doing it for the baby.

There it was again. Duty, honour and procreation. It transcended love. Andy was marrying because of it. My lids got heavy thinking about it. I decided to give them a little rest and closed them. I heard a voice in my ear.

—Get out of my bed.

It was Johnny's voice. He was standing by the side of the bed poking at Andy. What time was it? I had no idea.

—What time is it, Johnny?

—I don't know, I want to go to bed.

I shook Andy and at the same time I ran down the stairs to the kitchen. It was twenty to seven by Da's masterpiece. I ran upstairs and met Andy coming down.

—We're late . . . we're late.

Andy had the hall door open but I had no shoes on. I ran to the bedroom, grabbed them and started to put them on as I scrambled down the stairs. I tripped over myself and fell head first onto the landing where the ring spilled out and lodged under the weatherboard. I closed over the door to get it out but it only got stuck worse. When I did retrieve it, it was bent so badly I thought it was going to break.

Teresa and Catherine were waiting for us at the side entrance of the church. They didn't need to tell us we were in a mess. Our clothes were all creased and our hair was sticking out. It was all Teresa could do to stop herself from crying. In fairness, she looked beautiful and had obviously spent half the night putting her make-up on and organizing every strand of her beehive hair. Catherine looked perfection and as we made our way into the church it struck me as absurd that the wrong two people were getting married. Father Bingham was very welcoming with a distinct smell of wine from his breath. It was a small wedding, at a side altar, before a small crowd, in the small hours, but not to worry. Father Bingham made us feel big and important. The only glitch occurred when I handed Andy the ring and it wouldn't go on Teresa's finger until I took it back and bent it into shape. It was a twenty-minute Mass and we were out of there by five past seven, wondering what to do, when Father Bingham came around and took some photographs with his own camera. After that we went up town to the Del Rio for breakfast, but Catherine left early because she had to open the bakery. Andy paid for breakfast and I left him and Teresa to make their way to the train station. They were going out to Bray for their honeymoon. A day trip. Andy walked down the street with his hands in his pockets while Teresa waddled beside him, her bump pushed out to the world. Procreation. The driving force of the universe. I went home to talk to Sgt Pepper and see what he had to say about it.

*

The house was very quiet. Da was asleep in the armchair with a wet facecloth on his forehead. Beside him on the fireplace were his tablets and a glass of water. The television was on with the sound turned down. The reception was atrocious. There was no convincing him that it had had its day. I crept up the stairs. Ma was taking a nap. Beside her in the bed was Paul on one side and Gerard on the other. Paul was sucking a soother and Gerard had his thumb in his mouth. In the ashtray on the locker was a substantial butt

11

1968

The first sign Da was getting better was when he decided to dye his hair. Ita bought the bottle of Clairol in the chemist shop because he wouldn't go in and ask for it himself. The box promised jet-black hair with a before picture on the front and an after picture on the back. Black and white. He'd gone prematurely white and now he was taking remedial action. It had nothing to do with vanity. He wasn't trying to become a film star or turn back the clock. He just wanted his hair the colour it was before nature turned it upside down.

Ita washed his hair at the kitchen table. She made him sit in a chair and lean his head back into a basin just like in a women's salon. She took the bottle of dye and the sachet out of the box and had them ready at hand. Da issued his instructions.

—Half of everything.

—That's not what it says on the bottle.

—I'm not Italian, I'm Irish. I don't want it too dark.

—Warning. Use entire contents.

—Half the bottle, half the sachet, half the time. I know what I'm doing.

—Whatever you say.

Ita worked up a great lather and then covered his head with an old towel. He sat at the table and ate his tea with his head in a turban. He was running late so Johnny and I pushed the car out of the garage and had it ready for him to jump straight in and drive to the dogs. Ma cleared the table and Ita brought in a fresh basin of hot water to wash out the dye. As soon as his head met the H_2O there was a chemical reaction. The suds turned blue and his head seemed to glow red but it was difficult to tell because Ita's face went green before it turned grey and then went white. Da took his head out and knew there was something wrong from the expression on Ita's face. She stepped back and Da pulled himself up so that the coloured water ran down his bare back. No one knew what to do, whether to laugh or cry, reach out to him or pull away. Ma walked in from the scullery.

—Jesus, Mary and Holy Saint Joseph.

Da got up and looked in the mirror. His hair was inde-scribable, constantly changing colour from blue to red to purple and back to blue. In the end, the consensus came down on purple. Ita blow-dried it with the hairdryer while Ma went up to Sheriff Street to get help. I phoned Shelbourne Park and told the deputy manager that Da was sick.

—Is it his head again?

Mrs Hogan was crying at the sight of Da's purple hair. Her tears had everyone laughing. Da was lapping it up. He kept looking in the mirror and primping his hair with his hands. Mrs Hogan was telling him he should be on the stage.

—You should be in the Gaiety pantomime, Mr Sheridan.

—As what? One of the ugly sisters?

He walked over to the back door, took down Ma's coat and her scarf and came back into the centre of the room.

—I'm putting my hat and coat on, I'm fed up with all of you.

He had Ma to perfection. Every inflection. The sigh and the crucified look. When he started to put his hand into the coat that was too small for him, I got a pain in my chest laughing. I couldn't believe it when he tied the scarf under his chin and walked out the back door onto the street. He stuck his head in the air like a proper aul' wan and waddled up the street away from us.

—I'm going to the Ball Alley to get drunk. Have that house cleaned before I get back.

Ma came around the corner with the woman from the salon and saw Da walking towards her with her hat and scarf on. She looked him up and down in disbelief.

—Have you taken leave of your senses?

By the time Florrie from the salon had finished with Da, he looked Italian. Everyone was telling him it took years off him and that he was a ringer for Dean Martin. Publicly he brushed it aside but he was glowing inside. He adopted 'Little Old Wine Drinker Me' as his anthem. He sang it, whistled it, hummed it, all with attitude. He started slurring his words like he was drunk all the time. He resurrected some old songs and gave them the Deano treatment, including 'Mack The Knife' and 'Buòna Sera, Signorina' but he still couldn't sing his all-time favourite, 'Frankie and Johnny'. Ma was delighted with the Latin Da, and they started going back to the Liverpool Bar at night again. The late-night arguments followed but the old arrogance was gone. He was more thoughtful, more reflective. He seemed more concerned with action than with thought, with reality more than abstraction, with practice more than theory. He admitted that he'd sat in the front room and listened to *Sgt Pepper's* all the way through. Both sides. He thought The Beatles had a vision and expressed it very well. I asked him what his favourite track was. 'Fixing A Hole', came the reply, without the slightest hesitation.

I wanted him to sing it and slur the words but it was enough that he'd listened to it. It was his way of apologizing for saying they didn't play their own instruments. The question he posed and left dangling in front of us was where would the next Beatles come from? Would it be Leeds or

Glasgow, Manchester or Cardiff. Or could it be Dublin? Was he throwing down a challenge to Michael Maltese? He'd barred us from rehearsing in the garage. I couldn't let the moment pass.

—We might go places if we'd somewhere to rehearse.

*

We were sitting around the gramophone working out the chords to 'A Little Help From My Friends', when Da popped his head in the door and called me. Out in the hall he asked me to smarten myself up.

—Where are we going?

He said he had a hall for us to rehearse in and wanted me to come along. It was the first time in my life he didn't give me a note and send me on my own. We set off down Seville Place, turned right at the granite steps (he was a half yard ahead of me) and knocked at the Presbytery door. When the housekeeper answered, Da asked for Father Paul in a very affirmative tone. He came out, greeted Da, and they exchanged pleasantries.

—This is my son, Father. He has a band and they want to practise in the Oriel Hall.

Father Paul was very uneasy and invited us inside. He asked us would we like tea. Beware of Greeks bearing gifts. I knew what Da was thinking. He declined.

—I explained to your son that it was for parish activities only.

—My son is a parishioner.

—Yes, but—

—You're a priest.

There was an awkward silence. Da invited him to fill it.

—Yes, I'm a priest.

—It's a parish hall. Not a priest's hall. Two or three years you'll be gone from here. Am I right?

—I'll have to talk to the parish priest.

—I can wait.

The hair had started all this. He looked like my older brother. He'd put a colour in his hair and become another person. I didn't quite know who this person was but I couldn't wait to find out. Father Paul came back to the room and asked to speak with Da in private. I waited out on the front steps and looked down at the parish all around. Looked down from where Father Paul looked down every day of the year. You could get dizzy living this high up. The door opened and Da came out dangling the keys. He had a smirk on his face like he'd backed the winners of the Grand National, the Epsom Derby and the Cheltenham Gold Cup all in the one day. Back home we gathered up our instruments and got ready for the move to the Oriel Hall. Ma was ecstatic. She was following Da and punching the air around him like a boxer in the gym.

—It's civil rights, that's what it is, the start of civil rights.

We followed Da down Seville Place for the storming of the Oriel Hall. We didn't have to break down doors or scale any walls because we held the keys. We were entering it because it belonged to us. Da had claimed it on our behalf. We stood in the body of the hall and started to set up. Da advised us to practise hard because we were playing for the old folks in three weeks' time.

Up to that point, Michael Maltese had been a band searching for an identity. Now we had our first gig and a repertoire of only six songs, none of which was suitable for an audience of old folks. We only had one amplifier for two guitars and Andy's drum set consisted of a snare, a bass but no side drum and no cymbals. Plus we had no PA or microphones for Gerry Green's vocals or maracas. Our only hope of salvation was Ita. She'd gone out once or twice with a fella called Pat Stynes whose father managed a music store in town. It was crucial for the future of Michael Maltese that Pat Stynes be encouraged to marry Ita and provide the band with free equipment for life. Or provide the equipment first and marry Ita later.

Shea and Gerry Green took sick leave from work and I skipped school so we could rehearse. Andy, who neither worked nor went to school, was less available because Teresa wanted him around now that the baby was due. Worse than that, she was threatening to break up our rehearsals if Andy didn't find them a place to live. She was still at home with her mother and Andy was still in the flats. Andy thought if he could just get a flat from the Corporation Teresa would be happy for the rest of her life. To be eligible for accommodation, however, a couple had to have at least two children. The short-term solution was for them to squat and I agreed to help Andy find a place.

Shea and Gerry Green were detailed to approach Pat Stynes. The strategy was to enter the shop, buy a plectrum and get him into conversation. From there they'd work it round to rock bands and groupies and free love and Ita. Normally, I'd kill anyone who laid a hand on her – she was so small and fragile – but we were in a situation that called for sacrifices all around, and that included Ita.

Andy got a tip off about a ground floor flat in one of the old tenement houses. We stood outside number 2a Sean McDermott Street and watched people enter and leave the building. It was dusk. House lights started to come on all along the street. No light came on in the ground floor of 2a. The information seemed correct. The flat had been vacated and was a prime target for squatting. Our action would deny another family their rights but Andy hadn't created the housing crisis.

We entered the hallway, which was dark and dreary. There was a light fitting but no bulb. Andy knocked at the door of the ground floor flat.

—Anybody in?

There was no reply. We knew it was empty. To be really

certain, Andy gave the door a serious thump with his fist. I gave it one more for good measure. We stood with our heads resting against the door panels, listening. Andy pushed against it to test its resistance. He stood back and ran at it with his shoulder. It was no contest. The door sprung open like we'd been invited for tea. Andy turned the light on and I opened the window. The smell was overpowering. I turned to survey the room when I saw the figure on the bed. I almost jumped out of my skin. The old man was dead and decomposing. In his hand was a naggin of whiskey. It was a disgusting sight but I couldn't take my eyes off it. I went over and stood beside Andy or he came over and stood beside me, I'm not sure. We stood beside each other, the way you do at funerals, it's not easy to stand alone in the presence of death.

—The poor fucker.

—What a way to end.

I thought we should say a prayer for the repose of his soul. How could we abandon him, we who'd found him? He could be a saint in Heaven, just like Matt Talbot. Standing in that putrefied room, it didn't seem possible that the old man on the bed was looking down at us from anywhere. Heaven just didn't seem a logical explanation of what we were witnessing and what we were smelling. It was cruel and foul and we had to get out of there.

We tossed a coin and I lost. I rang 999, gave them the facts and hung up. We had a rehearsal in the Oriel Hall but Andy suggested going back to see the ambulance take the body out. Andy seemed determined to go back to 'the scene of the crime'. I laughed at the suggestion but Andy was serious. I got serious and Andy laughed at my seriousness. For a moment it felt like the old days when we were foolish and carefree, before procreation and housing lists, when we lived and played in the concrete playground of Sheriff Street. I wondered could the old man have been murdered. There was no sign of a break-in. No sign of a struggle. Not until we'd broken in. I'd opened the window. Andy had switched on the light. The place was crawling with our fingerprints. We could be possible suspects in a murder investigation. I decided to stay as far away from Sean MacDermott Street as I could and the Oriel Hall seemed as good a refuge as any.

*

The news from Pat Stynes was very good because Gerry Green couldn't talk about it.

—They were for nothing.

Shea smiled and made his ears move up and down, a trick he did when he was being cheeky.

—He fancies Ita big time.

It was all very mysterious. No one was saying much except Mahony who wanted us to start rehearsals and get the feel of the hall. No one paid the slightest attention to what he said. Three sharp blasts of a car horn sounded. Gerry Green went out the door of the Oriel like the proverbial bullet. There followed in the biggest speaker I had ever seen. Perched on four giant castors it glided into the hall with a personality all of its own. The man behind it stepped out and introduced himself as Pat Stynes. He looked at Mahony and told him to put it on the stage. Shea and Gerry Green followed in with more equipment – another giant speaker, an amplifier, two microphones, two stands and hundreds of yards of cable. Pat Stynes was a man in charge and we obeyed him like willing slaves. We plugged everything in and launched into our opening number. I did a three chord, two bar intro before Gerry Green stepped up to the microphone and did his Mick Jagger imitation. His voice bounced off the four walls, the ceiling, the floor. It was a total distortion of humanity.

Pat Stynes screamed at us to stop. He was not impressed.

Six attempts later he was still fine-tuning the levels, by which time Ita had come around to watch. She never came to our rehearsals. He sat beside her, put his arm around her shoulder and finally let us play all the way through. Gerry Green pouted his lips and screamed into the microphone. The words of the song were crystal clear.

Pat Stynes, Ita and Mahony looked up at him. Two beaming faces and one sad face. Two in the light and one in shadow. Mahony had been a good foil when we needed someone to tell us how great we were. In our hearts, we'd known we were rubbish. We practised in his bedroom and kept him up 'til all hours of the morning. It was a good arrangement for an insomniac. Things had changed utterly in one day. One hour. We were a real rock'n'roll band, making real rock'n'roll sounds, in our own rehearsal hall. There was no going back to dingy bedrooms. Halfway through our set, Mahony got up and left. He slipped out without saying a word, which only made his departure all the more obvious. He didn't come home that night. Shea and I said nothing because he'd taken the keys of the Oriel Hall with him. There was nothing sinister in it. He'd gone off with the keys because he was hurt. Ma and Da were worried when he didn't come in for his supper. He was so much a part of the family. He'd been very loyal to Da and Da put a great store by loyalty.

*

Shea and I went to Busaras the following morning. Mahony was behind the counter of the left luggage. He looked normal, in the abnormal way that was normal for him. He had his cap on back to front, which suited his baby face but wouldn't have you rushing up to entrust your luggage to him. Soon as he saw us he removed his glasses and started to wipe them with his shirt. He did it so we'd notice they were broken at the bridge and stuck with Sellotape. Shea

259

said we wanted to talk. Mahony hopped over the counter and marched out of the main entrance of the bus station for Keating's pub across the road. Shea and I followed at a distance. When we joined him in the pub he'd ordered three pints of stout. It was ten o'clock in the morning. I asked him to change mine to an orange. He wouldn't hear of it. When the barman brought the pints he ordered three whiskeys to go with them. Shea and I flatly refused. Mahony told the barman to put the drinks on his slate.

—If you make it big I'm going to sue the bollix off yous.

It was hard to drink to that even if he'd bought the round. I put the glass to my lips and licked the cream. Mahony leaned right into my face.

—I'm joking, serious face.

Mahony was right. I was too serious for my own good. My face felt like cement when all around me were laughing at the world. Mahony was a case in point. He felt jilted, but he was sitting down to have a few drinks and a laugh. Andy had nowhere to live and he took it in his stride. He was about to become a father but he didn't get bogged down with self-defeating thoughts of how he was going to cope. I needed to let go more. I looked at Shea who smiled and absorbed Mahony's negativity in his stride. Did he persecute himself remembering Frankie every day? I envied Shea. I needed to let go like he did. I lifted the pint glass to my lips and started to drink. I didn't stop but kept pouring it down. I poured beyond the point that was human because I didn't want to be human. I saw the end of the glass come into view. I drank until the glass was empty, then I slammed it down on the table.

—I'll have that whiskey now.

I matched Mahony drink for drink while Shea explained to him that Pat Stynes was our technical manager. He, Mahony, was our real manager unless he was stepping down. Or failed to secure gigs, excepting the old folks' gig which

260

had been secured by Da. Mahony agreed to stay on and promised not to sue us. We shook hands on it outside the bus station. As soon as I let go of his hand I felt there was something wrong with the street. I made to cross it and started to go sideways. Shea grabbed me and put my arm across his shoulder.

—You're drunk!

I tried to speak but I couldn't form the words. My brain was fine, it was my mouth, my mouth was the problem, why wouldn't it do what I wanted it to? We'd forgotten to get the Oriel keys from Mahony. I mumbled it as best I could. Shea seemed to understand.

He put me sitting in a doorway and went off, to get the keys, I don't know, I fell asleep. I don't remember walking home. Don't remember any of it. How I got into 44, who carried me up the stairs and put me to bed. I only remember waking up. Under the covers. Vest, underpants and socks. Nothing else. Well, yes, a terrible thirst. My saliva gone and my tongue stuck to the roof of my mouth. My lips like cinders out of the fire. No one to bring me a glass of water. I couldn't shout and I didn't have the will to get it myself. It was dark outside but didn't feel like night. My bones were young but they felt old. I was too young to be doing the right thing all the time. I wanted to do the wrong thing. I didn't care if it made me old, I didn't want to be the same me all the time.

*

The old folks' gig was a partial success because none of them actually suffered a cardiac arrest. After my two bar intro to 'Everybody Needs Somebody', I looked out and saw the entire audience raise their hands and cover their ears. Some of them clutched at their chests and fell sideways. When we adjusted the volume downwards they got back into their seats and clapped politely because they were still alive. We worked through our repertoire of six songs and when we'd finished they clamoured for a singsong.

—Give us 'Ramona', son. Yous must know 'Ramona'!

We stood paralyzed on the stage of the Oriel Hall while a hundred senior citizens shouted out the names of their favourite songs. From a dark recess of my brain, a little house of pain where I stored bitter memories, I launched into 'She'll Be Coming Round The Mountain'. Andy quickly provided a rhythm and Shea added the bass notes but Gerry Green was totally lost.

—I can't sing, I can't fucking sing.

By the end of the first verse they were all singing along. By the end of the tune they were standing, clapping, singing and dancing in the aisles.

Da was over the moon. He got up on the stage to a great round of applause. It wasn't that he'd found a second wind, more like he'd found a second life. A public life. It was as though the years of argument around the table in 44 had been a preparation for this stepping out into the community. Standing on the stage of the Oriel Hall, his black mane against his white skin, he looked like a Roman senator.

He complimented the old folk on their singing and dancing. He promised them they'd have an opportunity to learn some modern steps very soon. He announced the start of a Sunday afternoon hop for the teenagers of the parish and he asked for volunteers from the old folks' club to man the cloakroom, the mineral bar and the toilets. The profits from the Sunday dances would go towards setting up a drama club – the St Laurence O'Toole's Musical and Dramatic Society – which would be holding auditions in the coming weeks. He reminded the audience that the Oriel Hall was where the young Sean O'Casey had his first plays produced, whereupon Mrs Murphy from Abercorn Road stood up and shouted at Da.

—I sued that oul' reprobate for putting me in one of his plays and got twenty pounds off him.

Half of the old folks gave her a clap and the other half told her to shut up and sit down. I knew Mrs Murphy from the Legion of Mary paper round. I wasn't surprised Sean O'Casey put her in a play. Once she opened her hall door it was impossible to get away from her. She had an opinion on everything, especially the Government, and I could only imagine that whatever play she was in the other characters would have no chance of getting a word in edgeways.

The Sunday dance in the Oriel attracted the toughest crowd in Dublin. Sheriff Street, the Buildings, Summerhill, Ballybough and East Wall all claimed it as their own. It should have led to a civil war, and it always felt like warfare was about to break out, but the presence of so many old folks somehow seemed to calm the potential violence. Fellas who carried knives and used them in the dance halls up town, seemed reluctant to produce them in a hall where the bouncers carried walking sticks.

The other reason was Da. He got to know everyone who came to the dances by name. Git Walsh, Joe-Joe Lennon, Billy Boy Brennan, Scissors Kane, Ocky Nolan, Hard Head Hogan, Cattler Caulfield, Mousey Mitchell and Mickabird Langan. Da never addressed them by their nicknames. To Da they were Christopher, Joseph, William, Seamus, Noel, John, Kevin, Anthony and Michael. When rows broke out, Da would enlist the help of the hard men to break it up. He also encouraged disabled teenagers to come to the dance and the hard men took great pride in adopting these for their special protection. When Skinny Gildea, who had a normal body but a tiny head, got off with Tina Hurson, who was a midget, no one called them names on the dance floor by order of the hard men. There was a spot prize of ten Major cigarettes for the best jiving couple every week, and the biggest cheer ever heard in the Oriel Hall was when Da presented Skinny and Tina with the packet of smokes. It was little things like this that set the Oriel apart from other dances in Dublin.

I wasn't sure about the Musical and Dramatic Society. We read Shakespeare in school and learned speeches off by heart to quote in exams. It wasn't my idea of how to pass a Tuesday evening, not when there were still songs I hadn't mastered from *Sgt Pepper's*. Saint Laurence O'Toole's Musical and Dramatic Society. It wasn't as good a name as Sgt. Pepper's Lonely Hearts Club Band but I was curious as to how many would turn up for the auditions. Da, like Mr Kite, promised a splendid time for all. His enthusiasm was infectious.

There were twenty people in the Oriel Hall. To my surprise, Catherine Griffin was there. I sat a good bit away from her and gave her a wave. I knew she wouldn't come near me and she didn't. I'd long lost my opportunity with her. When she left the wedding breakfast early it confirmed it in an unequivocal way.

Da welcomed everybody and made a speech about the parish and its great literary past. James Joyce, Sean O'Casey and Brendan Behan had all lived within a radius of a mile. He distributed three copies of a play called *Shadow of a Gunman* and we all crowded round to read it out. The first thing I saw was Da's handwriting. 'This book is the property of Saint Laurence O'Toole's Musical and Dramatic Society. Return to Secretary please and oblige.' He went down the list of characters and assigned the parts. I was reading Tommy Owens. Catherine was reading Minnie Powell. Da was reading Seumas Shields. Mahony was reading Maguire. Big Ben Lalor was reading Donal Davoren. One of the old folks, Mrs Cremin, was reading Mrs Grigson. She insisted on offering everyone a drink from her bottle of Sandeman sherry before the reading started. Everyone refused but she made Da take a sup because, in her opinion, he was a lifesaver. She knew it was only her opinion but her opinion was as good as anyone else's unless anyone wanted to disagree. Mrs Cremin held us up for ten minutes trying to get an answer to her question. Eventually we got going. From the moment Donal Davoren spoke the opening lines of the play the reality of it engulfed me. It invaded my brain and my heart like nothing had ever done before. Everything about it was genuine Dublin. The words, the dialogue, the situation, the characters. There was no artifice anywhere. This was a community of people caught in a drama, talking to each other, and it unfolded in the most natural and logical way I had ever encountered.

My character was a mouth. A braggart. He wanted to die for Ireland but spent all his time in the pub. Catherine's character was entirely dismissive of me which seemed appropriate. Her focus was the gunman, Davoren. He was also a poet but the real attraction for Minnie was his association with the gun. He fulfilled her fantasy of the dynamic hero.

The play was forty years old but a perfect reflection of life. Da's character was a peddler who sold knick-knacks and whose world was contained in a suitcase. He also had an outside toilet. I could picture it. For the tenement room he shared with Davoren read the kitchen of 44. At night, Shields philosophized on the meaning of life from the safety of his bed. Not budging from that location, he sent others on messages he wouldn't do himself. Da had no need to act it. He understood every nuance of it in that first reading.

I didn't get to meet Da in the play. I did meet Mrs Madigan, however. It was Mrs Murphy from Abercorn Road made flesh. She walks in and takes over the tenement room and doesn't stop talking until she leaves it again twenty minutes later. No wonder Mrs Murphy sued the author and won.

The play ends in tragedy. Minnie is killed because she trusts in the gunman who turns out to be a fake. He lets her go to her death because he cannot face the truth about who he really is. He is a poet but he is hollow because he has no soul. He is all veneer. The appalling outcome is that the young idealist, Minnie, dies on his behalf and he lives on.

The play had me that I couldn't stop thinking about the man in 2a Sean MacDermott Street. He had died poor and alone in a street named for a gunman. Sean MacDermott was one of the leaders of the 1916 Rising. All around the city we paid homage to the gunmen of the past. All around the city poverty was everywhere. People living in tenement rooms dedicated to heroes of the past. Pearse, Connolly, Markiewicz, Plunkett and MacDermott. They were all honoured with slums in their names.

When the reading was over Da announced a date for the production of the play in the Oriel Hall. We would perform it for three consecutive nights with the proceeds going to the establishment of a boys' and girls' swimming club. Mrs Cremin, who was out of her mind on sherry, wanted to know how she could get tickets. She wanted them immediately. Da told her he had blank tickets and a rubber stamp ordered from a shop in Capel Street. He expected to have the stamp within the week. That seemed to satisfy her and she shut up. In the silence, he announced that Shea would direct the play. Then he handed out copybooks and pens so we could write out our individual parts from the play script. Mrs Cremin couldn't remember what part she was playing and got obstreperous. I worked away on my own in a corner. I wrote out my first line in my best handwriting.

Tommy: I seen nothin' – honest – thought you was learnin' to typewrite – Mr Davoren teachin' you. I seen nothin' else – s'help me God!

I paused and thought about what was happening on the stage when I walked into the room. Davoren and Minnie were about to kiss. I looked over at Big Ben Lalor and Catherine. They were stuck beside each other just like in the play. Writing and giggling. Maybe they were giggling in the play. I called Shea over.

—What's happening when I come into the room? Do you think they're giggling?

—That's not important.

He seemed very dismissive. Maybe he didn't know.

—All that matters is what's going on in your head.

—What do you mean?

—What do you expect to see?

—Davoren the gunman.

—What do you actually see?

—Davoren and Minnie. About to kiss.

—How does that make you feel? Happy? Disappointed? Think about it.

I thought about it to the point where I couldn't think about anything else. It took over all my thinking cells. This character who'd existed on a page up until a few hours previous, now seemed as real as I was. His world as touchable as my world. In the play the characters paraded into the tenement just like so many had paraded into our lives in the kitchen of 44. Lodgers and neighbours. Mahony and Minnie. Tommy Owens and John Charles Gallagher. People searching for father figures and heroes. Sitting there writing out the lines of Tommy Owens, I realized he had as much of a history as any living person. He brought it with him onto the stage. That was the meaning of Shea's direction to me. It was an unexpressed history but real nonetheless. The author's genius was that he encapsulated all this within the time frame of the play. It was like ten years of 44 realized in under two hours.

I became obsessed with rehearsals. I hated when they finished at night and I couldn't wait for them to come around again. I was interested in every aspect of the play and not just my scenes. I was as obsessive about Act Two in which I didn't appear. It was fascinating to watch Shea rehearsing with Da, drawing him out, building a character that was based on a knowledge of Da himself. What amazed me the most was that Da never saw himself in any of the suggestions made.

The entire cast were shocked when Shea announced that the gun of the play was a penis and all the characters, with the exception of Minnie, were afraid of it. This was the subtext of the play. It was more important than the actual lines of dialogue.

O'Casey was a Protestant, an outsider, but he could clearly see all the Catholic guilt and hypocrisy. His father died when he was a boy and he'd been raised by his mother. The women were the strong ones. They were stronger than the men. Minnie was the strongest. Davoren was the weakest. Minnie was the only one who wasn't afraid to grasp the erect penis. The men were impotent. Her virility reminded them of their own failure. The men were afraid to act, afraid to take responsibility and Irish society continued to reflect that failure.

Mrs Cremin took another slug of her sherry and asked Shea what drugs he was on. A lot of the cast were worried. Why did we have to bring sex into it? Why couldn't he just direct it as it was written? There was no mention of penises in the text. Catherine was one of the grumblers. I wasn't surprised because I knew how religious she was. Catherine said she wouldn't do anything that went against her conscience or the teachings of the church. I could see Shea biting his lip. Da said it was an interesting angle and if it helped the production then it could only be good. Big Ben Lalor said he wasn't impotent and couldn't play an impotent man. He had to kiss Minnie and kiss her he would but nobody was putting a hand or anything else on his penis. There were whistles and everyone looked at Shea.

—The kiss is important but Minnie is in control of that.

She's in control because the women are in control. She allows you to kiss her. Do you get me?

Big Ben Lalor, Catherine and I got up on the stage. We rehearsed it from my exit. I said my line, walked out the door and left them alone on the stage. Catherine walked towards Big Ben Lalor. Shea shouted up to her.

—Make him come to you. You're in control.

I stood in the tiny corridor at the side of the stage and watched them. Catherine with her big brown eyes and her open face. She looked down from the stage at Shea who was telling her to feel her power. Not to give it away.

—Have you ever had a fella on a string and dangled him?

She looked at Shea like she didn't understand. The truth was she understood perfectly.

She enjoyed watching Shea explain himself, scrunching up his face and scratching his head at a hundred and eighty miles an hour. She was feigning innocence. I remembered the night she asked me did I want to give her a good-night kiss. She was in control then, as now. Getting Shea to explain himself was part of that control. When the talking was done, Catherine played the scene to perfection. All innocence and light on the outside, cunning and control on the inside. Catherine made to leave the room. Big Ben Lalor followed her and put an arm on her shoulder.

—Minnie, the kiss I didn't get.

—What kiss?

She said her line looking down at the floor. Then she slowly raised her head and looked provocatively into his eyes. In the silence, I thought I heard Big Ben Lalor's heart beat. It was my own. Big Ben Lalor laughed out of nervousness. Then he said his line.

—When we were interrupted, you know, you little rogue, come, just one.

—Quick then.

But it wasn't a quick one. It was a long, slow kiss, because

Catherine made it that way. She pulled away from him, by way of reasserting her control, and silently left the room, leaving behind a panting and passionate Davoren. When she opened the door, I looked away. A round of applause broke out in the hall. We stood beside each other in the semi-darkness of the wings. Neither of us spoke. She'd made the poet feel like a man. She made him feel like a gunman and she was going to have him. We did the scene from my exit again. When it got down to the kiss, Catherine's boyfriend, Billy Boy Brennan, came bursting in the door of the hall. He fell over a chair because of the darkness and as he hauled himself up off the floor he ordered Catherine to come down off the stage. She tried to calm him but it only made him worse.

—They're a pack of fucking weirdos, get out of here.

Catherine left the hall with him in a temper. A major depression descended on the cast. We were within a week of opening night and had lost our Minnie Powell. I suggested Ita for the part.

—She's a bit on the small side.

Big Ben Lalor was six foot three. Ita was four foot ten. It would look funny. Mrs Cremin suggested her daughter, Isolde. She was thirty-five. We thought it could work.

Then we learned that she lived in Germany. We were starting to make a list of names when Catherine came back in with Billy Boy in tow.

—Billy Boy has something to say, Mr Sheridan.

—I'm sorry for interrupting your rehearsals and calling yous weirdos.

Catherine put him sitting on a chair and went back up on the stage to rehearse. She was not about to let Billy Boy Brennan interfere with her career as an actress.

Shadow of a Gunman played to a packed Oriel Hall for three performances and a special Saturday afternoon show for the kids who'd joined the swimming club. They were a great audience because they shouted things up and told the characters what to do. When Big Ben Lalor discovered the bombs in Act Two, Dazzler Brennan, Billy Boy's younger brother, rushed up to the front of the stage and offered to hide them in the flats. After the curtain came across on the Saturday night, the party started. Volunteers stacked the chairs and Pat Stynes moved in with his equipment. Mrs Cremin got the drinks table ready and the old folks put out the sandwiches and the apple tarts. Father Bingham went around from group to group taking photographs. Gerry Green and Mahony were stuck in a corner laughing their heads off – I reckoned they'd smoked a marijuana cigarette. Billy Boy Brennan was wrapped around Catherine and they were in conversation with Big Ben Lalor. Shea was talking to a white-haired man from the *Evening Press* who wrote a theatre column and had been a great friend of O'Casey in the early days. He'd come all the way from his home in Drumcondra to see the play. Da was sitting at a small table by the entrance, balancing tickets against money and writing the results into a ledger. He was just like his character in the play, Sheumas Shields, who started every morning making an inventory of his wares. He was like Shields, no doubt, but he was different from him, too. Shields could never have brought a whole community together like Da had done. I wondered how long he'd carried this love of the theatre in his heart? How many tickets had he handed out for the mystery train and dreamed of himself in a play? How often did he stand in the booking office and curse the hours he gave to the GNR (Great Northern Railway). Why did he have to lose Frankie before he realized that his dreams might come to nothing? He had been so angry all his life. Did Frankie have to die for him to lose his anger?

I saw him put his hand in his pocket and take out his headache tablets. He slipped two from the bottle and popped them in his mouth. He swallowed hard but they didn't go down. I walked over and put my bottle of orange on the table. I asked him did he want anything. He shook his head, but then picked up the bottle and took a large slug. It was pure Da. I turned to walk away and he called me back.

—Just a second, son.

He put the money in the cash box and locked it with the key. He handed it to me with the accounts ledger and asked me to drop them home. I knew I could refuse. I could say, sorry Da, I'm busy. I have to tune my guitar. There was no principle involved in taking the cash box home. We seldom clashed over principles these days. I didn't mind being his messenger as long as he knew I could refuse.

I was thinking about *Sgt Pepper's Lonely Hearts Club Band* on the way home. I'd spent years trying to get him to listen to The Beatles and eventually he did. If he'd asked me to read *Shadow of a Gunman*, I'd never have done it. Only for the organized reading in the Oriel Hall, it would have passed me by. Now I was in love with it, it was my all-consuming passion and it seemed deeper and more relevant than *Sgt Pepper's*. It had more emotional truth. When I walked into the kitchen Ma was sitting at the table crying. I could see black soot on her hands and there were two black lines down her cheeks to her chin. I asked her what the matter was.

—Just having a little cry, that's all.

Ma was twenty-five years in Dublin but when she was upset or excited she spoke with the thickest Dundalk accent you could imagine. I loved the sound of it but not against tears. She asked me how the play went and I told her. I put the cash box and the ledger on the shelf above the door. While I was standing on the chair she asked me to hand her down a paper bag. I gave it to her and she pointed to the fire grate.

—Gather up them conkers and give them to some youngster, will you, son?

In the grate were a dozen black balls that had once been conkers. They were dried up and brittle, not a smidge of brown splendour remained. I picked one up and squeezed it. It disintegrated in my hand. I put the dust in the bag, picked up the other conkers and put them in beside it.

—They're gone, Ma.

—Are you sure, son?

—I'm certain. They're no use to anyone.

—I suppose you can throw them out so.

The tears flowed down Ma's cheeks unchecked. She'd stayed strong all those months with Da's headaches. She was the strong one. She'd made us all better. Now it was her turn to grieve.

12

1969

Ma refused to join the Saint Laurence O Toole's Musical and Dramatic society. We were casting for our second production, *Juno and the Paycock* by Sean O'Casey, a natural choice after the success of *Shadow of a Gunman*. We needed a Juno and Ma was the obvious choice because of her passion. Da was playing the Paycock so with Ma opposite him the sparks were sure to fly. Ma was the best actor in the house, we all knew that. She was the required age, too. Looked at from every angle and in every conceivable way, Ma had been born to play the part. The night Da asked her at the tea table, she ignored him. She did that when she was looking for attention. It was a good sign. Da repeated the offer and Ma put on her posh voice.

—I heard you.

Shea weighed in and pleaded with her. She never refused him anything.

—We need you, Ma.

—I've enough to do here.

Shea explained that it was just like real life. He was playing Johnny, her son. Da was her husband, the Paycock, Jackie Boyle. All she had to do was learn the lines and say them. She didn't have to act. She'd get over the stage fright, if she had any, which we all doubted.

—You can't refuse your eldest, Ma.

Ma looked down at the rissole on her plate while Shea

goaded her to say 'yes'. In the play, Juno's son is executed by the IRA as an informer. I thought of the scene where she finds out and cries out to God in her grief.

—Where were you when me darlin' son was riddled with bullets?

Could Ma play that scene and stay sane, I wondered? Would she be able to separate the tragedy in the play from the tragedy in our own family? It was almost two years since we'd buried Frankie. It was Ma who'd held the house together for us all to come to terms with it. We were all starting to live again, except for Ma. She seemed worse now than at the time of his death. Every day was a day that brought her closer to being reunited with him in Heaven. She lived permanently with one foot in the hereafter. She hid it well. I'd never have known only I stumbled across her with the burnt conkers. We never referred to it but it seemed to bring us closer. The fire grate became our way of remembering him without having to say his name. When Paul wrote his letter to Santa he dragged Ma in from the scullery to put it up the chimney for him. She knelt in the fire grate and a look descended across her face. Paul shouted in her ear.

—Is he up there, Ma? Can he hear us?

She held the letter in her hand and stared at the grate. She made no attempt to do anything with it. Paul started to pull at her sleeve but Ma didn't respond. I walked over, took the letter from her, reached up into the chimney-breast and posted the letter on the ledge that had held the conkers. From then on I was always looking at her for signs of vulnerability. I watched her face a lot. She caught me staring at her and got annoyed with me. I couldn't look at her or do anything but she sensed an ulterior motive. I couldn't sit at the table or butter the bread but I was up to something. We'd been brought closer together but now Ma wanted some distance. She wanted isolation, and I knew she couldn't get it in the hurly burly of 44. Neither could she be persuaded to take on Juno. In the end she turned to Shea and with emotion in her voice said:

—I'm not from Dublin, let's leave it at that.

In that moment, she was a child again, standing in a hayfield outside Dundalk, looking up at her father who was sending her to an aunt in Belfast because he couldn't cope without her mother, who had died while having her.

Catherine Griffin was twenty years too young but made an authentic Juno based on her own mother. I was twenty-five years too young for Joxer Daly so I shaved the front of my head and made myself bald. Ma had a fit and asked Da where these dramatics were leading to. When I told her I was 'serious about my art', she raised her hand and struck out at me for the first time since I was a child. Everyone in the cast, apart from Shea, thought I had gone too far, which convinced me that I'd made the right decision. I knew they were concerned about vanity – how I looked in school, at home, at the Oriel dance, at Mass, only they couldn't understand I had no vanity where the play was concerned. The play was the thing and no sacrifice was too much to make the audience believe. How could I hold a mirror up to nature if I looked like the Paycock's son rather than his buddy? I had to transform myself, acquire the correct physical attributes so that I ended up thinking like the character. I had to work from the outside in. Joxer was described as a shoulder shrugger and a man with a permanent grin. Shoulder shruggers were common around the flats. Permanent grins were harder to find. The only one I knew was Ostler Doyle who drank in the Railway Bar. He wore a grin twenty-four hours a day. I copied him and got a pain in my face. It was hard work smiling all the time. Ma kept asking me what I was smiling at. I wouldn't tell her.

—I'll put that smile on the other side of your face.

I told her I didn't mind if she did.

—I'll give you something to smile about, I'm telling you.

Ma turned to Da for support.

—Where are these dramatics leading to, Da?

Da turned to me, his buddy in crime.

—Now, Joxer, that's enough.

I went out to the scullery and checked my pencil moustache. I was growing it to age me. It was too fair. I got out the black polish, took a piece on my finger and rubbed it along the hairs. It made a huge difference. I smiled at my reflection. It was a Joxer smile. I held it and went back to the table. Shea was eating his dinner with one hand. His other one was inside his shirt and bent behind his back to conceal it. He ate in character at all meals. He picked up his knife and tried to cut his meat. It was hopeless. He plunged his fork into it and put it to his mouth where he tore at it like a lion. Ma looked at him but said nothing. She saw me and immediately turned to Da again.

—Look at that fella smiling.

We played *Juno and the Paycock* for seven performances in the Oriel Hall before taking it out on the road to the amateur drama festivals. Our first competition stop was up the mountains in Roundwood, County Wicklow, Ireland's highest village. It must have been the lack of air up there because there was an energy in the performance that felt like another character in the play. We were all carried along in this adrenalin rush. The culmination was the scene where Johnny sees a ghost in his bedroom. Shea had always been good at working himself into hysterics. In Roundwood he reached such a pitch that several people ran out of the hall in fright. He looked like he was completely out of control, completely epileptic.

Some of the cast were livid with Shea but by the end of the week that all changed when he was awarded the Roundwood Cup for best supporting actor. We continued on our way to Carnew and Wexford, where I won a medal for my performance as Joxer.

*

Andy and Teresa were living in 2a Sean MacDermott Street with their son, Matthew, and another one on the way. It was funny seeing a little replica of Andy smiling up at me from the pram. It wasn't something I had ever imagined.

Andy seemed paralyzed by his circumstances. He seemed as trapped in this room as he had been in school. Brother Denehy had predicted that Andy would end up in a one-room tenement. I felt angry that Andy had fulfilled his prophesy. In truth, his situation was worse because he wasn't an official tenant. He was a squatter without rights. His electricity came via a cable connected to the hall light and illegally brought to his room through a hole in the wall. His only hope of salvation was that he'd get offered one of the new high rise apartments opening out in Ballymun, on the fringes of the city.

For now it was 2a and cream cakes. Matthew, Andy and Teresa lived on cream cakes from the Kylemore Bakery. Catherine brought the cream cakes and the Vincent de Paul brought the double bed and the baby's cot including the blankets. I wondered was that an encouragement for them to multiply? I decided I would lose my virginity to a prostitute. It was the perfect solution to the conundrum of procreation. Sex without responsibility.

Andy started to write original songs in school copy books using block capital letters. They were all in verses of four lines and in between each line, in different coloured pen, he wrote what he thought were the appropriate chords. He played out a rhythm on the arm of the chair to give me the tempo, I picked it up on the guitar and Andy sang the song.

Ninety per cent of them were love songs. I will give to you/if you will give to me/a heart to make you true/a love

278

to set you free. It was hard to concentrate with Matthew constantly screaming for cream cakes and Teresa wanting to know when we were getting paying gigs. None of it bothered Andy. He smiled and went at the next song like it was the best he'd ever written. Out of the hundred or so songs he'd penned, there were probably two worth considering for the Michael Maltese repertoire. Andy was anxious for us to rehearse them and get them down. In reality, the drama had taken over and despite my encouragement for him to get involved, the only place he could see himself on a stage was sitting behind a set of drums.

*

The first split in the Saint Laurence O'Toole's Musical and Dramatic Society came after the run of *Juno and the Paycock* ended. Big Ben Lalor suggested that it was time for the group to take a break, to take stock, to look at pooling our resources, human and material, to take on *The Plough and the Stars*, the final part of the O'Casey trilogy. His proposal was seconded by Sheila Loughman. She had played Mary Boyle and Big Ben Lalor had played Charles Bentham in *Juno*. They were boyfriend and girlfriend in the play and had become boyfriend and girlfriend in real life. Naturally, they wanted to play the lovers, Jack and Nora Clitheroe, in *The Plough* and they wanted time off before we went into rehearsals.

Shea and I didn't want a break. We had momentum, why let it dissipate? We had few supporters due to tiredness, but, to my surprise, Da took our side in the debate. Normally the embodiment of caution, he thought we could cater for both factions. He proposed that the next production, whatever it was, be mounted under a different name and that we retain the Saint Laurence O'Toole's Musical and Dramatic Society for the next major outing. Da proposed that we buy a rubber stamp for the new production out of the Society's funds. The opposing group proposed that the money for the rubber stamp come out of independent funds. A three-hour argument developed over the rubber stamp. In the end, the opposition won and the meeting broke up in acrimony.

SLOT Players was formed to do *Waiting for Godot* by Samuel Beckett. It was avant garde and ambitious for an amateur group. I loved the title of the play and it reminded me of Gerard at our back door 'waiting for Frankie'. It was set on a country road somewhere but it felt remarkably like the dump out in Donabate. The two tramps, Vladimir and Estragon, were two picaroonies looking for something they were never going to find. They might even have been looking for a television valve. If *Shadow of a Gunman* and *Juno and the Paycock* had spoken in a unique way about Seville Place and its environs, then *Waiting for Godot* was the family equivalent of that for us. Frankie wasn't coming back but we still had to go on. *Waiting for Godot* was a two-hour blues song of unbearable pain. It wallowed in its own shit and came out the other side laughing. Just like Leadbelly and Howlin' Wolf and Sonny Boy Williamson. This was a bitch of an earth and things didn't get better. There was only waiting and passing the time. In the meantime, nothing happens, nobody comes, nobody goes, it's awful. But things did happen in the play, unnatural things, like the tree sprouting leaves overnight. In a single night covered in leaves. And Pozzo, the ring master of the first part becomes the slave of the second, all in a single day. Lucky, the slave of the first part, becomes the eyes and ears of his blind master, Pozzo, in the second. Da was natural casting as the bombast Pozzo and with Johnny as the hapless Lucky it brought a father/son dimension to this terrifying relationship. I played Vladimir, the thinking tramp and Shea directed, so with Tim Rogers as Estragon the only non-Sheridan, the production became a catharsis for our recent family history. Every night during Act Two of the play, Da stepped into Frankie's grave in Glasnevin to deliver Pozzo's riposte to my repeated questioning of when he went blind.

—*Have you not done tormenting me with your accursed time! It's abominable! When! When! One day, is that not enough for you, one day like any other day, one day, one day he went dumb, one day I went blind, one day we'll go deaf, one day we were born, one day we shall die, the same day, the same second, is that not enough for you? They give birth astride of a grave, the light gleams an instant, then it's night once more. On.*

It was Da singing the blues in the recently dug grave of his dead son, my brother. In that moment on the stage I realized as Vladimir that I could be saved. The possibility of redemption is there, if fleetingly, and I turn to Estragon for confirmation, only for Estragon to destroy the moment with his doubts. I am plunged once more into uncertainty. I am utterly alone in the world. As Vladimir and as myself. Just like I was alone after Frankie when I realized that no one could cry my tears for me. Samuel Beckett had given me something that eased the burden and lessened the pain. It was a precious relief for me, for Da, for Shea, and for Johnny, a relief born out of true compassion for the human condition.

*

In August the North of Ireland exploded and Ma came back to life. Whole streets were on fire, and they were Ma's streets – Cromac and Bombay and Leeson and Falls and Ormeau and Antrim. Her people lived in these streets, abandoned for fifty years now. They weren't even second class citizens, they had no status. Now the roof over their heads was ablaze and their belongings in ashes. Where were the IRA, Ma wanted to know? Someone said the letters stood for I Ran Away.

—Where's the bloody IRA?

Where's the Irish Army? Our troops should be over that border defending our kith and kin. Were we going to do nothing? It was better to do something than nothing. What about our Government, what were they going to do?

—We will not stand idly by!

The man on the television with the bald head and the fat pipe looked sleepy and bewildered. No one believed him, especially Ma.

—That fella's worse than useless.

All aerials turned towards Belfast. We sat glued to the set from one broadcast to the next. We were the centre of the universe. The nation held its breath.

—We are interrupting this programme to bring you a newsflash.

Belfast was ablaze, Derry, too. Ma cursed the man who called it Londonderry. Disorder was general all over the North. It lit up the sky and rained down on the blackened people.

—The Protestant bastards are burning them out.

British troops arrived on the streets. Catholic women hugged them and gave them tea. Barricades went up dividing Catholic from Protestant. The Falls from the Shankill. In Derry the police battered an unarmed man to death. Samuel Deveney. The people of the Bogside had had enough and declared a 'Free Derry'.

—We will not stand idly by.

News from the North became our nightly serial. We watched it and shed our guilt. A group of dockers armed with hurley sticks set out for the conflict and ended up in a drunken ditch in County Cavan. There were reports of other such forays and still the burnings flourished. We found new words to explain what was happening – pogrom and bigotry and B men. On the border the Irish troops stood idly by and watched those too frightened to go home take up residence in makeshift tents. One Friday night in early September we returned from a performance of *Waiting for Godot* to find a note on the kitchen table in Ma's handwriting. It detailed the new billeting arrangements. Due to the arrival of refugees from Belfast, Shea and I would be on a settee in the kitchen until further notice.

Who were these wild men who'd been assigned to our room? I had never seen a refugee in the flesh. We'd watched the North plunge towards civil war on our televisions, now it had marched south and tramped into our house. We were a part of history and we had to sacrifice our room for the war effort. We had escaped the Second World War but now 44 felt like it was a military zone. It was general HQ and Ma was Commander-in-Chief. I had the strongest intuition that the men in our room were members of the long-lost Irish Republican Army.

I stole up the stairs past the bathroom. Somebody was inside having a bath. I carried on up to our room and paused at the door. I decided not to knock. If they were IRA I might catch them in the middle of something. Then again, if they were IRA and I walked in, I could be in trouble. It was my house, I was entitled to walk into my bedroom and get my pyjamas. I opened the door slowly but with authority and looked in the direction of my bed. Standing beside it was a naked woman pulling a nightdress over her head. She was tiny but had a wide arse. I was frozen in the doorway looking at her back.

—How was your bath, love?

She turned around and screamed at me. I stepped back and pulled the door closed. She screamed again. I heard the sound of feet splashing from the bath and fingers pulling at the lock. I decided to play innocent and saunter down the stairs. I had done nothing wrong, nothing with malice afore-thought. The bathroom door flew open and a young girl about fifteen or sixteen with a towel wrapped around her, looked at me for the briefest second before closing the door again and screaming. Da came running up the stairs and I explained what happened. He tried to calm them down.

—You have nothing to worry about, do you hear me?

—Who are you?

—I am Pozzo.

—Pozzo? Who's Pozzo?

I hadn't the heart to wait for Da's explanation. I ran into the kitchen and grabbed Shea by the arm. I didn't know whether to laugh or cry. Shea kept asking me what the matter was.

—I can't talk, I can't fucking talk.

By the time I'd calmed down sufficiently to tell him, Ma was in the back door. I told her about the awful happening but she brushed it aside. It was of no importance to her. She was a wild dog leading her pack. She had the scent of something and she wasn't going to lose it. She was a bitch, a right bitch, a proper bitch and nothing would deflect her from her goal. That goal was civil rights for our refugees. She'd gone to Amiens Street and gatecrashed the Fianna Fail cumann meeting demanding justice for Mrs McErlean and her daughter, Anne. Wee Anne. Burnt out because her father was a Protestant. Wee Mrs McErlean, defenceless Mrs McErlean, victim of a mixed marriage, burnt out of her home by her Protestant neighbours. Ma brought their Irish passports to the cumann meeting and wanted to know what they meant when they said they would not stand idly by. Somebody at the meeting said they needed more on-the-ground information. Ma gave them ground. She took them up the Falls Road, the Springfield, the Whiterock and the Grosvenor. She took them to Andersonstown, Ballymurphy, Turf Lodge and Tiger Bay. Ma asked them what the Catholics were meant to defend themselves with. Sticks? The talk turned to guns. Defence committees were being organized, street by street, of the ones still standing. Was there anyone in Fianna Fáil prepared to provide the committees with what they needed to defend themselves?

Mrs McErlean and wee Anne were much more ordinary

than the people on the television. They had very little to say, bordering on almost nothing. It was hard to imagine they did anything to deserve being burnt out. If they had taunted their Protestant neighbours it must have been by sign language. Getting information out of them was painful. Wee Anne was Mrs McErlean's only child by Tommy McErlean, a wee Protestant chimney sweep. He swept Catholic and Protestant chimneys without bias (chimneys were strictly non-sectarian), until August set Belfast ablaze and men who were fiercely loyal slit his throat and set his house on fire. Miraculously, he survived and was recuperating in the Royal Victoria Hospital. Ma extracted all this information from Mrs McErlean.

—They gave you five minutes to pack before they torched the house?

—That's right, Mrs Sheridan, they did.

What happened to Tommy McErlean brought home in a very real way the tribal hatreds of Belfast. I was very sorry about it but I wanted my bed back. As long as he was in hospital, I figured, there was every chance that mother and daughter would return to be at his side. Wee Anne was bound to be homesick. It was normal at sixteen to miss your friends. Just as normal as missing your bed at eighteen. If she missed her friends as much as I missed my bed, her heart was breaking.

Ma got Mrs McErlean a job cleaning offices. She got wee Anne a job in the kitchen of a hotel in Talbot Street. They were over the moon. Wee Tommy seemed a million miles from their thoughts. By the end of the month we had two more refugees. A second mother and daughter who shared with the McErleans. Mercifully, they didn't get on. It was a great relief that Catholics could hate Catholics and they were gone in a week. There were whispers that Mrs McErlean and wee Anne were looking for a flat because wee Tommy wanted to come to Dublin and make a new life for the family.

I prayed for the wee man, lots and lots of wee prayers for him to stay where he was. It was the first time in my life I said genuine prayers for a Protestant.

*

The end of the sixties crept up on us. I had finished school and registered at Trinity College. I decided on Trinity because I could walk there from 44. They had a good drama society with a famous little theatre called Players. Shea quit his job in the bank and registered at University College Dublin. He was going to check out their drama society. If neither was any good we were going to stick with SLOT Players. We still had the rubber stamp. There was also an Arts lab belonging to Trinity in a lane off Lincoln Place. Nobody knew who was in charge of it and nobody wanted to be in charge of it, it was a hip, cool place and very San Francisco. I knew the importance of having the keys so I got a hold of them and the Arts lab became ours. We started to improvise there and met a fella who knew about the Stanislavsky method and we got a free class from him. He never showed up again. I figured he committed suicide, he was so serious. We improvised stuff about the North, about 44. I lay on a table and pointed at the others . . .

—I'm Elvis Presley, you're not Elvis Presley!

It cracked them up. Shea gave us each a name, a definition. I was Ter. Gerry Green was Less, and Shea was Karak. Put together in the right order it was Karakterless. When Gerry Green figured what it meant he couldn't talk for four days, it was just too brilliant. Andy came to a couple of the sessions but he just watched. He seemed to get bored by the constant repetition. It couldn't have been more boring than looking at the four walls of 2a Sean MacDermott Street. There was pressure at home and Andy didn't seem to be able to laugh at it the way he'd always done. Then there was money. Andy's interest in money turned to obsession. Everything was reduced to pounds, shillings and pence. He wanted to know how much our university fees were and he wanted to know who got them. Who got the loot? I explained that I was on a scholarship from Dublin Corporation and I didn't actually see any money, it was paid directly to the college on my behalf. Who was it paid to? I told him I thought it was the Bursar.

—So how much would the Bursar take home every week for his wages?

Sometimes Andy was funny, sometimes he went on too long and it got boring. Sometimes we told him to shut up, but he still went on and I detected a resentment towards us. He was asking questions, not for answers, but to point up differences between him and us.

Once we discovered improvisation there was no stopping us and we could rehearse anywhere. On the street, in a pub, on a bus, in a shop, we could throw out an idea and work on it there and then. Band rehearsals suffered. It was easier to play at being Karak, Ter and Less than to drag all our equipment around to the Oriel Hall and set up to rehearse. We were on a different journey now and Andy suspected it was one we'd be making without him. He withdrew into writing his songs and started to learn the guitar. I lent him mine to help the process along and in no time he'd mastered the major chords. His song-writing, in consequence, improved in leaps and bounds.

*

Ma and Da decided to throw a New Year's Eve party. It was the beginning of a new decade. The end of an old one. The sixties making way for the seventies. We'd never say nineteen sixty anything again. It would take getting used to. In a day the sixties would be over. It didn't seem possible. There was the roaring twenties and the hungry thirties. What would people say of the sixties? How would they describe it? What would they remember first, *Sgt Pepper's Lonely Hearts Club Band* or Belfast burning? Everyone was talking about the permissive sixties and I was still living in hope. The division of time into decades was arbitrary. It was a convenience for historians, nothing else. When I looked back on the sixties I would think of two childhoods coming to an end – mine in the toilet of the Killarney train and Frankie's in a ward of Temple Street Children's Hospital. Neither would be recorded in history books. At midnight on 31 December, the world would grieve for the passing of the sixties but it would not be real; real grieving was done alone, it wasn't a public thing and no one could do it for you.

We needed a celebration in 44, it had been three years since we rang out the old and brought in the new. From seven o'clock, people started arriving and there was the sweet tingle of excitement all over the house. Ita was on duty at the front door with Pat Stynes, letting people in. Johnny was in charge of collecting and washing glasses and Gerard was berating people to eat sandwiches because 'there's millions of them'. Shea was supposed to be in charge of the gramophone but Gerry Green had decided on two solid hours of Jim Morrison and The Doors.

All the aunts and uncles were there and the two eldest children of each family. We had to have some limit on numbers. Neighbours and friends from all around the parish were there, and lodgers past and present, Mahony wearing his porter's cap back to front and offering to take the women's handbags. Some of Da's colleagues from the booking office in Amiens Street were there and one or two from Shelbourne Park. Ma was working her way from group to group with Mrs McErlean and wee Anne, explaining what was needed to end the trouble in the North. Da was talking to Big Ben Lalor and Sheila Loughman about the influence of the music hall on Sean O'Casey's plays while I collected their coats and headed for the stairs. When I put my foot on the first step the lights in the house went without warning. Darkness and shouts and then silence. Television, gramophone and talking all came to an end. Ma called out to Ita for candles that were in the cup she won for Irish dancing when she was ten. Da made his way out of the hall door and around to the garage where he had several lamps and dozens upon dozens of dead batteries, saved for such an occasion as this. The candles provided very little light and we all stood and waited for Da's anticipated return. Then there was the laugh. The laugh that bred a hundred laughs, pale imitation laughs, laughs that paid homage to the one, true, universal laugh of Uncle Paddy.

—Where's the fuse board?

Da was back with a rusty bicycle lamp in time to bring Paddy to the source of all power. Big Ben Lalor put Uncle Paddy on his shoulders and Da handed him the lamp. In the gloomy shadows he looked like an Indian Rajah on an elephant. He steered his way into the cubby hole cloakroom and examined the dead fuse board.

—You may have to cancel the party.

There was a huge groan, but Uncle Paddy's self-satisfied laugh subdued it easily. Lights, television and Jim Morrison all came on together and a huge cheer went up. Big Ben Lalor refused to put Uncle Paddy down and he was mobbed by everyone in the house who wanted to know how he'd fixed it.

—Faulty switch . . . it was a faulty switch . . .

Catherine Griffin arrived with Billy Boy Brennan. He brought a dozen stout but refused to give me his coat. Catherine brought an enormous cake and did give me her coat. Rumour had it they were getting married. It certainly looked that way. The cake was a complete giveaway. There was no sign of Andy and it was getting on for ten. I decided to call round and see if anything was wrong. Andy came to the door and said he couldn't come. I begged him. He couldn't leave Teresa and Matthew on New Year's Eve. I told him they were all welcome, all invited. The baby was asleep, he couldn't come. I told him he was the only one missing. The answer was still no. I stood on the steps and grinded my teeth until my face hurt.

—Just give me the guitar so.

—I don't have it.

I looked at him and knew he didn't have it.

—Where is it?

—I lent it to someone.

Someone? He doesn't have a name? You lent it to a nameless person? I knew it was a lie. My best friend was lying to me. I couldn't let him do this. I cared about the guitar but I cared a hell of a lot more about Andy lying to me.

—Tell me what you did with my guitar.

—I told you.

—Tell me the truth, please don't lie to me.

I stared down at the steps to make it easier for him.

—I pawned it.

I nodded my head and absorbed his words. That was all. There was nothing to say, really.

—I pawned it for the Christmas toys, I'm sorry.

I told him it was all right, that we'd redeem it after Christmas. But it wasn't all right. I wanted to kill someone. I wanted to kill whoever was responsible for reducing him to this. I didn't blame Andy. I just hated seeing his spirit ebb away. He'd always been a fighter. He fought his father, he fought school, he fought Artane. Now he was giving in and I wanted to kill the people who were making him surrender. In reality, I knew it was me. That was what really hurt. For the first time I felt like his oppressor. I knew I was going to give my life to the theatre and that was a rejection of him. He had to reject me in turn and pawning the guitar was his way of doing just that.

Walking home through the tenement streets of Dublin, it seemed that a lot of things had resolved themselves. The path ahead suddenly seemed straightforward and clear. 44 was too overcrowded, even for me. Ma needed her refugees and I was glad she had them. I would leave home soon and find my own field of battle. I could see myself in Belfast. I knew the streets even though I'd never walked them. It seemed the only place to be right now.

I went in by the back door, where they were glued to the television. They were watching snow. I looked at their rapt faces and the black and white lines that mesmerized them.

—What are you watching?

—The moon.

I looked again at the screen. If I squinted my eyes I could make out the shape of a man descending a ladder. It was Neil Armstrong.

'One small step for man, one giant step for mankind.'

It was News Highlights of the Year but it wasn't news in our house. We'd had it for a decade on our television.

—What's on the television?

—The moon.

Maybe that's where Frankie was now. Maybe that's what he'd seen with his damaged brain, his lunar home. The moon symbolized love and imagination because they both came out at night. Our aerial had gone up and connected to the cosmic imagination a decade before. Maybe he could see us now and was sending this picture back via the astronauts to let us know he was okay. Maybe Frankie would do something at the turn of every decade to let us know how he was.

We poured up to the front room for the countdown to twelve. Ten, nine, eight . . . Da made everyone link arms . . . five, four, three . . . Uncle Paddy shouted faulty switch and the room collapsed in chaos . . . no one heard two or one but hugging and kissing broke out and fog horns sounded and bells were rung and door knockers were knocked and car horns hooted and the community of Seville Place danced out on to the road to bring the new decade to life. A half an hour into the New Year we were back inside for the sing-song. By common acclaim it was Da to sing first. He looked over at Ma and I wondered would he do it.

—It's your song, Da!

He hadn't sung it in a long, long time. He cleared his throat and for a split second I thought I heard him say 'Frankie'. And maybe he did, but when the words came out it was one of his Dean Martin specials, 'Little Old Wine Drinker Me'.

He performed it with gusto. When the clapping died down he made a noble call for me to play something of The Beatles on guitar. It was the start of a sing-song that went on through the night and well into the day.

*

Ma finally despaired of the television ever being repaired, went up to McHugh Himself and rented the latest model. Everyone in the house was delighted. Gerard and Paul had only ever known interference. They didn't know you could have pictures without snow. It was nice for Ma to see Perry Mason again, even if he was a good bit older than the last time she saw him. Da was distraught and cut off communication with everyone. I caught his eyes once or twice when something on the television provoked laughter in the house and it was as if nails were being driven into his hands.

—God save me from dames. Dames with ideas.

Ma suggested giving the old television to Garrity, the scrap man.

—Keep your hands off that television if you value your life.

It was strange having the old television on the shelf specially made for it and the new one taking up half the table and blinding us while we ate. Da wouldn't hear of a swop because in his opinion the situation was a temporary one and the rented set would soon be making its way back to Mr McHugh. In the meantime, Da sat where he couldn't see the television because, in his own words, it 'exacerbates the headaches'.

The first Tuesday of the new year we set out for the dumps. We never came home empty-handed but never came home with what we'd set out to find. I wondered sometimes would it go on for ever. How long could I keep that up for?

Passing by a farmhouse on the back road out to Donabate, Da spied a toilet pan in a field. It was sitting on its own surrounded by nothing. Sitting on a grass mound with nothing for company. At that distance and travelling at the regulatory twenty-five miles an hour, Da could tell it was a perfect match for his cracked one at home. Da told me to make a note of the exact location so we could pick it up on the way home. I told him to stop taking the piss. He didn't see the humour in it. I explained it to him, by which stage it didn't seem funny any more, only slightly crude.

Donabate was the healthiest dump in Dublin because of its proximity to the sea. The ozone and the rotting debris were constantly at war with each other. It was the battle of good and evil. Some days I wished the ozone would disappear and just let the stench get on with it.

We turned off the back road onto a boreen and almost ran over two magpies in front of us. Da was delighted because they were good omens. Seconds later, the car started to splutter and then to lose power altogether. He knocked it into second gear and released the clutch but there was no response. The Anglia trudged to a stop and my first instinct was that we'd run out of petrol. But no, the gauge was showing a quarter full. Second choice was dirt in the carburetor. Da got out and interrogated the usual suspects – battery, spark plugs and points – before he proclaimed with supreme authority that it was the accelerator cable.

293

—The spring has snapped in half.

He went to the back of the car and took out his bits and pieces tin. He fished through it and came out with a spring that had once belonged to the twin tub washing machine. He stretched it with his finger.

—It'll get us out of gaol.

We were standing there contemplating our situation when a carload of picaroonies from Ringsend sailed straight past us grinning from ear to ear. Da had only one word for them.

—Worms.

A lorry came down the track towards us. The driver stopped and offered us a lift. He took us right to the spot where he discharged his load. We put on our masks and stood back. He tipped his truck and a cloud of dust rose up into the sky. I turned away because it was blowing in my direction. When I thought it was safe to turn back I looked around and there was Da in the middle of the pile pulling debris out of his way like he'd heard a human voice coming from inside it. He picked up a piece of kitchen lino and held it over his head like he meant to throw it. It froze there and he dropped it behind him. He bent down and picked up a television the same as the one at home. The glass at the front was cracked and the on/off button was missing. Da turned it over face down, pulled a screwdriver from his pocket and went at the screws that held the back cover in position. Inside was a perfect-looking television with a complete set of valves. Da knelt beside it and stroked it gently with his hand.

—Let's get her home.

We carried her, coffin fashion, to the car. When we got there, I opened the passenger door and tilted the seat forward. Da leaned in and put it face down on the back seat before covering it with the red tartan blanket.

He got to work under the bonnet and removed the broken spring. Fitting the replacement from the washing machine was a bastard. It was the wrong size and it was tighter. I pulled the spring apart and held it while Da tried to fit the holding screws. We were getting in each other's way.

—That's it, son, just hold it a few seconds longer.

Our fingers were almost sticking together with the grease and the oil. My hands were as big as his now. My thumbs had filled out and my fingers had stretched from playing the guitar. Being so close to him brought me back to my childhood.

—Turn it towards ten o'clock.

He finally got the screw in, put the key in the ignition and turned the car over. It sounded like an aeroplane. The engine was turning over at ten times its normal speed. The roar of it was so intense that every species of bird known to man was suddenly flying away from us in all directions. Da was undeterred. He put the car in gear and we were travelling at fifty miles an hour before he touched the accelerator. By the time we were in fourth gear the car was averaging seventy with no sign of it ever slowing down. I crawled into the back with the television to stop it jumping around and Da turned on the radio to try and counteract the deafening noise of the engine. We passed the landmarks for the farmhouse and I pointed them out to Da.

—Fuck the toilet pan, who gives a shite?

As we came off the back road towards the city we met other cars, all of which we left behind. Coming up to traffic lights, Da pressed on the horn and kept it pressed. Miraculously we made it to the North Strand without hitting another car. How were we going to make the ninety-degree turn at Seville Place, that was the question? Cleverly, Da switched off the engine and pulled up the hand brake. It got us around the corner and from there he let the car free wheel under the railway bridge and brought it to a standstill right outside the front door of 44. We carried in the television and took out the required valve. Da placed it with extreme care into the back of the old set. He switched it on and after a few minutes the BBC test card appeared in all its pristine beauty. It was the clearest it had ever been. No snow. No interference. No lunar landscapes. Just a perfect television picture.

He went upstairs and had a bath. I sat on the stairs and listened to him splashing. He started to sing. No Dean Martin imitation. Just Da singing, in Da's voice. The song he hadn't sung in a long, long time.

—*Frankie and Johnny were lovers,*
 Oh, Lordy, how they did love,
 Swore to be true to each other,
 Just as true as the stars above,
 He was her man, but he done her wrong.

He'd found what he was looking for. He'd replaced the faulty valve. But it was more that that. Much more. The valve was the genetic flaw that had killed Frankie.

He changed into his Sunday suit, came down to the scullery and had a slow, methodical shave. He came in and told Ma he was going around to the booking office for the afternoon. She went to the press and took out his headache tablets. He waved her away.

—Just in case, Da.

—I don't need them.

He went out the back door whistling and Ma looked at me.

—What's come over him?

—He's better, Ma, that's all, he's better.